SEPARATING CHURCH AND STATE

A volume in the series

Religion and American Public Life
Edited by R. Laurence Moore and Darryl Hart

A list of titles in this series is available at cornellpress.cornell.edu.

SEPARATING CHURCH AND STATE

A HISTORY

STEVEN K. GREEN

CORNELL UNIVERSITY PRESS
Ithaca and London

First published 2022 by Cornell University Press

Library of Congress Cataloging-in-Publication Data

Names: Green, Steven K. (Steven Keith), 1955– author.
Title: Separating church and state : a history / Steven K. Green.
Description: Ithaca [New York] : Cornell University Press, 2022. | Series: Religion and American public life | Includes bibliographical references and index.
Identifiers: LCCN 2021042170 (print) | LCCN 2021042171 (ebook) | ISBN 9781501762062 (hardcover) | ISBN 9781501762079 (pdf) | ISBN 9781501762086 (epub)
Subjects: LCSH: Church and state—United States—History. | Religion and state—United States—History. | Religion and law—United States—History.
Classification: LCC KF4865 .G7375 2022 (print) | LCC KF4865 (ebook) | DDC 342.7308/52—dc23/eng/20211001
LC record available at https://lccn.loc.gov/2021042170
LC ebook record available at https://lccn.loc.gov/2021042171

Contents

Preface

As the United States enters the third decade of the twenty-first century, religion clause jurisprudence is in flux. As discussed in this book's introduction, a majority of the current justices on the US Supreme Court apparently reject the longstanding rule against public funding of religious institutions, including houses of worship, which until recently was the mainstay of the principle of separation of church and state. At the same time, controversies have arisen over whether operators of secular businesses—bakeries, floral shops, pharmacies—should be able to raise religious objections to neutral nondiscrimination laws that govern public accommodations generally and, as arose during the COVID-19 pandemic, whether houses of worship were subject to neutral social-gathering restrictions. During these and related controversies, the value of church-state separation has been questioned.

The purpose of this book is not to engage in these contemporary controversies, as I have otherwise been able to do in my capacities as a teacher, attorney, and commentator. In this book, I speak through my preferred voice as a historian in the hope of providing background and context to the principle of separation of church and state, a concept that has long informed the understanding of the religion clauses of the Constitution. Accordingly, I eagerly accepted the invitation of Larry Moore and Darryl Hart to contribute a book on the history of church-state separation for Cornell University Press's Religion and American Life series. I thank them and the staff of Cornell University Press for this opportunity. I also wish to acknowledge the support I received for this project from the deans' office at Willamette University College of Law through its summer faculty research grant program. Finally, as with all of my writing projects, I appreciate the patience and support I receive from my wife, Cindy, and our daughter, Elizabeth.

SEPARATING CHURCH AND STATE

Introduction

> The greatest achievement ever made in the cause of human progress is the total and final separation of church and state.
>
> David Dudley Field, "American Progress in Jurisprudence"

Church-state controversies have played a prominent role in the US Supreme Court's docket since the 1940s. Every term, it seems, the Court decides one or more cases that implicate the Constitution's religion clauses contained in the First Amendment. And in most terms, those church-state cases involve controversial and contentious issues, such as whether a professional photographer or bakery shop owner can refuse to serve LGBTQ customers based on the proprietors' religious beliefs. This has long been true. Even the more conventional church-state disputes involving public funding of religious institutions or religious exercises in public schools have elicited strong feelings on opposing sides, with the Court's decisions in the early 1960s striking school prayer and Bible reading provoking attempts to amend the Constitution.[1]

Not only have the Court's specific church-state holdings proved to be controversial; so, too, has the Court's chosen standard for adjudicating many church-state conflicts: Does the government's involvement with religion or religious entities violate the *separation of church and state*? Commonly understood, the notion of church-state separation means that government cannot promote religion, financially or otherwise, or employ its coercive and persuasive powers to make people be more religious. Applied with rigor, it would mean that religious institutions and actors would be excluded from receiving grants and other benefits that flow to comparable secular entities (e.g., to fund public schools but not religious schools) and that the government would be prohibited from making religious proclamations or employing religious imagery, such as maintaining Ten Commandments monuments on courthouse grounds. As will be seen, the apparent rigidity in the phrase "separation of church and state" has rarely been applied with exacting rigor. Still, critics of church-state separation have often charged that the principle is hostile toward religion and that it privileges a regime of secularism.[2]

Church-state separation has an affirmative quality aside from its restrictive quality. The Court has identified a strain of separationism that protects religious institutions from intrusive governmental regulations, particularly when those regulations interfere with the autonomy and decision making of religious institutions about matters of doctrine and internal organization. When considering these "church autonomy" cases, the justices have rarely used the phrase "church-state separation," though they have acknowledged that this rule of independence is grounded not only in free-exercise principles but in nonestablishment principles as well.[3] Here the idea of separate zones of authority—a concept that goes back centuries—insulates religious institutions from too much government oversight. For some people, this internal tension within the principle of church-state separation—sometimes restricting while other times protecting the role of religion—illustrates a larger tension between the two religion clauses themselves, one affirming the value of free exercise of religion (religious pluralism) with the other embracing the value of nonestablishment (secularism). One can interpret the two clauses as working in tandem to advance the principle of religious freedom *writ large*, but others see an inherent conflict between the two clauses.[4]

This uncertainty over the meaning and application of the principle of church-state separation can be seen in three Supreme Court decisions in 2020.[5] Two of the cases implicated the religious autonomy strain of separationism. In one decision, *Our Lady of Guadalupe School v. Morrissey-Berru*, the Court held that lay teachers at Catholic schools fit within a judicially created "ministerial exception" to employment nondiscrimination laws.[6] Eight years earlier a unanimous Court had ruled that religious entities had an absolute say in selecting their religious leaders, even if it appeared the entity had otherwise discriminated on the basis of a protected status—race, gender, age, disability—in its employment decision. In that case, Chief Justice John Roberts had written that any restriction on that privilege "interferes with the internal governance of the church, depriving the church of control over the selection of those who will personify its beliefs," interests that are protected by both the Free Exercise Clause and the Establishment Clause.[7] Whereas the plaintiff in that earlier case was also a teacher, she held the title of "commissioned minister" and preformed significant religious duties; in contrast, the plaintiff-teachers in *Our Lady of Guadalupe School* met neither of those criteria. Nonetheless, the Court majority extended the ministerial exemption to block the teachers from bringing age and disability discrimination claims against the Catholic schools, reemphasizing the autonomy of religious entities in deciding matters of faith and the importance of insulating those decisions from oversight from civil authorities, including courts. Although neither the majority nor concurring opinion employed the language of "separating" church functions from those of the state, that principle underlay the holding.[8]

In contrast to affirming the concept of separationism in *Our Lady of Guadalupe School*, the Court took a different tack in *Bostock v. Clayton County*. There a majority interpreted the prohibition on sex discrimination under the 1964 Civil Rights Act to include banning employment discrimination on the basis of gender identity, thus expanding protections to members of the LBGTQ community. Even though none of the parties in *Bostock* was a religious entity, numerous religious groups filed *amicus curiae* ("friend of the court") briefs arguing that expanding the definition of "sex" to include gender identity would interfere with their autonomy to make and maintain employment decisions consistent with their religious doctrines. Justice Neil Gorsuch's majority opinion acknowledged that that possibility existed but held that such a claim was not before the Court at that time. Again, neither the justices nor the parties used that language of church-state separation, but the concept was implicated in the holding.[9]

In the third case in 2020, the principle of church-state separation was not simply implicated; it was also front and center in the holding. *Espinoza v. Montana Department of Revenue* involved a state tax credit for donations that paid for tuition at private schools, including religious ones. The Montana Supreme Court had voided the credit on the basis of a "no religious funding" clause in the state constitution, citing the state's interest in "separating church and State 'more fiercely' than the Federal Constitution." A narrow majority of the US Supreme Court rejected that interest as justifying the exclusion of religious schools from receiving the financial benefit. The majority brushed aside the long-standing precedent of prohibiting government funding of religious education, one reaching back to the early nineteenth century, holding that to deny funding to a religious entity constituted discrimination against religion. The majority and concurring opinions bristled with hostility to Montana's reliance on church-state separation and its insistence that the principle of not funding religious education advanced religious freedom writ large. Chief Justice Roberts called that claim an "ill-defined interest" and then added that "we do not see how the no-aid [to religion principle] promotes religious freedom."[10] And in his concurrence, Justice Clarence Thomas asserted that church-state separation represents a "distorted view of the Establishment Clause" and declared that "this Court's adoption of a separationist interpretation has itself sometimes bordered on religious hostility."[11]

In their dissenting opinions, Justices Stephen Breyer and Sonia Sotomayor defended the bona fides of the no-funding rule and separation of church and state. As Justice Sotomayor wrote, the Court's decision "'slights both our precedents and our history' and 'weakens this country's longstanding commitment to a separation of church and state beneficial to both.'"[12] When viewed in conjunction with a decision three years earlier where the Court held that a state could not rely on the no-funding principle to deny a renovation grant to a church, *Espinoza* was remarkable: a majority of justices rejected the principle of church-state separation that the Court itself had been so instrumental in crafting some seventy-five years earlier.[13] This reversal led constitutional scholar Erwin Chemerinsky to write that the trend was "unprecedented in American history: Never before had the Supreme Court held that the government is required to provide assistance to religious institutions. . . . The noble and essential idea of a wall separating church and state is left in disarray, if not shambles."[14]

The concept of church-state separation seems to be experiencing an identity crisis as one strain of separationism is ascending while the other is declining. It is with this latter, more conventional notion of separationism where there has been the greatest movement in recent decades. Not only has the Court backed away from its own jurisprudence of church-state separation with issues concerning aid to religion, upholding grants to religious nonprofits to conduct family planning counseling, instructional materials that can be diverted for religious uses, tuition vouchers for religious schools, and grants to houses of worship for facility renovations; a Court majority has also turned a kind eye to invocations at city council meetings and the government's use of religious symbols such as the Ten Commandments and Latin crosses.[15] Only with respect to officially sponsored devotional activity in public schools has the Court not retreated, though it has allowed student-led "Bible clubs" and other religious activities conducted by outside groups immediately following the school day.[16] The future of church-state separation appears to be in doubt.

What has led to the decline of church-state separation as a legal construct? As noted, the Court's embrace of separation of church and state has been controversial from the beginning. In 1947, the justices adopted church-state separation as the operative legal standard for judging Establishment Clause violations. *Everson v. Board of Education* involved a challenge to a state reimbursement for transportation costs associated with sending children to parochial schools. Even though the Court voted 5–4 to uphold the reimbursements based on public safety grounds, the justices unanimously agreed that separationism was the controlling legal rule. Writing for the majority, Justice Hugo Black set out what famously became known as the "no aid" rule:

> The "establishment of religion" clause of the First Amendment means at least this: Neither a state nor the Federal Government can set up a church. Neither can pass laws which aid one religion, aid all religions, or prefer one religion over another. . . . In the words of [Thomas] Jefferson, the clause against establishment of religion by law was intended to erect "a wall of separation between Church and State."[17]

A year later, in a case striking religious instruction in the public schools (*McCollum v. Board of Education*), the Court reaffirmed its commitment to church-state separation. Writing again for the majority, Justice Black reasserted that the Establishment Clause "erected a wall between Church and State which must be kept high and impregnable." In their concurring opinions, other justices added their own modifiers to describe the rigor of the separationist principle: "complete and uncompromising separation," "a spacious conception," "eternal separation," and "strictly apart." The object of the Establishment Clause "was broader than separating church and state in [a] narrow [institutional] sense," wrote Justice Wiley Rutledge. "It was to create a complete and permanent separation of the spheres of religious activity and civil authority." This rhetoric left little doubt that the justices considered separationism to be the controlling principle behind church-state relations and to represent a constitutional rule.[18]

Public reaction to the Court's adoption of church-state separation was generally favorable, with the *New York Times* praising the justices' pronouncements, though not the specific holding in *Everson*. Legal journals such as the *Harvard Law Review* also endorsed the Court's embrace of separationism, calling it "a towering issue of our time—the relation of the state to religious minorities in a democratic society."[19] Not all reaction to the Court's embrace of separationism was positive, however, particularly following the *McCollum* decision, with Protestant theologian Reinhold Niebuhr charging the principle would "greatly accelerate the trend toward the secularization of our culture." Catholic archbishop Richard J. Cushing went further in his criticism, labeling church-state separation a "phony plea" and a "smoke screen for secularism or bigotry." And a handful of conservative scholars challenged the justices' historicism, with one particularly harsh critic calling church-state separation a "fictitious principle." But overall, Americans appeared to accept the idea of church-state separation, at least in principle.[20]

By the mid-1950s, the status of church-state separation seemed so secure that one commentator declared that the "separation principle has become axiomatic in American thought." Another observer remarked that church-state separation, "with its comforting connotations of certainty and security, now seems to occupy a central—for some even a dominant—position in the dialogue on church and state." Thomas Jefferson's iconic wall of separation also came to epitomize the principle: "If a single metaphor dominates American thinking about church and state it is the metaphor of a wall of separation," opined a commentator. More than being a compelling visual representation, the "metaphor of a 'Wall of Separation' between church and state has become an enduring element of First Amendment analysis."[21] Even conservative Protestants endorsed separationism. Contained in the Doctrinal Statement of the National Association of Evangelicals, along with affirmations of the Bible's infallibility and of Jesus's divinity, was the goal of the "preservation of separation between church and state." As a result, John F. Kennedy's iconic 1960 statement "I believe in an America where the separation of church and state is absolute" was not that remarkable, even coming from a Catholic, as it reflected a near consensus among Americans, Protestants, Jews, and rank-and-file Catholics.[22]

For three decades following the *Everson* and *McCollum* decisions, the Court largely took a separationist approach to church-state controversies, albeit with a few exceptions. In the early 1960s, the Court struck down the common practice of prayer and Bible reading in public schools, and then in the 1970s it issued approximately a dozen rulings on public aid for religious education, striking the bulk of the programs. At times, the justices reaffirmed church-state separation as the constitutional touchstone, while at other times they simply let the separationist result speak for itself.[23] The Court's separationist approach seemed to align with, and reinforce, the growing secularization of the culture, represented by an increasing consumerism and the social revolution of the 1960s. While some people criticized specific separationist holdings—such as the prayer and Bible-reading decisions—few condemned the concept. This apparent consensus led church-state lawyer and scholar Leo Pfeffer to write in 1975 that "[t]he principle of separation . . . is as alive and well as it was in 1791, when the First Amendment was added to the Constitution. Indeed, there are many who claim that it is now more vigorous than [ever]."[24]

Pfeffer's confidence was shortly proven wrong. By the late 1970s, lingering opposition to the Court's school prayer and abortion decisions, and to a perceived cultural secularism and relativism, led to the rise of the Christian Right that accompanied, if not facilitated, a conservative political backlash that resulted in the election of Ronald Reagan as president. Among other items, Reagan proposed a constitutional amendment to guarantee prayer and Bible reading in the nation's schools, criticizing church-state separation in the process. Reagan declared at one event that the drafters of the First Amendment "sought to protect churches from government interference" but "never intended to construct a wall of hostility between government and the concept of religious belief itself."[25] At the same time, a new round of scholarly commentary arose criticizing the Court's promotion of church-state separation. In 1982, political scientist Robert L. Cord wrote an influential book, *Separation of Church and State: Historical Fact and Current Fiction*, that excoriated the Court's historicism and its separationist holdings. Cord's book was followed by a series of critiques, popular among political and religious conservatives, that attacked the principle as much as its applications, with Richard John Neuhaus of the journal *First Things* charging that church-state separation had created a "naked public square." Yale law professor Stephen Carter offered a similar critique, declaring that "[o]ur jurisprudence of church and state has become almost silly, a satire on itself, struggling to enforce an ahistorical fantasy." The result, wrote Carter, was that "separation of church and state, in its contemporary rendition, represents little more than an effort to subdue the power of religion, to twist it to the ends preferred by the state."[26]

Before long, criticism of church-state separation appeared in the opinions of conservative Supreme Court justices, those appointed to the bench by Presidents Reagan and Richard Nixon. On one level, the criticism was not new; the sole dissenter in the *McCollum* decision, Justice Stanley Reed, had warned that a "rule of law should not be drawn from a figure of speech."[27] Still previously, accommodationist justices, including Byron White and Warren Burger, had declined to attack separationism directly, preferring instead to qualify its understanding. As Burger had written in the 1971 decision in *Lemon v. Kurtzman*, "Our prior holdings do not call for total separation between church and state; total separation is not possible in an absolute sense. Some relationship between government and religious organizations is inevitable."[28]

By the mid-1980s, however, the tone in judicial opinions began to shift from hesitancy to hostility. Justice William Rehnquist had consistently taken a nonseparationist approach in church-state cases since being appointed by Nixon to the Court in 1972. Chiefly in the minority for over a decade, Rehnquist allowed his disdain for church-state separation to boil over in a dissenting opinion from a 1985 decision striking a state statute providing for silent prayer and meditation in public schools (*Wallace v. Jaffree*). Rehnquist attacked the concept of church-state separation at length, calling the wall metaphor "misleading" and "mischievous" and "all but useless as a guide to sound constitutional adjudication," concluding that it "should be frankly and explicitly abandoned."[29] Shortly, other justices joined in Rehnquist's broadside, with Justice Antonin Scalia likening separationism (as represented in the *Lemon v. Kurtzman* test) to a ghoul from a late-night horror film that refuses to die. Justice Thomas also condemned what he termed "extreme notions of separation of church and state."[30] This judicial criticism of church-state separation accompanied a rising number of nonseparationist holdings after the 1980s, approving greater forms of financial aid to religion and the official use of religious symbolism and rhetoric. This evolution led church-state scholar Ira Lupu to write an article in 1994, "The Lingering Death of Separationism," that argued the legal regime of separation of church and state was not only in decline but was also effectively existing in a terminal medical condition, being kept alive by its resiliency as a "stock phrase."[31]

Affirmations of separation by liberal justices also declined in the mid-1980s, possibly reflecting a reluctance to highlight a controversial—and for some, divisive—issue. In fact, the last majority opinion to acknowledge church-state separation as a controlling rule was *Lynch v. Donnelley* (1984), where Chief Justice Burger offered a tepid endorsement: "The court has sometimes described the Religion Clauses as erecting a 'wall'" between church and state. . . . The metaphor has served as a reminder that the Establishment Clause forbids an established church or anything approaching it. But the metaphor itself is not a wholly accurate description of the practical aspects of the relationship that in fact exists between church and state."[32] Thus, by the 1990s, few church-state opinions openly embraced the idea of church-state separation. A principle that had been at the heart of an important area of constitutional law was now openly reviled by opponents and all but abandoned by supporters.[33]

Paralleling separationism's decline among members of the judiciary and academy were voices of popular discontent, the harshest critiques coming from commentators and authors associated with the Christian Right. Televangelist Pat Robertson, a one-time Republican presidential candidate, charged on more than one occasion that the Constitution "says nothing about the separation of church and state," while noting that the phrase appeared in the Soviet Union's constitution. (Although true, the term "separation of powers," acknowledged in numerous Court decisions, also does not appear in the Constitution.) In 1992, the legal arm of Robertson's ministry, the American Center for Law and Justice, circulated a newsletter titled "Tear Down This Wall" that compared the wall of separation between church and state to the Berlin Wall, demanding that the former also be demolished.[34] More recently, Focus on the Family, a religious advocacy group founded by James Dobson, published an analysis, "Cause for Concern: Church and State," that asserted that the "so-called 'wall of separation between church and state' has done more damage to America's religious and moral tradition than any other utterance of the Supreme Court." Raising a familiar complaint, the analysis charged that the Court's "misuse of the 'separation of church and state' phrase has fostered hostility toward, rather than protection of, religious freedom." Asserting that America was founded as a "Christian nation," the analysis concluded that church-state separation is "an unconstitutional doctrine."[35] Fueling these attacks has been a veritable cottage industry of popular works criticizing church-state separation—best represented by David Barton, author of several pseudo-histories, including *The Myth of Separation*—that have charged that the concept is antireligious and lacks a historical basis.[36]

Criticism of separation of church and state, both scholarly and popular, has centered on three charges. The first is that the Court's choice of separationism to represent the meaning of the religion clauses is ahistorical or, in the words of Justice Rehnquist, amounts to "bad history."[37] This critique, which has existed since *Everson* was decided in 1947, has two interrelated parts: that the justices selectively emphasized the contributions and writings of Jefferson and James Madison to the exclusion of other members of the founding generation (with critics frequently noting that Jefferson was minister to France during the drafting of the Constitution and Bill of Rights, such that his input was minimal) and that the majority of people during the founding period never expressed fealty to separationism but articulated alternative ideas about church-state ordering. As historian Philip Hamburger writes, contemporaries "adopted many different conceptions of the relationship between church and state, but they did not ordinarily, if ever, propose a separation, let alone a wall of separation." Accordingly, "the constitutional authority for separation is without historical foundation."[38] While agreeing with Hamburger's critique, Daniel Dreisbach has argued that even Jefferson did not believe in the phrase he helped coin, that his statement was motivated out of political considerations rather than sincere conviction, and that Jefferson's record as Virginia governor and president does not demonstrate a commitment to church-state separation. Robert Cord also highlighted several inconsistencies between the writings of Jefferson and Madison and their public actions, which were more accommodating of church-state intermixing.[39]

The second complaint about separationism is that it conflicts with the nation's religious traditions and the beliefs of its people and, when applied with any rigor, is hostile to religion. This critique relies on a similar analysis about the historical record, one that emphasizes the ubiquity of religious discourse during the founding period, including official acknowledgments of religion, such as Thanksgiving proclamations and the appointment of chaplains in Congress and the military. It maintains that the founding lacked a strain of anticlericalism, absent the inclinations of figures such as Jefferson and Thomas Paine, and that most people considered religion essential for fostering public virtue. It then argues that the Court's pronouncement of separationism has led to a "brooding secularism" that hamstrings religious practice and expression today. As one critic charged following the *McCollum* decision, the Court had "taken sides with the secularists in their campaign to drive religion out of public life under the specious pretext of separation of church and state." Hamburger concurs that the phrase "penalizes religion and discriminates against religious groups," thus "undermining the Constitution's religious liberty." As discussed, religious conservatives have embraced this argument.[40]

A third criticism of separationism, popularized by Hamburger and Thomas Berg, is an extension of the first two critiques. It asks, How did church-state separation become an established constitutional principle if it was generally alien to members of the founding generation? The answer, according to Hamburger and Berg, is that it arose in the mid-nineteenth century as a Protestant response to Catholic immigration and was used to impose a Protestant cultural hegemony on Catholics. "[S]eparation became a popular vision of religious liberty in response to deeply felt fears of ecclesiastical and especially Catholic authority," Hamburger maintains. Nativists "popularized separation in America in the nineteenth century, and, during the first half of the twentieth, they continued to distinguish themselves as the leading proponents of this ideal." Then, as Berg continues, "the late 1940s and the early 1950s saw a resurgence in fear and distrust of Catholicism, and these contributed to the rise of church-state separationism in constitutional decisions, especially in decisions limiting aid to religious, overwhelmingly Catholic, schools." Agreeing with this critique, Stephen Carter asserts that "nobody seriously argued that aid to religious schools was unconstitutional until the argument became a useful tool in the nativist campaign against Catholicism." According to this third critique, church-state separation is not only ahistorical; it is a perverse and illiberal concept that should be rejected as a constitutional standard. In the words of Justice Thomas, it is a principle "born in bigotry [that] should be buried now."[41]

One can acknowledge that church-state separation developed in the United States chiefly as a Protestant concept without necessarily considering it to be anti-Catholic. While today church-state separation has a secular orientation—meaning that government policies and programs must have secular purposes and effects beyond being merely neutral among religions—it is clear that the early idea of separationism reflected Protestant presuppositions. Church-state separation presumed and valued several distinctly Protestant values: freedom of religious conscience, voluntarism or "soul liberty" on matters of faith, and a suspicion of clerical authority and ecclesiastical power.[42] As will be seen, these assumptions underlying church-state separation ensured that its early application would be consistent with Protestant worldviews and less assessable to Catholics, who sensed, even absent Protestant-oriented practices such as Bible reading in the public schools, that church-state separation favored Protestant perspectives to the detriment of Catholic ones. This presumptive Protestant understanding of separationism continued into the mid-twentieth century, reflected in part on the creation of Protestants and Other Americans United for Separation of Church and State (POAU) in 1947 to resist perceived Catholic incursions on church-state separation. (POAU's founders initially proposed naming the organization "Protestants United for Separation of Church and State" but added "Other Americans" so as not to appear too sectarian.)[43] It is no coincidence that as church-state separation began to reinforce more secular-oriented values, matching a growing secularization of the overall culture, support for church-state separation declined among religious conservatives. To an extent, the current controversy over whether separationism is the appropriate referent for adjudicating church-state controversies reflects a broader cultural division over the role of religion in American public life and whether government policies should promote a regime of secularism or reflect an ethic of Judeo-Christianity.

Although much of the debate over church-state separation has been ideologically driven, other criticism has centered on semantics. Because "separation of church and state" represents a legal principle, the question arises how closely the words, "separation," "church," and "state" should define the concept. Few commentators have interpreted the phrase literally but as interdicting various degrees of intermixing of religion and government authority. Few people argue that the word "church" should not include synagogues, temples, or mosques. But some have maintained that Jefferson, as the main promoter of the concept, was chiefly concerned about the tyranny of ecclesiastical institutions and of government control of the same—that he purposefully used the narrower word "church" rather than "religion" so as not to prevent the government from patronizing religion generally. Jefferson, according to legal scholar Steven Smith, was addressing "the problem of the church."[44] If the principle of separation of *church* and state is chiefly to prevent government control of institutional religion and to guard against the latter's incursions into democratic governance, then the words may make a difference. Justice Reed advocated this position early on, writing in his *McCollum* dissent that the prohibitions on a religious establishment "may have been intended by Congress to be aimed only at a state church." Under Reed's view, church-state separation "do[es] not bar every friendly gesture between church and state." That position did not persuade the other justices, however, with Justice Rutledge responding that "the object [of disestablishment] was broader than separating church and state in this narrow sense. It was to create a complete and permanent separation of the spheres of religious activity and civil authority by comprehensively forbidding every form of public aid or support for religion."[45]

Relatedly, commentators have argued that separation of church and state is a term of art that speaks of a relationship of *separation* of the two spheres, which is impossible in a religiously pluralistic culture. Several decades ago, religious historian Sidney Mead wrote that if one considers "Jefferson's concepts of 'church,' 'state,' and a 'wall,' the image that is conjured up is two distinct and settled institutions in the society once and for all times separated by a clearly defined and impregnable barrier which has solid foundations in the Constitution." Mead asserted that the more apt metaphor was a "line," a term used by Madison, so as to indicate a boundary rather than a barrier. (In the same letter, however, Madison called for the "entire abstinence" of interference of either entity with the other "in any way whatever.") Relatedly, Hamburger claims that while members of the founding generation spoke about preventing a "union" of church and state, few if any demanded "separation" between the two spheres.[46] On that point, Hamburger is essentially correct; the historical record indicates that people more commonly wrote about *preventing* a "union of church and state" than *ensuring* a "separation" between the two entities. That phrasing should not be surprising considering that a "union" had existed under the established Church of England and the immediate concern was to prevent another such union. The strength of this argument also turns in no small degree on an assumption that contemporaries distinguished between the two phrases and purposefully used the word "union" to represent a more limited concept rather than the word "separation." As will be seen, members of the founding generation used a variety of terms to describe the goals of disestablishment, and there is little to suggest they viewed the phrases "union" and "separation" as mutually exclusive terms of art.[47]

Semantics aside, separation of church and state—a principle that has long been a cornerstone of constitutional law and societal ordering—appears to be on the ropes. It is attacked from various sides, and a majority of Supreme Court justices seem ready to jettison it outright or at least ignore it into irrelevance or obscurity.[48] Yet separationism's demise has been predicted before. Only four years after *McCollum*, the justices retreated from that holding in *Zorach v. Clauson* by upholding the practice of releasing students for religious instruction, provided it occurred off school premises. There, Justice William O. Douglas famously declared that "[w]e are a religious people whose institutions suppose a Supreme Being," while he asserted that the government could accommodate the "spiritual needs" by "cooperat[ing] with religious authorities." Pundits quickly announced the demise of separationism, and even Justice Robert Jackson wrote fellow Justice Felix Frankfurter that "[a]s a legal doctrine, separation is gone."[49] Then, a decade later, the Court reaffirmed separationism in the prayer and Bible-reading decisions, with Justice Tom C. Clark repeating the earlier line that the Constitution required "a complete and permanent separation of the spheres of religious activity and civil authority."[50]

Despite the repudiation of separation by members of the judiciary and academy, church-state separation remains popular in the cultural mainstream. A 2011 opinion survey indicated that 67 percent of Americans either "strongly or mildly agree that the Constitution requires 'a clear separation of church and state.'" Those figures far outstrip the percentage of Americans who are progressive Christians or Jews or self-identify as atheists or agnostics.[51] Even some conservatives remain wedded to the concept, though they disagree with the way courts and public officials may have applied the principle. In a 2018 contribution to *Time* magazine, Republican senator James Lankford and Rev. Russell Moore, president of the conservative Southern Baptist Ethics and Religious Liberty Commission, wrote that "[s]eparation of church and state is too important a concept to be misused." The principle, they asserted, "ensures both that the government does not show preference to a certain religion and that the government does not take away an individual's ability to exercise religion. In other words, the church should not rule over the state, and the state cannot rule over the church." According to Lankford and Moore, "[t]he concept of a 'separation of church and state' reinforces the legal right of a free people to freely live their faith, even in public, without fear of government coercion."[52]

Popular support for the concept may say less about agreement with the Court's pronouncements than about the public's familiarity with the phrase and the protean quality of the concept that allows people to read various meanings into the idea. As Hamburger has quipped, separation of church and state "is a pleasingly rotund phrase that seems innocuous to many Americans."[53] Researchers have documented a disjuncture between abstract views about church-state separation and its concrete applications. The 1988 Williamsburg Charter Survey found that the "American public is generally ambivalent about the relationship between church and state, tending to favor a strict separation in theory, while accepting a strong blending of the two in practice." Another study concurred that there is "strong support for a high wall of separation between church and state, but the public is almost equally divided on whether government should help all religions equally or not help religion" at all. As that study concluded, "[i]t may be that much of the rhetoric of church-state separation is primarily symbolic."[54]

This book considers the ongoing controversy, both culturally and legally, over the concept of church-state separation and the metaphor of a "wall of separation." Its purpose is not to provide a polemical defense of separationism but to examine it as a legal and historical/cultural construct.[55] It examines the origins of the concept and what led to its rise as a popular concept, to its adoption by the Supreme Court, and then to its fall into disfavor among many Americans. Several claims are made. First, the idea of separationism as a model for church-state relationships has a stronger historical pedigree than critics acknowledge. The rhetorical use of a "wall" to represent the concept also has notable historical bona fides. Second, even though popularity of the concept during the nineteenth century was partially in reaction to Catholicism and Mormonism, that alone does not fully explain the widespread public embrace of the principle. A reactionary view of separationism also does not explain its adoption as a legal principle. Third, notwithstanding its provenance, the Supreme Court's adoption of the wall metaphor in 1947 was an afterthought—it was not essential to the Court's holding or to its adoption of separationism as a jurisprudential standard. However, in short time, several justices came to embrace the metaphor as epitomizing the idea, defending it against critics. In essence, the justices became convinced by their own rhetoric.[56] This facilitated the modern embrace of separationism and the wall metaphor by the American public.

The reign of separationism was always tenuous, however, and its decline started more than a decade before the rise of the Christian Right and the appointment of conservative judges under the Reagan and Bush administrations, in part because of its association with secularism. Finally, because the metaphor was never indispensable for the Court's initial holdings, the contemporary battle over the idea of a wall of separation has essentially been a distraction. While groups such as the American Civil Liberties Union (ACLU) and Americans United for Separation of Church and State vigorously defend the metaphor against critics, the controversy over the wall has always been more symbolic than real.

In examining the origins, rhetoric, and applications of church-state separation, this book considers the concept broadly, not as a narrow term of art. This is appropriate because people for centuries have read various meanings into the concept, and there is not now and never has been one definition of separationism. As used in this book, "separation of church and state" stands for the idea that rejects models of religious and legal/governmental ordering where a religion or religion per se maintains a preferential legal status or where either entity exercises authority or influence over the other's operations, doctrines, or messaging. It also prevents the government from facilitating the religious ministries of any or all religious groups. With that definition in mind, the purpose of this book is to explore separation as a legal and cultural artifact and to analyze its development over time.[57]

One theme that this book seeks to clarify is the relationship between nonestablishment of religion and church-state separation. Justice Black's iconic statement in *Everson* equated the two concepts, raising the ire of critics. For a while, Black's equivalency seemed to prevail. Yet the idea of nonestablishment of religion can be both narrower and broader than that of church-state separation. As will be discussed, members of the founding period could have supported forms of disestablishment without advocating separation; at the same time, nonestablishment is a legal, institutional mandate, whereas separation may imply a broader constraint affecting public policy and cultural forces. (This book will use the terms "disestablishment" and "nonestablishment" as connoting similar principles; though closely related, disestablishment is *act* of severing, while nonestablishment is the resulting *status*.) In addition, disestablishment was "America's original contribution to religious liberty," as the subtitle to the anthology *No Establishment of Religion* proclaims. In contrast, the impulse for church-state separation did not arise in North America and has much deeper roots.[58]

The book is organized in the following manner. Chapter 1 traces the various historical antecedents for the idea of separation of church and state, both religious and secular. These were chiefly the Free Church movement arising out of the Reformation and the writings of the Enlightenment and Whig theorists of the eighteenth century.[59] For American colonists, Roger Williams, founder of Rhode Island, made important early contributions to the concept, advocating a "hedge, or wall" separating the two realms. Coinciding with this impulse, and running on a parallel track, were the works of Enlightenment and British Whig writers including John Locke, John Trenchard and Thomas Gordon, Richard Price, Joseph Priestly, and James Burgh, all of whom promoted greater forms of separation. Burgh also employed a version of the wall metaphor to explain his views of church-state separation. Chapter 1 does not maintain that separationism was the consensus or controlling model for church-state arrangements leading to disestablishment. Nonetheless, it was a familiar and increasingly popular concept during the founding period.

Chapter 2 examines the separationist impulse in relation to the American disestablishment at the state and federal levels. It considers the writings and actions of Jefferson, Madison, and other members of the founding generation who advocated forms of separationism, as well as countervailing views about church-state interaction. Chapter 3 then considers the early national period and the crucial election of 1800. Included within that discussion is the ongoing debate over how to interpret Jefferson's famous letter to the Danbury Baptist Association. Then chapter 4 examines the events of the nineteenth century where the Jeffersonian-Madisonian understanding of separation gave way to a pan-Protestant notion of the concept, leading to an era scholars have called a "Christian America" or the "Moral Establishment," when a Protestant ethos held sway over the nation's culture and institutions.[60] This era bore witness to the rise of moral reform movements, to nonsectarian instruction in public schools and the conflict over school funding between Protestants and Catholics (the "School Question"), and to the conflict between the federal government and the Mormon Church (the "Mormon Question"). Throughout these events and controversies, various groups and factions fought over the meaning of church-state separation.

Chapter 5 discusses the modern Supreme Court's adoption of church-state separation as the constitutional standard. It examines the cultural backdrop to *Everson v. Board of Education* and *McCollum v. Board of Education*, one in which mainstream Protestants and secular intellectuals viewed separationism as an essential American democratic principle. It analyzes how the wall metaphor entered into the justices' discussions. The chapter then traces how justices and commentators expounded on the metaphor, elevating its significance in the law and public discourse. Finally, chapter 6 examines how the idea of church-state separation evolved in the law and public imagination from the 1960s through the early 2000s. For the first part of that period, few people questioned the legitimacy of separation as a model or the usefulness of the wall metaphor. In the early 1980s, however, a reevaluation of both ideas began, spurred on by the expansion of social welfare programs and a resurgence of political and religious conservatism. The wall metaphor came to represent the dividing line between those who embraced the secularization of American culture and those who supported an ideal of religious pluralism and cooperation. Religious conservatives raised arguments that separationism was antireligious, while religious liberals, embracing the social welfare and nondiscrimination goals of the post-1960s, became less wedded to separationism as they saw the benefits of greater cooperation between the government and religious institutions. Whether the anti-separationist critique directly influenced members of the Supreme Court, that critique was reflected in the less separationist holdings of the 1990s and 2000s. Those holding have led to separationism's decline as a legal construct, although it continues to resonate in the popular culture.

Chapter 1

Historical Antecedents of Separationism

Writing ten years after the *Everson* and *McCollum* decisions at a time of heightened debate over the meaning of church-state separation, religious historian E. Bruce Thompson asserted that "separation of church and state is a comparatively recent development in the evolution of human society. In fact, it is a uniquely *American* contribution to political and religious philosophy." If Thompson was referring to the American version of church-state separation reflected during the 1950s, then he was correct. However, as Thompson's own essay on "the European background" to American religious freedom documented, the impulse for a separation between the authority of the church and that of the state has deep historical roots in Western civilization. As John Witte Jr. has remarked, "separation of church and state has a much longer history, and much more complex and wholesome pedigree, than some recent historiography allows."[1]

Scholars have commonly identified two sources for the separationist impulse, the older being religious and the more recent arising out of the Enlightenment. Although that assessment is essentially correct, this division risks creating the impression that these two strains of separationism arose independently from each other and reflected distinct concerns. Such a binary model obscures the fact that Enlightenment thought arose chiefly as a critique of the prevailing religious worldview of the time. Enlightenment theorists lived in societies saturated with religious doctrines and customs that controlled the most exacting aspects of human life. Theorists such as Francis Bacon and Isaac Newton sought to reconcile Christianity with science and reason, and even skeptics such as Lord Bolingbroke, Voltaire, David Hume, and Jean-Jacques Rousseau were responding to existing religious presuppositions. As such, central aspects of the Enlightenment—scientific inquiry, freedom of conscience, and religious toleration—meant little without considering the religious status quo. That said, by the founding period, figures as different as Thomas Jefferson and Baptist leader John Leland could identify two "distinct" strains of separationism: religious and secular.[2]

Religious Roots

By the seventh century, the Catholic Church was the established religion for most of the kingdoms of Western Europe).[3] That status did not mean that the two spheres maintained an amicable relationship. The history of the medieval church was one of conflict and competition with civil rulers, with each entity frequently seeking to exert authority over the other. That tension, beginning with the sack of Rome and later barbarian invasions, led church leaders to promote dualistic paradigms of authority to protect the independence of the church. Augustine, Bishop of Hippo, reacting in part to the fall of Rome in 410, was one of the first church leaders to assert a model of separate spheres. In his *City of God* (410–26?), Augustine advanced the model of two entities, one spiritual and the other temporal, each with separate authority and functions. Augustine went so far as to employ an image of two walled cities separated from each other as a means to protect the purity of the church and those destined for salvation from the sinfulness of the world and its political institutions. Later church leaders utilized this idea of separate powers and functions to forestall attempts by civil rulers to exercise authority over clerical activities. At the end of the fifth century, Pope Gelasius resisted Emperor Anastasius's efforts to encroach on spiritual authority by warning him that there were "two powers by which this world is chiefly ruled: the sacred power of the priesthood and the royal power. Of these the priestly power is the weightier, because it has to render account of kings of men [at the final judgment]."[4]

During what has been called the Papal Revolution of the eleventh and twelfth centuries, Pope Gregory VII modified the two-powers theorem into a model of "two swords" in which clergy wielded the spiritual sword and civil magistrates possessed the temporal sword. Gregory used this two-swords theorem to secure jurisdiction over not only church doctrine, liturgy, and patronage but also over various legal areas, including marriage, inheritance, and behavioral offenses.[5] Later Thomas Aquinas affirmed this dualism by writing that "Church and State are as two swords which God has given to Christendom for protection; both of these, however, are given by him to the Pope and the temporal sword by him handed to the rulers of the State." What this meant was that though the earthly and spiritual realms were separate, civil authority was subservient to that of the church, and civil magistrates were to enforce civil law consistently with canon law. Thus, although Catholic thinkers employed various imagery—two walled cities, two powers, or two swords—they concurred that the church and the state were separate entities with distinct powers and functions, though both were subject to God's supreme authority.[6]

This idea of separate authorities and operations belied the reality of medieval Europe, where princes selected bishops, clerics served as legal and political advisers, and church officials relied on government actors to enforce religious edicts. During the Reformation, Protestants rebelled against what they perceived as the papacy's autocratic exercise of both swords, seizing the two-swords theorem and "adding new accents and applications," in the words of John Witte.[7] Both Martin Luther and John Calvin distinguished spiritual from temporal authority and called for a division of labor between the two. Martin Luther adapted Augustine's two-cities theorem by distinguishing between "two kingdoms"—a spiritual kingdom and a temporal kingdom. For Luther, God had ordained the spiritual and temporal kingdoms for human activity, the former being the place where people operated in faith in anticipation of salvation, and the latter being civil society, which relied on reason, force, and law. Each kingdom had its own jurisdiction, and people were to be governed by both, even though the earthly realm was corrupted by human sinfulness. Although the kingdoms overlapped, and people operated simultaneously in both, they were distinct; Luther wrote of a "paper wall" that separated the "spiritual estate" from the "temporal state." Under Luther's schema, "the church was not a political or legal authority. The church had no sword, no jurisdiction, no daily responsibility for law."[8]

The other leading protagonist of the Reformation, John Calvin, advanced similar views. Calvin wrote in his *Institutes of the Christian Religion* (1559) that "Christ's spiritual Kingdom and the civil jurisdiction are things completely distinct" and, as such, "must always be considered separately" because of the great "difference and unlikeness . . . between ecclesiastical and civil power." These distinct realms did not mean, however, that civil authorities in Calvin's Geneva had no interest in ensuring that society functioned according to religious precepts. Likewise, Luther preached subservience to civil authorities and did not object to "Lutheranism" being established by local princes.[9]

Unlike Luther and Calvin, Protestants in the Anabaptist tradition—Mennonites, Hutterites, Brethren—took the theological idea of separationism to heart, seeking to separate their communities from the corruptions of the fallen world, declining to swear oaths of allegiance to civil authorities or otherwise participate in civic functions. The early leader of the Mennonites, Menno Simons, used the term a "separating wall" or "wall of separation" to illustrate the degree of separateness their faith required from the world. That Anabaptists disputed the legitimacy of temporal authority and of the established churches ensured that they were persecuted by Lutherans, Catholics, and civil officials alike.[10]

Most Protestant dissenters did not seek to isolate themselves from the corrupt world to the extent of the Anabaptists; as a result, they did not promote notions of separationism where the two realms would never interact. Thus, while many Protestants decried the "adulterous union of church and state," others, such as Presbyterians, promoted milder forms of establishment in which the regenerate organized a national church and where civil authorities enforced religious standards. Because of this prevailing arrangement, Philip Hamburger maintains that the "overwhelming majority of Protestants who criticized religious establishments and the union of church and state did not understand themselves as seeking separation."[11] That may be true as for advocating an absolute sense of that term, but that does not mean that Protestant dissenters did not promote versions of separation that were consistent with their particular needs and theology. Puritans—despite their reputation as theocrats—promoted notions of separation between the true church and the ecclesiastical authority of the Church of England, which served as a proxy for the British crown. Whereas English Puritans sought to purify the national church, their Separatist (Pilgrim) brethren went a step further, advocating a regenerate church that was separated from its temporal overlords. Early Baptists also employed the metaphor of separate spheres in their critiques of religious establishments.[12]

All of this indicates that separation was a familiar theme in the political-theological thought of many Protestants. While a greater number employed separationism as a rhetorical device rather than as a creed to be practiced, the idea—whatever its particular strain—was sufficiently prevalent in sixteenth-century Britain to draw the ire of Anglican theologian and apologist Richard Hooker. Hooker derided the concept of separationism, criticizing its appeal among religious dissenters. Dissenters, Hooker reproved, insisted on "a necessary separation perpetual and personal between the Church and Commonwealth." Hooker believed that separatists threatened to undermine the system that God had ordained by urging that "the Church and the Commonwealth are two both distinct and separate societies . . . and the walles of separation between these two must forever be upheld." On the contrary, the "episcopal form of government was the best for the Church of England. . . . Church and state were two aspects of the same Commonwealth," he asserted. The "difference therefore either of affayres or offices Ecclesiastical from secular is no argument that the Church and the Commonwealth are alwayes separate and independent the one from the other."[13] The point is that while a minority of religious dissenters promoted actual separation between the religious and civil realms, the concept was familiar to people in both orthodox and dissenting camps. Jefferson reputedly owned a copy of Hooker's *Of the Laws of Ecclesiastical Polity*, which provided the founder with one of several sources for the metaphor of a wall of separation.[14]

The idea of separationism made the transatlantic crossing with the early settlers of British colonial America, many of them being religious dissenters from the Church of England. As discussed, Puritans and their Separatist brethren promoted a separation between the offices and functions of the colonies and their church. William Bradford, the future governor of Plymouth Colony, wrote in 1605 that "no Ecclesiasticall Minister ought to exercise or accept of any Civill publique jurisdiction and authoritie, but ought to be wholly imployed in spirituall Offices and duties to that Congregation over which he is set." According to colonial historian Edmund S. Morgan, Puritans "were particularly insistent that the church, because it was charged only with the spiritual welfare of its members (and of them only), must not become involved in the activities of the state, even when those activities were directed toward spiritual ends. The church must not do the state's work." In like manner, civil magistrates, though members of the elect and responsible for protecting the church, were to stay out of religious affairs. When magistrates prosecuted heresy and enforced religious behavioral norms, they did so not as an arm of the church but because the transgressions threatened the order and survival of the colony and violated enacted laws, such as those contained in the *Lawes and Libertyes* of Massachusetts Bay Colony. As Morgan notes, the "relationship between church and state was one of the things that the Puritans knew they must get right." Yet despite the organizational formalism of the New England colonies, a "blending of spiritual and temporal authority penetrated to the lowest level of public life."[15]

Today the most famous proponent of church-state separation during the colonial period was Roger Williams, the founder of Rhode Island in 1636. Initially identifying as a Separatist, Williams later affiliated with Baptists, attracted to their strong theological aversion to religious establishments. Like Baptists, he perceived that state support and endowments of religion corrupted true faith. In correspondence with Puritan leader John Cotton, Williams advocated erecting a "hedge or wall of separation between the garden of the church and the wilderness of the world." Williams believed that such a model was not only necessary to protect the true church, but that it was biblically ordained because "the church of the Jews under the Old Testament" and "the church of the Christians under the New Testament . . . were both separate from the world." Williams's desire to erect a wall to protect the garden of the church from worldly corruptions led twentieth-century legal scholar Mark De Wolfe Howe to insist that his wall of separation was intended only to restrain the activities of the state but not those of the church (i.e., a "one-way" wall). However, as Williams biographer David Little correctly observes, the idea that separationism restricted only the actions of the state was inconsistent with both Puritan thought and Williams's modifications of it. As Little writes, "the wilderness Williams fear[ed] [was] the condition of an established religion where both church and state are mutually degraded and corrupted by failing to observe the critical distinction between the inward and outward forums." Although modern-day scholars credit Williams as an architect of the American idea of church-state separation with its wall metaphor, his writings were not generally known during the colonial period. Rather, his letters were rediscovered during the Revolutionary era by Baptist leader Isaac Backus, who, along with fellow Baptist John Leland, promoted the concept widely. It is therefore unlikely that Jefferson was familiar with Williams or had read his writings.[16]

According to historian Nicholas Miller, a strain of separationism was also evident in the writings of William Penn and in the operation of the colony he founded, Pennsylvania. If that is the case, then it would be of greater historical significance than the writings of Roger Williams. Penn was more widely known than Williams, and Pennsylvania, unlike Rhode Island, was a leading colony in British America, influencing the church-state arrangements in New Jersey and Delaware. People commended Pennsylvania's practice of religious toleration as a model to be emulated throughout the colonies. In 1670, shortly after converting to Quakerism, Penn wrote *The Great Cause of Liberty of Conscience*, which championed that principle. Penn argued that liberty of conscience involved not only "mere liberty of the mind" but also the "exercise of ourselves [as dissenters] in a visible way of worship." He called for obedience to government and laws "tending to matters of an external nature" but asserted that religious matters were "consequently wholly independent of the secular affairs" of the state. The believer had the right to private judgment about religion because God had not delegated that authority to secular governments. Miller maintains that these statements, and Pennsylvania's practice of toleration and lack of an establishment, demonstrated "Penn's commitment to the separation of church and state."[17] Although Penn envisioned separate spheres of governmental and religious authority, it amounted to a limited understanding of separationism. The Frame of Government of Pennsylvania (1682), written by Penn, asserted that "government seems to me a part of religion itself, a thing sacred in its institution and end." The colony's "Laws Agreed upon in England" (1682) required that all judges, sheriffs, members of the council and assembly, and all other public officers "possess a faith in Jesus Christ," and the same statue authorized magistrates to enforce Sabbath laws and "all such offenses against God," such as swearing, drunkenness, and gambling. Neither Penn nor his fellow Quakers viewed civil enforcement of such laws as infringing upon liberty of conscience. According to one historian of Pennsylvania's church-state legacy, even though the colony lacked a legal church establishment with accompanying forced tithes, Penn and his followers envisioned a colony where the "Society of Friends would occupy a position comparable to that of the Church of England. Friends would determine the laws and government and the tone of society. Others would be welcome, but they would have to be governed by Quaker principles." At best, Penn's experiment practiced a "separation of the institutional church from the state."[18]

By the mid-eighteenth century, the religious impulse teaching separation between religious and secular institutions and their respective authority was well established among dissenting faiths, which essentially meant all Protestant denominations other than the Church of England. Separation was necessary to prevent the worldly corruptions of the state and its authorities from blemishing the purity of true Christianity. While this version was initially concerned about ensuring church authority and autonomy, it also existed to protect individual liberty of conscience and the private right of judgment in religious affairs. As will be seen, leading founders—Thomas Jefferson, James Madison, George Washington—relied on this latter rationale as a justification for separation of church and state.

The Enlightenment Impulse

A related argument for church-state separation arose out of the Enlightenment's emphasis on scientific inquiry, freedom of conscience, and religious toleration. The Enlightenment perspective challenged accepted epistemological orderings with their assumptions of God as the source of knowledge; instead, it shifted the source as resting in the human mind and obtained through observation and reason. Leaders of the emerging scientific revolution, such as Bacon and Newton, sought to identify universal natural laws of science that operated free from the mysteries and constraints of religious dogma. Though always careful to assert their laws of nature were consistent with God's laws and his reality, they emphasized that freedom of thought and inquiry were necessary prerequisites for scientific discovery. Free inquiry and freedom of conscience also meant that civil authorities should have limited authority to enforce religious discipline and conformity.[19] Other writers championed freedom of conscience and free inquiry. John Milton, who defended freedom of speech and the press in *Areopagitica* and other writings, insisted that "[t]o judge [over religious matters] as a civil magistrate he has no right. Christ hath a government of his own, sufficient of itself to all his ends and purposes in governing his church, but much different from that of the civil magistrate." Though those within this group did not fashion their arguments in terms of separation, they did distinguish the different spheres of authority of religious and civil officials.[20]

One of the more influential political thinkers on the founding generation was John Locke. Political and religious figures of the revolutionary era regularly quoted and rephrased Locke's writings.[21] Locke's most comprehensive work on religious matters, including ideas on toleration and church-state separation, was his *Letter on Toleration*, though related discussions appear in his *Two Treatises of Government* and *Essay Concerning Human Understanding*. Locke wrote about religion against the backdrop of the religious conflicts of the second half of the seventeenth century, and he attributed much of the political and religious turmoil of the era to instability created by religious intolerance and the assumption of religious authority by civil officers.[22]

The leading themes in Locke's *Letter* were that there was a firm distinction between religious and civil authority, that civil authorities lacked all power over religious matters, that religious judgments could not be compelled, and that any attempt to do so would create more social disorder. Religious toleration was key to ensuring civil peace and freedom of conscience. Another key factor was to separate the functions and authority of the church and the state. Each entity had limited duties and powers. "I regard it as necessary above all to distinguish between the business of civil government and that of religion," Locke began, "and to mark the true bounds between the church and commonwealth." A political commonwealth was "constituted only for preserving and advancing [people's] civil goods." However, "the care of souls is not committed to the civil magistrate. . . . It is not committed to him by God . . . [n]or can any such power be vested in the magistrate by men." Accordingly, Locke wrote, "the civil power ought not to prescribe articles of faith, or doctrines, or forms of worshipping God, by civil law." But

Locke went further, tying his vision of state and church disengagement to concepts of separationism. The church, Locke asserted, must be "absolutely separate and distinct from the commonwealth and civil affairs. The boundaries on both sides are fixed and immovable." Locke's understanding of separationism was not one-directional, however. As civil magistrates had their sphere, so did religious societies. The ultimate "end of a religious society" was "the public worship of God." All authority to discipline communicants and "all ecclesiastical laws [were] to be confined within these limits. In this society nothing is or can be done that relates to the possession of civil or earthly goods." That force "belongs wholly to the civil magistrate."[23]

Locke's notion of a "fixed and immovable" separationism contained several wrinkles, however. First, Locke did not call for religious disestablishment, even though that seemed to be the logical conclusion of his writings. Provided the church kept to its proper sphere and practiced toleration, an established church could supply a stabilizing and unifying function against sectarian strife. Locke also concluded that suppressing religious dissent was unjust and counterproductive. As he argued in his *Letter*, "it is not the diversity of opinions (which cannot be avoided)" that was the cause of religious strife; rather it was "the refusal of toleration to people of different opinions." As Madison would echo a century later, stability of government relied on a multiplicity of sects existing under a regime of equal standing: "All the several separate congregations, like so many guardians of the public peace, well keep a sharper watch on one another's behavior, that no innovations be plotted . . . because they can hope for nothing better than what they already enjoy, that is equal conditions with their fellow subjects." Thus, a multiplicity of sects and a tolerant establishment could work in tandem in ensuring civil and religious peace.[24]

Second, Locke's conception of separate and limited spheres of authority did not deprive civil magistrates of all power over religious matters. For Locke, the primary purpose of separation and toleration was not necessarily to advance religious freedom; rather, it was to safeguard the safety and security of civil society. Even though churches exercised exclusive control over their individual doctrines and modes of worship, actions that were illegal or tended to undermine civil peace could be suppressed. Locke famously wrote that a church "is a free and voluntary society." On one level, that restricted the ultimate claims and power a church had over any person, who could essentially affiliate or leave as he pleased. On another level, however, that declaration diminished the stature of the church to the status of other voluntary societies that operated to the extent they were consistent with needs of civil society. "[N]o doctrines, incompatible with human society, and contrary to the good morals which are necessary for the preservation of civil society, are to be tolerated by the magistrate." Similarly, those clergy who attributed "to themselves, any privilege or power above other mortals, in civil affairs; or who on the plea of religion claim any authority over men who do not belong to their ecclesiastical communion . . . these have no right to be tolerated by the magistrate; as neither have those who refuse to teach that dissenters from their own religion should be tolerated." Thus, intolerant religion was a threat to civil society and not to be tolerated. Scholars have argued that, at its core, Locke's version of separationism implied the ultimate supremacy of secular authority over religion. According to Sanford Kessler, although Locke "seems to advocate the strict separation of the two bodies, he in fact empowers the government to further undermine religion by restricting and reforming it to meet the needs of civil society."[25]

Because Locke accepted religious establishments and promoted the ultimate supremacy of civil authorities over religious entities, some scholars maintain that modern-day separationists are wrong to promote Locke as a progenitor of church-state separation. To be sure, Locke's understanding of separationism was less developed than understandings during the twentieth and twenty-first centuries. What is important, however, is not how advanced or "separationist" Locke's schema of separationism was by modern standards but that he, as a writer who influenced the thinking of so many members of the founding generation, proposed an argument on behalf of church-state separation. Unlike earlier writers' embrace of separatism—even Roger Williams's—Locke's was not hesitant or subtle. His schema also introduced a second rationale for separationism: to protect civil society from encroachments by the church and clergy. This second rationale for separation would influence Enlightenment and Whig writers later in the eighteenth century as well as founders including Jefferson and Madison.[26]

Two other Enlightenment theorists who wrote about religion and influenced the attitudes of the founding generation were Baron Montesquieu and David Hume. Both theorists agreed largely with Locke about the "problem with the church" as a source of discord but offered divergent solutions to that problem. Montesquieu was likely the only Enlightenment writer to match Locke's influence among the founders, in no small part for his advocacy for separation of powers.[27] Like Locke, Montesquieu criticized the power of the clergy and the corruptions of church doctrine. Yet Montesquieu was ambivalent about religious establishments, voicing admiration for the union between civil and religious authority that had existed in early Rome. For his own era, however, Montesquieu advocated different spheres of authority. Those "things that prejudice the tranquility or security of the state . . . are subject to human jurisdiction," he wrote. "But in those which offend the Deity, where there is no public act, there can be no criminal matter, the whole passes between man and God, who knows the measure and time of His vengeance." Mischief arose when civil magistrates engaged the notion "of revenging the cause of the Deity." Instead, magistrates should "enforce also a toleration among these religions themselves. It is a principle that every religion which is persecuted becomes itself persecuting." It was therefore necessary, Montesquieu insisted, "that the laws require from the several religions, not only that they shall not embroil the state, but that they shall not raise disturbances among themselves." Montesquieu was concerned that religion could easily become a force of evil, which would necessitate its correction by the state.[28]

Hume's critique of the corruptions of organized clergy far surpassed those of Locke and Montesquieu, earning him the reputation of being a skeptic if not an atheist. For Hume, the chief threat to civil government was faction and then religious faction, which was fomented largely by clergy. Religious faction lay in religious differences and strife and through the acquisition of political authority by leaders of the religious establishment, which he called the "priestly parties and bigots who fought over abstract political principles."[29] "[A]fter Christianity became the established religion," Hume wrote, the "priestly government . . . engendered a spirit of persecution, which has ever since been the poison of human society and the source of the most inveterate factions in every government." One would think this problem would have led Hume to advocate for disestablishment and a strict separation between religious and civil authority. But for his perfect commonwealth, Hume proposed a highly structured religious establishment under which civil magistrates would impose severe limitations on the power of the clergy. As he wrote in his *History of England*, "there must be an ecclesiastical order, and a public establishment of religion in every civilized community." This was because every religion, except "true" religion, "is highly pernicious" and has "a natural tendency to pervert the true [religion], by fusing into it a strong mixture of superstition, folly, and delusion." Hume's proposed establishment was a Presbyterian model, with magistrates authorized to "name rectors or ministers to all of the parishes." "Without the dependence of the clergy on the civil magistrates, and without a militia, it is vain to think that any free government will ever have security or stability."[30] It is widely accepted that Hume was a leading source for Madison's ideas about human nature and faction—particularly on religious faction that the latter wrote about in Federalist No. 10 and No. 51. While Madison largely accepted Hume's framing of the problem—the "latent causes of faction" included "[a] zeal for different opinions concerning religion," Madison wrote in Federalist No. 10—he proposed a vastly different solution: political stability through the "multiplicity of sects" and a separation of religious and civil functions and authority.[31]

Aside from Enlightenment theorists, the writers who most shaped the political thinking of the founding generation were the Real Whigs (or Radical Whigs). Essentially, the Whigs were a loose group of British aristocrats, intellectuals, and opposition politicians who advanced ideas of liberty, rights, and republicanism in mid-eighteenth-century England. Many held dissident or radical religious beliefs. One idea that unified Whigs was their criticism of the political machinations and corruption of members of the established clergy. Another constant topic Whig writers discussed was freedom of conscience. They advocated for greater religious toleration and a lessening of dogmatism within traditional Christianity. The Whig idea of tolerance extended beyond dissenting Protestants to include Arians, Unitarians, atheists, Jews, Muslims, and, for Joseph Priestley, even Catholics.[32]

Two of the more influential Whig writers were John Trenchard and Thomas Gordon, authors of the *Independent Whig* and *Cato's Letters* (1720–23). One historian has described the *Independent Whig* as "anticlerical and antipapistical," the latter term not being reserved for the Catholic Church: "The anticlericalism of the *Independent Whig* [was] its most striking characteristic." According to Bernard Bailyn, the *Independent Whig* attacked "High Church pretentions and, more generally, the establishment of religion." A similar theme ran through *Cato's Letters*, which was subtitled *Essays on Liberty, Civil and Religious, and Other Important Subjects*. Firm believers in religious tolerance and freedom of conscience, Trenchard and Gordon opposed all authority over individual religious exercise, whether that came from church officials or civil authorities. For Trenchard and Gordon, the "High-Church Jacobite Clergy" was the greatest threat to liberty, and they warned about the combined powers of church and state. Writing in the *Independent Whig*, Gordon asserted that "Religion is a voluntary Thing; it can no more be forced than Reason, or Memory, or any Faculty of the Soul. To be devout against our Will is an Absurdity. . . . We have no Power over the Appetites of others, no more than over their Consciences. Neither a Man's Mind nor his Palate, can be subject to the Jurisdiction of another." Although Trenchard and Gordon did not use the language of separationism, their writings emphasized separate spheres of authority among the government, the church, and the individual.[33]

Later opposition writers who advocated political and religious reform included Richard Price and Joseph Priestley, two religious radicals who criticized Britain's religious establishment. Price, an Arian, was a clergyman, a founder of early Unitarianism who supported American independence, and a prolific writer of political pamphlets whose American friends and subscribers included Benjamin Franklin, John Adams, Thomas Jefferson, and Thomas Paine. Price wrote in one of his more popular pamphlets that "RELIGIOUS LIBERTY signifies the power of exercising, without molestation that mode of religion we think best, or making decisions of our own consciences, respecting religious truth."[34]

Joseph Priestly, the discoverer of oxygen, was also a leader in Britain's Unitarian movement, going a step beyond Price's Arianism to embrace Socinianism. Like Price, Priestly corresponded with many members of the founding generation before he fled Britain in 1791, and his writings were widely read in America. In an early book, *An Essay on the First Principles of Government* (1768), Priestley called expressly for disestablishing the Church of England, labeling any "union of civil and ecclesiastical power" an "unnatural mixture." On one level, the two entities possessed different spheres of authority: "Civil and religious matters . . . seem to be so distinct." It was, he noted, "impossible to name any two things, about which men are concerned, [that are] so remote in their nature." Building on that observation, Priestley insisted that "all human establishments, as such, obstruct freedom of inquiry in matters of religion, by laying an undue bias upon the mind. . . . They are, therefore, incompatible with the genius of christianity." Establishments were also unnecessary to ensure public morals. Salutary laws "might be obeyed very well without any ecclesiastical sanctions, enforced by the civil magistrate," he asserted. Priestley even objected to nonpreferential government support of religion: "if all the modes of religion were equally protected by the civil magistrate, they would all vie with one another, which should best deserve that protection." Even though he did not use the exact terminology, Priestley essentially called for a separation between the two spheres: "the junction of civil and ecclesiastical powers hath done much mischief, and . . . it would have been a great blessing to the bulk of the people, if their magistrates had never interfered in matters of religion at all." Any "*alliance between church and state* is only the alliance of different sorts of worldly minded men, for their temporal emolument" (italics in original). In his later book *A History of the Corruptions of Christianity* (1782) (which disputed biblical miracles and essential church doctrines), Priestly called for repealing the Test and Corporation Acts, which required all office holders, as well as students at Oxford and Cambridge, to be communicants in the Church of England. Priestly insisted that true religious freedom could only exist under a regime of disestablishment, which required a greater separation of religious and secular realms than Locke and others had advocated.[35]

A final Whig writer who was particularly influential among many founders was Scottish schoolmaster and radical propagandist James Burgh, author of *Political Disquietations* and *Crito*. Burgh was an admirer of Lord Bolingbroke and John Locke, invoking the latter frequently in his writings, along with the works of Trenchard and Gordon. Burgh was a staunch proponent of religious toleration, but unlike Locke he extended that privilege to Catholics and possibly non-Christians. Like other radical Whigs, Burgh condemned the power and wealth of the clergy and church hierarchy, labeling "ecclesiastical corruption, the most odious of all corruptions." He also condemned Britain's religious establishment, calling it in colorful language "a mixed-mungrel-spiritual-temporal-secular-ecclesiastical establishment." He warned of "a church getting too much power into her hands, and turning religion into a mere state engine." To prevent this, Burgh called for building "an impenetrable wall of separation between things sacred and civil. . . . [T]he less the church and state had to do with one another, it would be better for both." This was likely another source for Jefferson's famous 1802 letter to the Danbury Baptists, where he used the same metaphor. Burgh's fans and subscribers included not only Jefferson but also Benjamin Franklin, George Washington, John Adams, John Dickinson, Benjamin Rush, and James Wilson, a veritable who's who of the founding generation.[36]

Relying on both impulses, the political and religious leaders of the founding period were able to draw on a long-standing intellectual tradition that promoted a separation between the authority and functions of religious and governmental entities. That idea, whether originating out of religious or Enlightenment/Whig strains or a combination of both, did not necessarily presuppose religious disestablishment or the way in which religious and civil officials interacted on an informal level. The separationist impulse also did not mean that civil magistrates, or civil society writ large, had no interest in the maintenance of public morality. And for the majority of secular and religious proponents, separation did not disable civil officials from observing religious traditions and customs; the modern conceptions of a secular culture and the privatization of religion would have been alien to most early advocates of separationism.

On its own, however, this intellectual tradition was insufficient in bringing about the actual disestablishment of religion at the state and federal levels or motivating people to endorse separationism as the model for church-state ordering in the new republic. It took several events preceding and continuing into the founding period to add urgency to changing existing church-state arrangements and to give meaning to the idea of church-state separation.

The Great Awakening

The first event that influenced peoples' ideas about church-state arrangements and the notion of separationism was what has been called the First Great Awakening. The Awakening was a series of religious revivals that broke out up and down the Eastern Seaboard in the late 1730s, gaining in intensity during the first half of the 1740s. Historians agree that the Awakening was a transformative event for American religion, both theologically and organizationally.[37] Aside from the revivals being the birthplace of American evangelicalism, their personalizing impulse challenged the clerical authority of the settled churches. The right to private judgment—that is, the ability to decide for oneself about matters of faith—meant that Christians no longer had to follow the admonitions of clergy who claimed authority over doctrine. And because the only legitimate faith was faith voluntarily arrived at, religious compulsion was ineffective and unjust. Once these ideas were implanted in people's minds, they invited them to challenge other sources of authority, including the established churches and their temporal patrons, in what historian Gordon Wood has called a "massive defiance of traditional authority." The right of private judgment and the concept of voluntarism on matters of religious belief and church affiliation also meant that religious bodies had no need for government help but should rather operate by voluntary support. Under this new schema, religious establishments, which supported the religious orthodoxy, were anachronistic if not contrary to this concept of voluntarism.[38] Whether the Awakening also laid the groundwork for the democratic impulse of the American Revolution, it contributed to the eventual disestablishment of colonial state churches. As historian Thomas Curry concluded, the "attitudinal and structural changes [brought about by the Awakening] ultimately transformed Church-State relations in America, although the transformation did not fully manifest itself until the revolutionary period."[39]

The revivals that spawned the Awakening declined in the 1740s, and they would shortly be overshadowed by other events of the midcentury, such as French and Indian War (1754–63), the Bishop Controversy (discussed below), and the political crises surrounding the Stamp Act and Intolerable Acts. Still, the aftereffects of the Awakening were long felt, particularly in backcountry areas, through the growth of evangelical bodies such as the New Side Presbyterians and Separate Baptists, to be followed by the Methodists. Itinerate ministers spread out through the less populated frontier where they found a sympathetic audience, one that was not particularly beholden to the established churches.[40]

New Side Presbyterian ministers were the first to work their way through the Piedmont regions of Virginia and North Carolina in the 1740s, following the earlier migration of Scotch Irish farmers. In North Carolina, with a struggling Anglican establishment and an existing religious pluralism of Quakers and Mennonites, Presbyterians faced little opposition. Virginia was a different story. Presbyterian ministers found a receptive audience among the Scotch Irish who resented the Virginia gentry and their Anglican clergy, and the evangelists frequently stirred up trouble by preaching against the incompetence and decadence of the established clergy. Civil and religious authorities took note when Presbyterian itinerates began infiltrating the Tidewater area and attracting large crowds. Authorities insisted that before itinerates could preach and benefit from the Act of Toleration, they had to obtain licenses; otherwise, they were "liable to be bound to their good Behavior and treated as Vagabonds by the Justice of the Peace."[41]

One account demonstrates the hostility that Presbyterian ministers encountered from civil and religious authorities. In 1745, in James City Parish (outside the capital of Williamsburg), two brothers, Joshua and John Morris, publicly withdrew from the Anglican Church, becoming dissenters. They invited Presbyterian itinerate John Roan to preach in their house over the course of several days. According to an account, Roan "inveighed against the clergy of the Established Church with great freedom, charging them not only with neglect of their official duties, but with gross moral delinquencies." Lieutenant Governor William Gooch and Anglican clergy heard about the activity, and the latter secured an indictment against Roan for blasphemy and "vilifying the Established Religion in diverse sermons . . . before a numerous audience unlawfully assembled." Roan fled to Pennsylvania before he could be arrested, but the court nonetheless issued an order forbidding any meetings of "Moravians, Muggletonians, and New Lights." Several who had attended the informal meetings at the Morrises' house were fined for unlawful assembly.[42] Not until the late 1750s, with Presbyterians firmly entrenched in Virginia and rising in social standing, did officials give up on efforts to restrict their churches. Because Presbyterians were willing to obtain licenses and otherwise work within the system, Lieutenant Governor Gooch would later remark that he considered them "not only [to be] tolerated but acknowledged as part of the established church of the realm."[43]

The same happy resolution did not await the Separate Baptists, who began expanding into Virginia and North Carolina in the 1750s and 1760s. Baptist itinerates were usually less educated than Presbyterian ministers, and their evangelical message commonly appealed to people of lower social standing. Chiefly for theological reasons, Separate Baptists refused to petition authorities for certificates for their clergy or licenses for their meeting houses. Rhys Isaac has argued that in addition to defying civil authority, the austere Baptists raised the ire of the gentry and other Anglicans by condemning their lifestyles and social practices. As a result, Virginia's civil and religious authorities persecuted Baptists with a vengeance.[44] According to one account, on a Sunday in 1771, a Baptist meeting was interrupted by an Anglican parson accompanied by his clerk and the local sheriff. As the preacher, John Waller, led the congregation in a hymn, the Anglican parson ran "the but end of his whip into Waller's mouth and silenced him." When Waller then attempted to pray, the clerk dragged him from the stage and beat his head on the ground, with the sheriff horsewhipping Waller some twenty times, scarring him for life. That same year, four other Baptist itinerates were attacked and beaten at other meetings in Virginia. Later in 1771, officials imprisoned Waller and several Baptist preachers for forty-six days for "not having an Episcopal Ordination to Teach or Preach the Gospel" and for engaging in actions "Destructive to the Peace of Society to the subversion of all Religious establishments."[45] The violence Waller experienced may have been exceptional, but indictments and imprisonment of Baptist ministers persisted throughout the period, and Baptist communicants were regularly fined for "willfully absenting themselves from Divine Service at their Parish Church." Despite such persecution from religious and civil authorities, Baptists did not initially call for disestablishment or church-state separation; rather, they sought the abolition of compulsory assessments and licensing requirements, not to mention the persecution, which were more immediate concerns. But the religious persecution they encountered, coupled with the growing disrepute of the Anglican establishment and its civil patrons, later lay the foundation for such calls.[46]

Although Virginia Baptists of the 1760s and 1770s were not yet calling for church-state separation, their struggle impacted its development in one indirect but highly significant way. In early 1774, a young James Madison, recently returned to Virginia from college in Princeton, New Jersey, discovered that a handful of Baptist ministers had been arrested and were being held in a nearby jail. He described the encounter and his reaction to it in a series of letters to his college friend William Bradford. In one dated January 24, 1774, Madison bemoaned the ongoing religious persecution that was taking place in Virginia, writing that he had "nothing to brag as to the State and Liberty of my [colony]." He railed against the "Pride[,] ignorance and Knavery among the Priesthood and Vice and Wickedness among the Laity" of the established church in Virginia. But the corruption among the Anglican clergy was "not the worst I have to tell you," he continued. "There are at this time in the adjacent County not less than 5 or 6 well meaning men in close Gaol for publishing their religious Sentiments which in the main are very orthodox." "That diabolical Hell conceived principle of persecution rages among some and to their eternal Infamy the Clergy can furnish their Quota of Imps for such business," Madison wrote. "So I leave you to pity me and pray for Liberty of Conscience to revive among us."[47]

Bradford replied in March, commiserating with his friend that he was "sorry to hear that Persecution has got so much footing among you." "Persecution is a weed that grows not in our happy soil [Pennsylvania]," Bradford remarked, "and I do not remember that any Person was ever imprisoned here for his religious sentiments however heretical or unepiscopal they might be." Madison responded quickly upon receiving his friend's letter, revealing that he found the matter still troubling. He related that the Virginia Assembly was about to consider a petition from the "Persecuted Baptists," with possible support from the Presbyterians, "for greater liberty in matters of Religion." Madison doubted the petition would succeed because the majority of legislators were "too much devoted to the ecclesiastical establishment to hear of the Toleration of Dissentients." Railing again against the Anglican establishment, Madison remarked that "the Clergy are a numerous and powerful body [and] have great influence at home by reason of their connection with & dependence on the Bishops and Crown and will naturally employ all their art & Interest to depress their rising Adversaries."[48]

Historians have pointed to this episode as foundational for Madison's ideas about church and state. There can be little doubt that the Baptists' imprisonment impacted Madison's perspective; later in life, he recounted the event, writing that he "spared no exertion to save them from imprisonment, and to promote their release from it." The Baptists' stance for religious liberty, Madison wrote, "obtained for [me] a lasting place in the favor of that particular sect."[49] Yet Madison had been thinking about church-state questions even before leaving college in 1772. In an earlier letter to "Billey" Bradford, Madison asked his friend for his thoughts concerning "religious Toleration." Raising a rhetorical question that demonstrated Madison's reading of David Hume, he inquired, "Is an Ecclesiastical Establishment absolutely necessary to support civil society in a supream Government?" And, he continued, "how far is it hurtful to a dependent state?" Madison's later encounter with the imprisoned Baptists provided a concrete reality to his intellectual ruminations about church-state matters. The experience likely contributed to his developing views about the separation of church and state.[50]

The Great Awakening also impacted the church-state arrangements in New England. The religious enthusiasm of the revivals precipitated a schism within Congregationalism, resulting in orthodox "Old Light" and revivalist "New Light" congregations. The latter self-identified as Strict Congregationalists or Separatists, with most shortly reorganizing as Separate Baptists. The existing General Baptists, with Arminian leanings, generally spurned the revivals because of their strong Calvinist thrust. After the Awakening, the two Baptist bodies maintained an uneasy relationship during the decades preceding the Revolution.[51] In the 1740s, the General Baptists secured from the Massachusetts Assembly two successive religious tax exemptions for "Baptists," the second in 1747 designed to last for ten years. But with the incursion and steady growth of the revivalist Separate Baptists, the assembly rescinded the exemption after five years, then reenacting a more restrictive one in 1753 that excluded Separate Baptists. Civil authorities frequently insisted that the Separate Baptists, many of whom had recently been Congregationalists, did not belong to a separate denomination but were merely schismatics and not entitled to an exemption. In addition, exemption certificate requirements were complicated and easily manipulated by officials; at times they required two or three attesting signatures, the signature of a full-time minister (at a time when many Baptist congregations shared part-time ministers), and a declaration of full membership, not just frequent attendance. Throughout this period, Baptists were regularly imprisoned and/or had their property distrained for failure to satisfy one or more requirement.[52]

In their initial struggles to overcome religious persecution, Baptists did not advocate for disestablishment, let alone call for separation of church and state. As William McLoughlin notes, for Baptists prior to 1773, liberty of conscience and freedom of religion represented "essentially a self-centered and denominationally oriented goal rather than an absolute or clearly enunciated principle." At the time, Baptist leader Isaac Backus "did not argue on behalf of dissenters generally or join with other groups to work for separation on an interdenominational basis." Rather, their chief goal was to abolish compulsory assessments and licensing fees. McLoughlin maintains that because Baptists were willing to accept compromise measures, they were often "ambiguous and often ambivalent in their attitude toward the relations of church and state."[53]

In the early 1770s, the perspective and approach of Backus and other Baptists began to evolve. Witnessing the growing political conflict between the Sons of Liberty and royal authorities, Baptist leaders decided in 1773 to change tactics and refuse to comply entirely with the certificate exemption system. (This coincided with the expiration of the 1770 Massachusetts exemption law that year.) As a means of steeling fellow Baptists for civil disobedience and to make their case to the larger community caught up in the debate over civil liberty, Backus wrote a sixty-two-page pamphlet, *An Appeal to the Public for Religious Liberty*, where for the first time he argued for abolishing tax support for churches and for the value of church-state separation. (Likely not by coincidence, Backus had discovered and read Roger Williams's writings that year.)[54] McLoughlin describes Backus's *Appeal* as the "Declaration of Independence of the Separate Baptists against the ecclesiastical tyranny of the Standing Order," with it owing "something to John Locke, a little to Williams, [and] much to Backus' reading of the Bible." Delving into the Baptists' pietistic heritage, Backus articulated the concept of two spheres: "God has appointed two kinds of government in this world, which are distinct in their nature, and ought never to be confounded together; one of which is called civil. The other ecclesiastical government." Yet the "very nature" of an establishment "implies an acknowledgement that the civil power has a right to set one religious sect up above another," Backus wrote. An establishment "emboldens people to judge the liberty of other men's consciences . . . [and] tends to destroy the purity and life of religion." But because Christ's kingdom was not of this world, "this blending of church and state together can[not] be pleasing to him." In addition to being unscriptural and injurious of true faith, establishments were unjust and ineffective: "religion is a *voluntary obedience unto God*, which therefore force cannot promote." Finally, Backus argued that establishments were "very hurtful to [a] civil society [committed to liberty]: for by the law of Christ *every man*, is not only allowed, but also required, to judge for himself, concerning the circumstantials as well as the essentials, of religion, and to act according to the *full persuasion of his own mind*."[55] Backus's comprehensive argument foreshadowed points Madison later articulated in his *Memorial and Remonstrance*. Although Backus's understanding of church-state separation was essentially limited to denying that civil authorities could regulate rights of conscience or compel support of religion—he did not object to Sabbath laws or public pronouncements of religion generally—he nonetheless articulated an early form of separationism that would become an essential component of Baptist political theology.[56]

The Bishop Controversy and Anticlericalism

A second event that led colonialists to reconsider existing church-state relationships and embrace disestablishment involved the machinations of the Church of England, including a long-simmering controversy over appointing an Anglican bishop for the American colonies. Even though the Church of England was officially established only in the southern colonies, church officials in England and America insisted on the church's privileged status in the other colonies; they viewed other Protestants—Congregationalists, Presbyterians, Baptists, and Quakers—as dissenters from the Church of England. (Lutherans, Dutch Reformed, and Mennonites were just dissenters.) The colonial Anglican Church was under the authority of the bishop of London, and, in 1701, the See established the Society for the Propagation of the Gospel in Foreign Parts (SPG) to send missionaries to evangelize indigenous natives, slaves, and nonadherents. Before long, however, the SPG's mission expanded to extend Anglican authority throughout the colonies, including proselytizing members of dissenting Protestant churches.[57]

The Anglican Church's new aggressiveness, particularly its efforts to convert Congregationalists and Presbyterians, raised the ire of dissenting leaders in the middle and New England colonies. Those concerns only heightened in 1750 when rumors circulated that church officials in England were considering appointing an Anglican bishop in America to oversee the church's activities. The proposal, building on existing tensions between Anglicans and Protestant dissenters, ushered in a two-decade controversy that by its end convinced many colonialists of the evils of religious establishments. Two Congregationalist clergymen in Massachusetts led the opposition to the appointment of a bishop, while in New York a pamphleteer assumed the same mantel.[58]

The first gauntlet came from Jonathan Mayhew, pastor of the liberal and affluent West Boston congregation, who in early 1750 delivered a sermon, "A Discourse Concerning Unlimited Submission and Non-Resistance to the Higher Powers," which asserted that the powers of civil authorities were limited, such that people could disobey their unjust directives. As the sermon's title suggested, Mayhew cleverly affirmed that because civil and religious officials received their authority from God, they were normally entitled to obedience. But that "unlimited submission" was due only those officials who faithfully followed God's will: "no civil rulers are to be obeyed when they enjoin things that are inconsistent with the commands of God," Mayhew wrote. "All such disobedience is lawful and glorious; particularly if persons refuse to comply with any *legal establishment of religion*, because it is a gross perversion and corruption." The thrust of Mayhew's sermon was that based on recent events, the Anglican episcopate had exceeded its authority. "A spirit of domination is always to be guarded against, both in church and state, even in times of the greatest security." Even though Mayhew did not condemn religious establishments outright, he emphasized that "ecclesiastical tyranny" is "the most cruel, intolerable, and impious of any" form of tyranny.[59]

Mayhew's sermon, quickly printed in pamphlet form, caused a sensation in New England and throughout the colonies, even making "a noise in Great Britain." Mayhew's *Discourse* "was read by everybody; celebrated by friends, and abused by enemies," John Adams later recounted. For many people, *Discourse* first articulated the idea of resistance to tyrannical civil and religious authority. Writing to another acquaintance in 1818, Adams recommended that anyone who wanted to understand "the principles and feelings which produced the Revolution" should read Mayhew's sermon and James Otis's pamphlet *A Vindication of the Conduct of the House of Representatives*. To Adams, Mayhew was a "transcendent genius."[60]

On the heels of Mayhew's sermon, a related controversy broke out in New York over political maneuvering by Anglican authorities to secure their privilege and authority there. In 1748, Anglican clergy petitioned the New York Assembly for exclusive authority to perform marriage ceremonies. Although that effort failed, it exasperated relations with the Presbyterians and Dutch Reformed. Then, in 1751, Anglican authorities set their sights on seizing control over King's College, which the assembly had recently authorized for New York City.[61] The machinations elicited an outcry from New York's dissenting religious community, led by William Livingston, who founded a newspaper in 1752, the *Independent Reflector*, to expose official corruption and advocate for reform. In his broadsides, Livingston did not limit himself to criticizing the actions of the Anglican leadership but also attacked the practice of religious establishments themselves. Establishments were perpetuated "by the unutterable Miseries of PRIEST-CRAFT," which throughout history had "reduc[ed] Nations and Empires to Beggary and Bondage" and people to "Vassalage."[62] In a different article, Livingston explained his understanding of church-state relations:

> Matters of Religion relate to another World, and have nothing to do with the Interest of the State. The first resides in the Minds and Consciences of Men; the latter in the outward Peace and Prosperity of the Public. It is the Business of the civil Power, to see that the Common-Wealth suffer no Injury. . . . But provide he hurt no Man, every Subject has a Right to be protected in the Exercise of the Liberty of thinking about Religion, as he judges proper, as well as acting in Conformity thereto.

Livingston asserted that "Religious Opinions and Speculations come not therefore within the Design of cloathing the Magistrate with a Superiority over the Subject."[63]

A newly arrived Anglican apologist, William Smith, responded to Livingston's remonstrances. Smith disputed the value of a right to private judgment, asserting that "[i]f, according to the *Reflector's* Scheme, all Religions were equally favor'd by the Civil Power, none establish'd, and every Man left at Liberty to preach and practise what he thought proper, what a Scene of Confusion would thence arise . . . from such unbridled Liberty of Conscience." This "leveling Notion, [of] a perfect Equality among all religious Persuasions," Smith claimed, had no basis in British liberty, but rather "seems to have [been] borrow'd . . . from Voltaire." Smith also demonstrated his insensitivity to the concerns of non-Anglicans over the political implications of an establishment. Continuing, Smith sniped that only "a very shallow Politician" does not see "the Political Uses of national Establishments." Civil authorities had "always found it necessary for the Purposes of Government, to raise one Denomination of religions above the Rest to a certain Degree. This favor'd Denomination, by these Means, becomes as it were the Creature of the Government, which is thus enabled to turn the Balance and keep all in Subjection." Why would a government "give away the Power of bestowing its own Favors," Smith asked rhetorically, "and let all Sects and Persuasions be equally favor'd?" Whether intended or not, Smith confirmed the worst fears of American dissenters about the effects of consolidating Anglican authority through a robust establishment.[64]

The controversy over King's College continued several more years, perpetuating sectarian divisions in New York. It was eventually chartered as an Anglican institution but at a cost to the church's standing among dissenters. In retirement, Madison reflected how, when he was a student in Princeton from 1769 to 1771, William Livingston served as a trustee there and that students read copies of the *Independent Reflector*, which Madison "admired for the energy and eloquence of their composition."[65]

The Bishop Controversy resurfaced in the early 1760s following the appointment of Thomas Seeker as archbishop of Canterbury. In addition to overseeing the SPG, Archbishop Secker favored appointing a bishop for the American colonies.[66] Now the religious controversy became entangled with growing political tensions as American colonialists faced a parliamentary aggression that matched that of the Anglican Church. In order to pay for the recently concluded Seven Years War and otherwise raise revenue, Parliament enacted a series of taxes and duties, culminating in the Stamp Act and the Townshend Acts, along with a law that required colonies to provide for the quartering of British troops. The political protests over these measures transformed American attitudes toward the British government and lay the groundwork for the American Revolution. The cries of liberty against

British political tyranny quickly bled over into the religious arena. The various parliamentary measures demonstrated the dangers of expanded British authority in the colonies, which by implication included expanded ecclesiastical authority. According to one historian of the period, in the 1760s there was "a discernable shift in the American nonconformists' polemic against the Church of England." The "non-Anglican opposition to the Church of England accordingly fell easily into alliance with colonial opposition to Parliament." From that point on, "Church and government [were] castigated as joint opponents of American liberty."[67]

At the cusp of the political conflict, Mayhew published another missive, this time more condemnatory of the Anglican Church's actions. In his *Observations on the Character and Conduct of the Society* (1763), he attacked the SPG for sending missionaries into New England to convert Congregationalists. Now Mayhew tied the SPG threat directly to the proposed appointment of a bishop; the society had a "formal design to root out Presbyterianism, etc., and to establish both Episcopacy and Bishops" in New England, he claimed. Not mincing words, Mayhew charged that SPG missionaries were the "entering wedges" in "carrying on the crusade, or spiritual siege of our churches, with the hope that they will one day submit to an episcopal sovereign." A bishop would not just oversee the operations of the colonial Anglican Church by ordaining priests and directing SPG missionaries; rather, an episcopacy would include the entire apparatus of a religious establishment with church courts and bishops exerting political influence on colonial assemblies to tax non-Anglicans and exclude them from positions in government. This was "the true plan, the grand mystery, of their operations in New England," Mayhew asserted.[68]

Four years later, Charles Chauncy, the other leading light of New England Congregationalism, repeated Mayhew's charges. Early in 1767, the bishop of Llandaff had addressed the SPG in England, where he lamented the obstacles facing the SPG in America due to the lack of a supporting episcopacy. After excerpts of the bishop's remarks appeared in Boston, Chauncy published a *Letter to a Friend* to draw attention to Anglican designs. If bishops were appointed in the colonies, Chauncy asserted, they would exert their influence on the colonial assemblies to "force the growth of the Church" at the expense of dissenters and their voluntary religion. Echoing Mayhew's earlier accusations, Chauncy claimed that "[t]he conduct of the Society has, for many years, given us reason to suspect their MAIN VIEW was to EPISCOPISE the Colonies, but we never before, that I know of, told so in direct terms."[69]

Chauncy's *Letter* represented the opening salvo in the most active phase of the Bishop Controversy. Coinciding with Chauncy's *Letter*, Thomas

Chandler, rector of St. John's Church in Elizabethtown, New Jersey, wrote a vigorous defense of a colonial bishop, titled *An Appeal to the Public on Behalf of the Church of England in America*. Chandler asserted that Anglicans only desired the same privileges as other Protestants, including the ability to manage their internal church operations, including ordaining priests, which required a bishop. Seeking to address dissenters' concerns, Chandler insisted that any bishops sent to America "shall have no Authority, but purely of a Spiritual and Ecclesiastical Nature, such as derived altogether from the Church and not from the State." Their authority "shall operate only upon the Clergy of the Church, and not upon the Laity nor Dissenters of any Denomination," he asserted. Also seeking to rebut charges that an episcopate would include political powers, Chandler promised that "the Bishops shall not interfere with the Property of Privileges, whether civil or religious of Churchmen or Dissenters." In essence, an American episcopate would not create an established church as in England.[70] Chauncy responded the following year (1768) with his *Appeal Answered*, which, after refuting the need for a bishop, disputed that a bishop could exist without his normal authority as an officer of the state. "We are as fully persuaded," Chauncy wrote, "as if they had openly said it, that they have in view nothing short of a COMPLETE CHURCH HIERARCHY, after all the patterns of that at home." Chauncy then launched into a discussion about the evils of a religious establishment:

> We are in principle against all civil establishment in religion. It does not appear to us that God has entrusted the State with a right to make religious establishments. . . . [W]e claim no right to desire the interposition of the State to establish that mode of worship, [church] government, or discipline we apprehend is most agreeable to the mind of Christ. . . . Episcopalians . . . want to be distinguished by having bishops upon the footing of a state establishment. The plain truth is, by the Gospel-charter, all professed Christians are vested with precisely the same rights; nor has one denomination any more right to the interposition of the civil magistrate in their favor than another.[71]

Chauncy's *Appeal Answered* made several points. One was jurisdictional—that the government and the church possessed different realms of authority. A related point was that the voluntary church did not need assistance from civil authorities to promote church doctrines or modes of worship. And, finally, Chauncy asserted that all denominations existed on equal status in relation to government and were entitled to equal rights. Establishments contradicted the equal station of all religions.[72]

Over the next three years, Chandler and Chauncy exchanged a series of rebuttals in pamphlets, with neither convincing members of the opposing camps. It was in this climate that a young John Adams penned his own dissertation about the evils of church-state arrangements. *A Dissertation on the Canon and Feudal Law* warned its readers about the "infernal confederacy [of] ecclesiastical and civil tyranny." The most calamitous event for human liberty, Adams wrote, was the creation of the "wicked confederacy between the two systems of tyranny," ecclesiastical and civil authority. The latter had "contribute[d] every thing in their power to maintain the ascendancy of the priesthood," while "the spiritual grandees in their turn . . . employ[ed] their ascendancy over the consciences of the people, in impressing on their minds a blind, implicit obedience to civil magistracy."[73] Later in life, Adams wrote that that "the apprehension of Episcopacy contributed . . . as much as any other cause to arouse the attention, not only of the inquiring mind, but of the common people" to the patriots' cause. "The objection was not merely to the office of a bishop, though even that was dreaded, but to the authority of parliament, on which it must be founded." The proposed appointment of a bishop "spread a universal alarm against the authority of Parliament," Adams remembered, and "excited a general and just apprehension" throughout the colonies. Historian Patricia Bonomi claims that the Bishop Controversy "easily consumed as much paper as the Stamp Act dispute" of 1765.[74] The American Revolution brought an end to the controversy, but the episode was fresh on the minds of colonialists as they undertook steps toward disestablishment.

The antiestablishment perspectives engendered by the Great Awakening and the Anglican controversy and the way both events supported evolving notions of the right of conscience and religious equality—not just religious toleration—helped to set the foundation for disestablishment at the state and federal levels. These perspectives also complemented Enlightenment and Whig ideas of freedom of conscience and distrust of clerical authority. Together they would fuel the impulse for disestablishment and fuller conceptions of church-state separation.

CHAPTER 2

Disestablishment and Separationism

The dismantling of America's religious establishments took approximately fifty years, from 1776 to 1833. That time frame is misleading, however. Outside of New England, disestablishment occurred at an amazingly rapid pace considering the entrenched establishments that existed in many colonies and the idea, accepted by many people, of the duty of government to ensure public piety and morals. The transformation was truly remarkable. In a short ten-year period, from 1776 to 1786, the number of functioning religious establishments went from nine to three (or four, depending on how one interprets Vermont's arrangement). Although calls for church-state separation did not lead to that change, notions of separationism informed it. To appreciate that transformation, one must understand the church-state arrangements and dynamics of mid-eighteenth-century colonial America.

Colonial Establishments

In the eighteenth century, the Church of England was the officially established church in all lands of the British realm, Scotland excluded. Pursuant to the 1707 Act of Union, the Anglican Church was the only recognized and privileged church, and members of other religious bodies existed as nonconformists or dissenters subject to the Act of Toleration of 1689. Despite this legal establishment, the myriad church-state arrangements in the British-American colonies challenged the facade of religious conformity. Those arrangements depended in large part on the legal status of the colonies—charter, proprietary, or royal—and on the religious background of the initial settlers of each colony: Puritan, Dutch Reformed, Quaker, Catholic, or Anglican.[1]

By midcentury, nine of thirteen colonies maintained some form of a religious establishment. This meant that residents were taxed to support clergy salaries and houses of worship and that only established clergy could officiate quasi-legal functions such as performing baptisms, marriages, and funerals and supervising guardianships and estates. In addition, establishment frequently meant that the holding of public office and other civic opportunities were limited to communicants of the established church and that public officials exercised authority over creating new churches or parishes, determining clergy remuneration, and approving church doctrine and practices. Finally, an establishment usually meant that dissenting clergy and their congregations were required to obtain licenses or permits in order to preach or build their houses of worship.[2]

That definition belies the intricacies of the religious establishments that existed throughout the various colonies. In the southern colonies (Virginia, Maryland, Georgia, and North and South Carolina), colonial assemblies established the Church of England by law. All colonists were taxed to maintain Anglican churches and clergy, the latter also receiving glebe lands from colonial assemblies as supplemental income. As noted, only Anglican clergy could perform certain ceremonies, such as marriages, and only Anglican churches received legal protection and could own property. All other religious societies existed as dissenters, with their clergy frequently harassed by officials, ineligible to partake in the benefits of being officially recognized. The "benefits" of being officially established flowed in both directions, however. The absence of an Anglican bishop in the colonies meant that colonial assemblies exercised authority over the immediate operations of the Anglican churches. Assemblies created parishes, determined clergy salaries, and delegated authority to parish vestrymen, members of the local planter elite, to select clergy and oversee doctrinal compliance.[3]

Unlike the other southern colonies, Maryland had not been founded with the presumption of maintaining an Anglican establishment. Its founders, the Lords Baltimore (George and Cecil Calvert), were converts to Catholicism who established their colony essentially as a commercial venture. Still, they envisioned a colony where Catholics and Protestants could peacefully coexist, and they insisted that their representatives promote a degree of religious toleration unmatched in the other colonies at the time. Unlike other early colonies, Maryland imposed no religious test for voting or officeholding. In 1649, facing a hostile British Parliament controlled by Puritans, the Calverts directed the Maryland Assembly to enact the Act Concerning Religion, which memorialized the de facto policy of religious toleration. The act, the first of its kind in America, provided that "noe person . . . professing to believe in Jesus Christ, shall from henceforth bee any waies troubled, Molested, or discountanenced . . . for . . . his or her religion or in the free exercise thereof . . . nor any way compelled to be beleife or exercise of any other Religion against his or her consent." The assembly rescinded the act when the Calverts lost control of Maryland during the Commonwealth but reinstated it after the Calverts regained control with the Stuart Restoration. Following the Glorious Revolution (1688) and the deposing of the Catholic King James II, disgruntled Maryland Protestants seized power, raising false claims of Catholic intolerance. The new royal governors instituted a series of laws disenfranchising Catholics, requiring public worship according to the Anglican *Book of Common Prayer*, and, in 1702, formally established the Church of England. Maryland's brief experiment in religious tolerance came to an end, a victim of the Anglican establishment.[4]

The Anglican establishment operated most effectively in the Tidewater and near-Piedmont regions of Maryland, Virginia, and South Carolina. In the backcountry, particularly in expansive North Carolina, the Anglican establishment was all but nonexistent. Beginning in the latter seventeenth century and continuing into the next, Quakers and Moravians migrated down to the Piedmont areas of Virginia, North Carolina, and South Carolina. Around the same time, Charleston experienced an influx of French Huguenots and then Jews from England and the Dutch Republic, whereas Georgia became a haven for other religious groups—Lutherans, Moravians, and Scottish Presbyterians—also fleeing political and economic distress. Then, beginning in the 1740s, southern colonies experienced the effects of the religious enthusiasm resulting from the Great Awakening. New Side Presbyterian and Separate Baptist itinerates traveled the same Piedmont path, holding revivals and accumulating converts in the backcountry, adding to the colonies' religious pluralism and setting the stage for future religious discord.[5]

Founded by Puritan dissenters from the Church of England, the New England colonies of Massachusetts, Connecticut, and New Hampshire maintained a different form of establishment. Their colonial assemblies enacted laws providing for "orthodox" ministers and authorizing towns to impose taxes for their support and to maintain meeting houses. At the same time,

Puritan officials persecuted and banished religious dissenters such as Baptists and Quakers. Puritans generally denied that they operated a religious establishment—a term they identified with the Church of England—although in 1692 the Massachusetts General Court enacted a law for "the Establishment of the Christian Religion." The 1692 Act for the Settlement and Support of Ministers and Schoolmasters established each town as a parish and required residents to hire "an able, learned, orthodox minister" for it, to be supported by an annual tax on all inhabitants. "Orthodox," of course, meant a Congregational (or possibly Presbyterian) minister. Connecticut followed suit, enacting its Saybrook Platform in 1708.[6] Dissenters—Baptists, Quakers, and even Anglicans—were taxed to support the local Congregational church and the minister selected by the parish members. Facing ongoing complaints by Anglican clergy and church officials in England, the Massachusetts and Connecticut assemblies enacted laws in 1727 exempting Anglicans from supporting the settled church, followed shortly by laws exempting Baptists and Quakers as well. In Massachusetts, the exemption laws were at first temporary, requiring dissenters to file new petitions with the General Court for extensions while facing the threat of imprisonment and distraint of property in the interim. When in effect, these exemption laws technically created a "multiple establishment" system, where a person's assessment could be assigned to the religious society of his choosing. In reality, the system favored Congregational churches, as non-Congregationalists had to convince assessors they were bona fide members of another church with a minister certified by authorities.[7]

A third form of religious establishment existed in New York, which had been founded as New Netherland by the Dutch in 1624. The Dutch Reformed Church was established as the official religion, with the 1640 charter providing that "no other Religion shall be publically admitted in New Netherland except the Reformed," which by default allowed Presbyterians and Independents (Puritans) to support their own congregations. Before long, Dutch Calvinists were outnumbered by immigrants who were lured to the colony by its tolerant policies and generous land grants. Commenting on the colony's growing religious pluralism, a Dutch Reformed pastor wrote in 1655 that "[w]e have here Papists, Mennonites, and Lutherans among the Dutch; also many Puritans or Independents, and many Atheists. . . . [I]t would create still further confusion, if the obstinate and immovable Jews came to settle here." The colony's religious diversity led the intractable Governor Peter Stuyvesant to strike out against non-Reformed groups, particularly Quakers, but his actions were rebuked by the directors of the Dutch West India Company, who viewed religious intolerance as contrary to their commercial interests.[8]

In 1664, the British seized New Netherland, renaming it New York in honor of its new patron, the Duke of York (the future King James II). New York was already the most religiously diverse colony in the Americas, a title it would retain through to independence. In order to reassure residents and ensure commercial stability, James directed the new assembly to enact the Duke's Laws (1665), which afforded rights of worship to all Christians and abolished religious tests for officeholding. The law also required each town/ parish to build a church and call a Protestant minister according to the preference of the majority of town residents. Following the Act of Toleration (1689), Anglican leaders insisted that the Church of England was established in New York, with other denominations relegated to the status of dissenters under the act. Other denominations were not about to go backward, so they petitioned the assembly for redress. In 1691, the assembly enacted a law protecting the rights of conscience and public worship and then in 1693 enacted the Ministry Act, which directed towns to select a "good sufficient Protestant" to be supported by a local assessment. Despite ongoing claims by Anglican authorities that the Church of England was legally established, the act's failure to mention any denomination by name ensured that a majority of town residents decided whether their settled church would be Dutch Reformed, Presbyterian, or Lutheran rather than Anglican. Only by exerting political pressure did the royal governor succeed in having the newly founded Trinity Church (Anglican) designated the established church of New York City in 1697. After the city's Dutch residents complained, British authorities granted a charter to the Dutch Reformed Church, effectively exempting it and its members from supporting the city's Anglican establishment. As a result, by the eighteenth century, New York operated two putative religious establishments: an Anglican "establishment" in the lower four counties surrounding Manhattan (with the Dutch Reformed effectively exempt) and then a multiple, local-option establishment for the rest of the colony.[9]

In the four remaining British-American colonies, a religious establishment never took root, either by plan or default or a combination of both. Rhode Island was founded in 1636 by Roger Williams and other dissenters from Puritanism who had either fled persecution or were banished from the New England colonies. Williams's strong theological inclinations, having transitioned from being a Puritan to a Separatist to a Baptist, led him to reject any temporal authority over spiritual matters. For Williams, this meant complete freedom of conscience about theological matters and the absence of any religious establishment. Rhode Island became a haven for religious dissenters but also for social misfits, none of whom were inclined to agitate for a connection between civil government and religion. Nonetheless, Rhode

Island was rife with religious and political discord as churches divided and towns quarreled, leading outsiders to point to the consequences of rejecting a religious establishment. The colony existed on a tenuous legal status until it secured a royal charter in 1663. The charter did not expressly disclaim religious establishments, let alone declare church and state to be separate as Williams believed; rather, it declared that "noe person within the sayd colony . . . shall bee any wise molested, punished, disquieted, or called in question, for any differences in opinione in maters of religion [provided he] doe not actually disturb the civill peace of our sayd colony." The closest the charter came to disclaiming government authority over religious matters was a clause that asserted that the above rights would remain inviolate against "any lawe, statute, or clause . . . [or] usae or custome of this realme, to the contrary hereof, in any wise, notwithstanding." Despite rejecting an establishment and guaranteeing a fair degree of religious freedom, Rhode Island did not serve as a model for other colonies, chiefly because outsiders had difficulty distinguishing its religious experiment from its reputation as a haven for social and political disorder.[10]

The colony that members of the founding period held out as a model of religious freedom was Pennsylvania. Like Williams, William Penn's convictions for religious liberty sprang from his theological beliefs. As a Quaker, Penn believed that all knowledge of God came from uncovering an inner spark of the divine ("inner light") that every person possessed, which did not come from external sources. This required absolute freedom of conscience. All attempts at religious compulsion or uniformity were profane and contrary to God's will and interfered with the ability of people to discover that inner light. In his work *The Great Cause of Liberty of Conscience*, Penn insisted that religious compulsion was not only unjust; it was also unscriptural, noting that "imposition, restraint and persecution for conscience sake, highly invade the Divine prerogative." The Frame of Government of Pennsylvania therefore decreed that all persons who "acknowledge the one Almighty and Eternal God . . . shall, in no ways, be molested or prejudiced for their religious persuasion, or practice in matters of faith and worship, nor shall they be compelled, at any time, to frequent or maintain any religious worship, place or ministry whatsoever."[11] Motivated by these theological convictions and a desire to attract people to his colony for it to prosper, Penn and his agents recruited religious dissenters to migrate to the colony, distributing advertisements throughout Britain and the German Rhine Valley, where Pietists were suffering at the hands of Lutheran and Catholic princes. These latter groups—Mennonites, Moravians, Brethren, German Reformed—immigrated to Pennsylvania seeking religious freedom and economic security, quickly making it a very religiously diverse colony. As a result, creating a religious establishment in Pennsylvania would have been both theologically inconsistent and practicably impossible. Yet even though Penn believed that religious matters were "consequently wholly independent of the secular affairs" of the state, he still envisioned an informal Christian commonwealth, one in which Quakers would set the moral tone of society.[12]

The final two colonies, New Jersey and Delaware, were both strongly influenced by Pennsylvania's experiment in religious toleration and nonestablishment. In its early years, New Jersey operated under the control of Quaker proprietors, including William Penn, whereas Delaware was created out of lower Pennsylvania in 1701. Quakers never constituted the majority in either colony, and although Scottish Presbyterians and Congregationalists predominated, neither colony created a religious establishment. New Jersey's Fundamental Constitution of 1683 borrowed language from Pennsylvania's Frame of Government saying that no person shall "be compelled, at any time, to frequent or maintain any religious worship, place or ministry whatsoever," and in 1697 the New Jersey Assembly rejected an attempt to set up an assessment system for ministers. Similarly, Delaware's 1701 charter provided that no one would be "molested or prejudiced . . . because of his or their conscientious Persuasion or Practice, nor be compelled to frequent or maintain any religious Worship, Place or Ministry, contrary to his or their Mind."[13]

Thus, entering the founding period, the American colonies offered a variety of church-state arrangements, ranging from single-church establishments (Virginia), to de facto establishments (Massachusetts), to multiple establishments (New York), to no establishments (Pennsylvania). No colony, however—even those without an official establishment—practiced full religious freedom, even by eighteenth-century standards. All colonies enacted and enforced behavioral laws—regulating Sabbath activities or requiring church attendance, prohibiting public swearing, blasphemy, adultery, drunkenness, and gambling—and restricted officeholding and civic participation to Protestants. Outside of Rhode Island, entrenched religious majorities imposed official and unofficial barriers to prevent equal opportunities for religious minorities. Mere toleration of dissenting religious believers was the rule up and down the Eastern Seaboard.[14]

State Disestablishment

In May 1776, the Second Continental Congress enacted a resolution recommending to "the respective assemblies and conventions of the United

Colonies . . . to adopt such government as shall, in the opinion of the representatives of the people, best conduce to the happiness and safety of their constituents." Despite the open-ended language in the resolution, Congress expected the various colonies to reorganize as *states* and write constitutions grounded on republican principles. They needed little encouragement, as that year eight states enacted constitutions, with three more following suit in 1777, one being the new breakaway state of Vermont. One issue the new state assemblies had to address was what to do with their existing church-state arrangements. Some states had an easier time of it than others.[15]

Connecticut, Massachusetts, and New Hampshire did not interpret Congress's recommendation to write constitutions as an invitation to abolish their religious assessment systems, which ostensibly operated as multiple establishments. (By virtue of continuing under its royal charter, Connecticut did not reconsider its assessment system until it adopted a constitution in 1818. Massachusetts will be discussed in more detail below.) New Hampshire responded immediately to Congress's recommendation, becoming the first state to draft a constitution. Its constitution of 1776 was exceptionally brief, chiefly declaring the state's independence, leaving its religious assessment unmentioned. The New Hampshire Constitution of 1784 contained more detail, providing that "morality and piety, rightly grounded on evangelical principles, will give the best and greatest security to the government, and . . . the knowledge of these, is most likely to be propagated through a society by the institution of public worship of the Deity, and public instruction in morality and religion." The constitution merely continued New Hampshire's system of multiple establishments, where each town would "make adequate provision" through a general assessment "for the support and maintenance of public protestant teachers of piety, religion, and morality." Dissenting Protestants could designate their taxes for their own ministers, provided their churches were incorporated by the state; noncooperative dissenters were forced to pay for the majority denomination. This was the New England way.[16]

In New York, the colonial religious establishment had also been controversial. In April 1777, a convention adopted a constitution that guaranteed "the free exercise and enjoyment of religious profession and worship without discrimination or preference." As in most states, the constitution authorized the continuation of the common law but expressly stated that those "parts thereof, as may be construed to establish or maintain any particular denomination of Christians or their ministers . . . hereby are abrogated and rejected." An earlier draft of that article had specifically forbidden any establishment of the Church of England, indicating that many delegates still resented the earlier machinations of the Anglican Church, but in the end they substituted the broader phrase "any particular denomination of Christians." Additional evidence of residual ill will is found in another provision, which declared that because "the bigotry and ambition of weak and wicked priests and princes have scourged mankind," the people must "guard against that spiritual oppression and intolerance" that flowed from an establishment. If that statement was not sufficiently clear, the constitution then declared that priests and ministers of the gospel were ineligible to hold any civil or military office in the state. The delegates to the New York convention were making an unmistakable point about their disdain for religious establishments.[17]

Elsewhere, the new North Carolina Assembly quickly abolished its moribund establishment, declaring that there "shall be no establishment of any religious church or denomination . . . in preference to any other." In order to prevent any misunderstanding that such language permitted a multiple establishment, the article also provided that "neither shall any person . . . be compelled to attend any place of worship contrary to his own faith or judgment, nor be obliged to pay for . . . the building of any house of worship, or the maintenance of any minister or ministry," constituting one of the earlier stated "no compelled support" clauses. North Carolina, too, was making a point.[18]

Aside for North Carolina, lawmakers in the new southern states struggled with whether and how much to disestablish. During the Revolution, the Anglican establishments had become essentially inoperable, a fallout from the transition from colonial to state governments. Many patriots also held an unfavorable view of the Anglican Church due to its close association with the British government. Those facts, however, did not dissuade lawmakers from addressing the issue. Not surprisingly, with their long tradition of an Anglican establishment, southern states were initially hesitant to fully disestablish, with Georgia, South Carolina, and Maryland ostensibly creating multiple-establishment systems in their respective constitutions. In Georgia, delegates wrote a constitution in 1777 that guaranteed the free exercise of religion, while declaring that no person, "unless by consent, [shall] support any teacher or teachers [of religion] except those of their own profession." That last provision authorized a state-levied assessment, and in 1785 the assembly enacted a law for "the regular establishment and support of the public duties of Religion." The statute's preamble pronounced that the "regular establishment and support [of Christianity] is among the most important objects of Legislature [sic] determination," and it additionally provided that every county with at least thirty families could select a minister to receive the assessment. There is no indication that this law ever went into effect. A new constitution in 1789 reaffirmed that no persons were "obliged to contribute to support any religious profession but their own," but again no assessment ever occurred. Finally, in 1798, Georgia's third constitution formally disestablished, relieving the obligation of church-goers from having to financially support their own churches.[19]

The Anglican establishment in colonial South Carolina had been healthier than in its neighbors to the north and south, and interest remained in maintaining some form of an establishment. What resulted in the 1778 constitution was a paradox. In a lengthy provision, article 38 announced that the "Christian Protestant religion" was deemed "constituted and declared to be, the established religion of this State." Unwilling to allow just any Protestant church to claim the status of "established," the article required that as a prerequisite of receiving incorporation, each church had to subscribe to five doctrines of faith:

> 1st. That there is one eternal God, and a future state of rewards and punishments.
> 2nd. That God is publicly to be worshipped.
> 3nd. That the Christian religion is the true religion.
> 4th. That the holy scriptures of the Old and New Testaments are of divine inspiration, and are the rule of faith and practice.
> 5th. That it is lawful and the duty of every man being thereunto called by those that govern, to bear witness to the truth.

Finally, only persons and religious societies "who acknowledge[d] that there is one God, and a future state of rewards and punishments . . . shall be freely tolerated" or eligible for public office.[20]

Although article 38 created the appearance that South Carolina was regressing on the issue of an establishment, its language was chiefly hortatory. At the same time that article 38 imposed a religious test for officeholding, it allowed a witness to swear "in that way which is most agreeable to the dictates of his own conscience," thereby including Quakers and Mennonites. Most significant, the article concluded by providing that "[n]o person shall, by law, be obliged to pay towards the maintenance and support of a religious worship that he does not freely join in, or has not voluntarily engaged to support." By omitting a provision for enforcing that "freely joined" obligation and substituting notions of voluntary support in lieu of forced taxation, the 1778 constitution all but gutted the understanding of an establishment. Although Protestant churches still maintained a public role, South Carolina's "establishment" amounted to "a method of incorporating churches, and no church received public tax support."[21]

The Maryland Constitution of 1776 also reflected uncertainty over what was the appropriate church-state arrangement in a republican government, and the constitution included three provisions that touched on the matter. Article 33 initially proclaimed equal religious liberty to all professors of Christianity, renouncing the legal disability that had been imposed on Catholics and other dissenters in 1702. The article then provided that no person "ought . . . to be compelled to frequent or maintain, or contribute, unless under contract, to maintain any particular place of worship, or of any particular ministry," language that appeared to abolish the collection of religious assessments. The next sentence then inconsistently authorized the legislature to "lay a general and equal tax, for the support of the Christian religion," allowing each taxpayer to designate his assessment to a "particular place of worship or minister, or for the benefit of the poor of his own denomination." This created a multiple establishment, not dissimilar from what ostensibly existed in New England. Yet, unlike the rationale for assessments in the New England states, this tax was not to support "public teachers" of religion or advance a common morality but was an assessment to maintain *churches*. But as in Georgia, no religious assessment ever went into effect. Despite creating the framework for an assessment, Maryland voters in 1785 rejected a proposed tax, preventing any mechanism for an establishment. The state formally repealed the provision in article 33 in 1810.[22]

Vermont's path to disestablishment was closer to Maryland's than to its neighboring New England states. As in Maryland, the Vermont Constitution of 1777 contained contradictory language regarding religious assessments. Article III initially affirmed the "natural and unalienable right [of people] to worship . . . according to the dictates of their own consciences and understanding." Emphasizing a principle of voluntarism, it continued that "no man ought, or of right can be compelled to attend any religious worship, or erect or support any place of worship, or maintain any minister, contrary to the dictates of his conscience." Taken together, these two clauses appeared to forbid any religious tax and to guarantee disestablishment. Yet the same article also declared that every denomination should observe "the Sabbath or Lord's day, and keep it up, and support, some sort of religious worship, which to them shall seem most agreeable to the revealed word of God." Local officials interpreted this latter provision as authorizing towns to continue to assess religious taxes. To alleviate any confusion over the matter, the legislature enacted a law in 1783 that clarified how towns were to collect the taxes and how religious dissenters could obtain exemption certificates. Then, in 1786, with statehood secured, the Vermont legislature revised the 1777 constitution, removing the obligation in article III to "support" religious worship.

The same revision also omitted a clause limiting rights of conscience only to "profess[ors] of the protestant religion." Again, the constitution seemed to forbid compelled religious assessments, now going so far as to repudiate any legal preference for Protestantism in the state. But in a general revision of the laws in 1787, the legislature left intact the 1783 law authorizing religious assessments. This enabled Congregationalist-controlled towns to collect taxes over the objection of Baptists and other dissenters. Complaints that the law was inconsistent with the 1786 constitutional revisions fell on the deaf ears of the Federalist/Congregationalist -controlled legislature, and assessments continued sporadically for another twenty years. Finally, in 1807, with the ascent of the Republican Party in Vermont and a growing number of dissenters, the state legislature abolished all statutory authority for collecting assessments. So, unlike the other New England states, Vermont operated an unconstitutional religious establishment for three decades, or at least allowed towns to do so.[23]

All in all, what the examples of Georgia, South Carolina, Maryland, and Vermont indicate is that people's attitudes about the benefits and necessity of publicly supported religion were evolving. Initially many lawmakers were unwilling to disturb the assumptions that underlay establishments, seeking instead to correct what they perceived to be their more offensive aspects, chiefly preferentialism. But shortly, lawmakers and voters realized, as one critic observed, "to establish all denominations by law, and to pay them equally" while ensuring religious equality, was "absurd and impossible." Outside of New England, there was little enthusiasm for maintaining religious establishments of any kind.[24]

The disestablishment "fever" even affected those new states that had not experienced colonial establishments. The constitutions of Pennsylvania, Delaware, and New Jersey all included provisions that guaranteed disestablishment, if for no other reason than to quell any such sentiments in the future. The Pennsylvania Constitution of 1776 provided that no person could "be compelled to attend any religious worship, or erect or support any place of worship, or maintain any minister, contrary to, or against, his own free will and consent." As if to emphasize the complete lack of governmental authority over religious matters, the article continued that no civil official "can or ought to be vested in . . . any power whatever, that shall in any case interfere with, or in any manner controul, the right of conscience in the free exercise of religious worship." The revised constitution of 1790 restated those two provisions, adding a third stating that "no preference shall ever be given, by law, to any religious establishments or modes of worship," thus removing any doubt about Pennsylvania's stance on church-state relations. According to one historian, Pennsylvanians could have been forgiven for thinking "they had arrived at the apogee of religious liberty" through their constitutional pronouncements.[25]

The constitutions of Delaware and New Jersey followed Pennsylvania's lead in making strong statements favoring disestablishment. Delaware's revolutionary constitution of 1776 was relatively concise, providing merely that "[t]here shall be no establishment of any one religious sect in the State in preference to another." Revisions in the constitution of 1792 provided more detail, declaring that no person could "be compelled to attend any religious worship, to contribute to the erection or support of any place of worship, or to the maintenance of any ministry." In addition, the provision affirmed that "no power shall . . . be vested in or assumed by any magistrate . . . [to] interfere with, or in any manner control, the rights of conscience, in the free exercise of religious worship." In contrast, New Jersey's constitution of 1776 was express from the beginning. Like Delaware, it declared that "[t]here shall be no establishment of any one religious sect in [this State] in preference to another," and like Pennsylvania, it contained a "no-compelled support of religion" clause. As if to clarify what that latter clause meant, the constitution provided in detail that no person shall:

> ever be obliged to pay tithes, taxes, or any other rates, for the purpose of building or repairing any other church or churches, place or places of worship, or for the maintenance of any minister or ministry, contrary to what he believes to be right, or has deliberately or voluntarily engaged himself to perform."[26]

Because both constitutions used language prohibiting the establishment of "any one religious sect . . . in preference to another," those provisions could be interpreted as potentially authorizing the states to create a nonpreferential establishment. Indeed, such antipreferential language was common in early state constitutions, appearing in those of Georgia, New York, Pennsylvania, and North Carolina. Relying on this language, some scholars have argued that the prevailing attitude toward disestablishment during the founding period was to avoid the government's preference of any particular religion but not to bar assistance to all religions equally.[27] To be sure, exclusive religious establishments as had operated in the southern colonies were considered the greater evil; preferential establishments, whether officially declared or operated by default, constituted the prevailing pattern that members of the founding generation had experienced. But there are several reasons not to rely too heavily on the antipreferential language. The revolutionaries were overthrowing the embodiment of all preferential establishments—the Church of England—and their most immediate goal was to keep that from reoccurring in any state or nationally; for them to memorialize opposition to preferential establishments did not necessarily translate into support for nonpreferential ones. Opponents of proposed nonpreferential establishments also used such terminology out of habit and because they feared that any multiple establishment would inevitably favor some denominations over others. Even James Madison, who opposed all forms of establishments, exclusive and nonpreferential alike, employed preferential language at times. Two years after Virginia had rejected a nonexclusive general assessment (see discussion below), he remarked that "[f]ortunately for this commonwealth, a majority of the people are decidedly against any exclusive establishment—I believe it to be so in the other states." As historian Thomas Curry has noted, those who engaged in the various disestablishment controversies "used the concept in diverse and loose ways, without much debate or without forming in their minds a clear distinction between an exclusive and a non-exclusive establishment."[28]

Second, there is nothing in the history of Pennsylvania, Delaware, and New Jersey—and North Carolina for that matter—that indicates that legislators were inclined to create or provide for a general assessment for all religions when they had never had one before or had never acquiesced to that practice. That they intended to leave the door open for a nonexclusive establishment in the future makes no sense, as it would have represented a step backward.

Disestablishment efforts in two remaining states have yet to be discussed, chiefly because the events in Virginia and Massachusetts have grown in significance over time, particularly with the former state's experience being memorialized in the *Everson* and *McCollum* decisions.

In June 1776, the Virginia legislature adopted the Declaration of Rights, which provided that "all men are equally entitled to the free exercise of religion, according to the dictates of conscience." George Mason's original language had guaranteed only "the fullest *toleration* in the exercise of religion," but Madison substituted the phrase "free exercise of religion." In addition to offering that substitution, Madison recommended a provision that "no man or class of men ought, on account of religion to be invested with peculiar emoluments or privileges." If approved, this provision might have barred a religious establishment, particularly an exclusive establishment as had existed with the Anglican Church. Even though the convention did not adopt Madison's second proposal, the declaration's free exercise clause raised questions whether a religious assessment would violate freedom of conscience. Creating additional uncertainty, the House of Delegates refused to act on a number of petitions by Baptists and Presbyterians seeking a recension of the assessment. Instead, the assembly simply suspended religious assessments during the war, so the future of the state's Anglican establishment remained unclear.[29]

In 1779, two proposed bills reignited a debate over disestablishment in the Virginia Assembly. First, Thomas Jefferson introduced his Bill for Establishing Religious Freedom, which provided that "no man shall be compelled to frequent or support any religious worship, place, or ministry whatsoever," then adding that "noone shall be enforced, restrained, molested, or burdened in his body of goods, nor shall otherwise suffer on account of his religious opinions of belief." This language would have made support of religion completely voluntary, ending Virginia's religious establishment and preventing even a nonpreferential system. Because a battle over disestablishment would have divided Virginians at a time of war, Jefferson's bill was tabled, leading him to remark later that despite his effort to make "protection of opinion . . . universal," the bill "still met with opposition."[30] Later that year, supporters of the Anglican Church introduced an Act Concerning Religion, based on article 33 of the South Carolina Constitution, declaring that the "Christian Religion shall in all times coming be deemed, and held to be the established Religion of this Commonwealth." As in South Carolina, the bill would have recognized only those denominations that followed five articles of faith and obtained an incorporation. But unlike South Carolina's paper establishment, the bill included an assessment to pay for Christian (Protestant) ministers. Even though this latter bill had greater support, it, too, was tabled for the remainder of the war.[31]

At the conclusion of the Revolution, people petitioned the assembly to clarify the status of Virginia's religious establishment, with some proposing a "general and equal contribution for the support of the clergy." Anglican clergy—having reorganized their church into the Protestant Episcopal Church—were desperate for financial support and, with their conservative vestry, railed against the decline in public morals since the advent of the war. In October 1784, Patrick Henry introduced a modified version of the 1779 assessment bill to "pay a moderate tax or contribution annually" for the support of the Christian religion. In order to garner wider support, Henry and his allies had the bill recast as Establishing a Provision for Teachers of the Christian Religion and included a provision to allow taxpayers to designate the Christian denomination to receive their tax or to allocate nondesignated funds to "seminaries of learning." Henry's bill also omitted the earlier reference to creating an establishment, likely reflecting discomfort with the term or the belief that a nonexclusive assessment did not constitute a "religious establishment." (At the same time, supporters of the Episcopal Church secured a law for incorporating the church, thus allowing it to retain title to its property, buildings, and glebe lands.)[32]

Initially, the general assessment bill had widespread support, with Presbyterian leaders reversing their earlier opposition to a religious tax, "seduced by the prospect of state support."[33] After a preliminary version passed the House by a vote of 47–32, Madison secured the bill's postponement so he and other assessment opponents could mount a petition drive. (Madison also supported Henry's election as governor in order to remove his rival from the assembly.) During the delay, Madison wrote his famous *Memorial and Remonstrance* to rally support for the petitions. The *Memorial* raised fifteen arguments against religious establishments, making three essential points. The first was jurisdictional—a term Madison actually used—affirming that religious and civil entities operated in separate spheres and exercised distinct authority. "[I]n matters of religion," Madison wrote, "no man's right is abridged by the institution of Civil Society and that Religion is wholly exempt from its cognizance." Henry's bill falsely implied that "the Civil Magistrate is a competent Judge of Religious Truth, or that he may employ Religion as an engine of Civil policy." The first proposition, Madison insisted, was "an arrogant pretension," while the second was "an unhallowed perversion of the means of salvation." "If Religion be not within the cognizance of the Civil Government," he asked rhetorically, "how can its legal establishment be necessary to Civil Government?" The second point was that religious establishments violated notions of religious equality and a society based on "equal conditions." Here Madison did not distinguish between exclusive and multiple establishments; all forms of religious assessments violated rights of conscience and constituted a religious establishment: "Who does not see that the same authority which can establish Christianity, in exclusion of all other Religions, may establish with the same ease any particular sect of Christians, in exclusion to all other Sects?" Madison's third essential point was that religious establishments, rather than advancing Christian piety, harmed religion: they were "adverse to the diffusion of the light of Christianity." Indeed, the "fruits" of legal establishments historically had led to "pride and indolence in the Clergy, ignorance and servility in the laity, [and] in both, superstition, bigotry and persecution." Although Madison did not call for separation of church and state in the *Memorial*, in his discussion about distinct realms of civil and religious authority, he analogized to the idea of separation of governmental powers, remarking that the "preservation of a free Government requires . . . that the metes and bounds which separate each department or power be invariably maintained." Both matters—civil and religious authority—called for creating a "great Barrier which defends the rights of the people." Maintaining a separation between the authority and functions of religion and civil government is a unifying theme in the *Memorial*; in the words of historian Donald Drakeman, the *Memorial* was "an eloquent call for strict separation between church and state."[34]

Madison's *Memorial* was not the only memorial submitted against the assessment bill, but it helped turn public opinion against it. Opponents sent fifteen hundred petitions to the assembly, many signed by evangelicals—including Virginia Presbyterians who changed their position again—and the legislature permanently tabled Henry's bill. Madison then took advantage of the bill's demise to introduce Jefferson's Bill for Establishing Religious Freedom, which passed overwhelmingly. So, in a period of ten years, Virginia went from maintaining the most entrenched religious establishment in the colonies to instituting full disestablishment, pausing only briefly to consider a nonexclusive establishment.[35]

The controversy over disestablishment in Massachusetts matched, if not exceeded, that in Virginia, though it produced a different result. After failing to adopt a revolutionary constitution in 1778, Massachusetts enacted its constitution of 1780, which formalized the state's previously decentralized multiple establishment. That outcome was not a foregone conclusion, as opposition to an assessment was strong in the state, which forced the Congregationalist Standing Order to defend its system against calls for greater religious equality and freedom of conscience. According to one historian, the "most vitriolic political issue in Massachusetts during the Revolution was the public support of the ministry." The Massachusetts experience confirmed that religious establishments were controversial throughout the new United States.[36]

As the state assembly undertook writing a constitution after 1778, Isaac Backus renewed his calls to abolish the assessment system, rather than simply to reform it. Those calls led Rev. Phillips Payson to challenge dissenters such as Backus who sought to upend the existing establishment. In an election sermon, Payton declared that the "importance of religion to civil society and government is great indeed, it is of special importance in a free government." Any changes to the "[e]stablished modes and usages in religion, more especially the stated public worship of God," which "conformed to the spirit and simplicity of the gospel, may be esteemed very dangerous experiments in government." For that reason, Payson continued, people should "guard against every innovation that might tend to overset the public worship of God, though such innovations may be urged from the most foaming zeal," the last remark likely a snub toward the enthusiasm of evangelicals.[37]

Backus responded to Payson's sermon in his pamphlet *Government and Liberty Described and Ecclesiastical Tyranny Exposed* (1778), which built on his *Appeal* from five years earlier. Backus asserted that he was, "in principle, against all civil establishments in religion," quoting directly from Charles Chauncy's 1768 response to Thomas Chandler. By relying on Chauncy, Backus was equating the errors of Massachusetts's assessment system with an exclusive establishment of Anglican design. Backus charged that claims of equality under the state's nonexclusive assessment was illusory; the system distributed tax monies only to "orthodox" ministers and government-recognized churches, thereby "impower[ing] the majority to judge for the rest about spiritual guides, which naturally causes envying and strife." "How can liberty of conscience be rightly enjoyed, till this iniquity is removed?" Backus asked. "The word of truth says, why is my liberty judged of another man's conscience? Let every man be fully persuaded in his own mind."[38] Backus also refuted Payson's claim that an assessment for ministers and public worship was necessary to ensure virtue and maintain civil society. "I am as sensible of the importance of religion, and of the utility of it to human society, as Mr. Payson is," Backus wrote. "But I am so far from thinking, with him, that these restraints would be broken down, if equal religious liberty was established."[39]

The exchange between Payson and Backus was merely one salvo in the "vigorous political debate in the newspapers" over the public support of religion in the lead-up to the constitution.[40] Assessment proponents, such as Rev. Samuel West, writing as "Ireneus," argued that the support of public ministers ensured "the peace, safety and happiness of the community" through the promotion of public morals. Although public piety was a legitimate concern of government, West wrote, the primary justification for an assessment lay in its benefits to *society*.

Thus, state support of public worship was a *civil*, not religious, duty within the authority of civil government. To abolish public worship, as Backus and others advocated, would lead to "impiety, irreligion and licentiousness."[41] Other assessment proponents denied that Massachusetts's assessment system constituted a religious establishment. "Mr. Backus's ideas of a *religious establishment* appear to be prodigiously obscure," wrote "Hieronymus" in the *Boston Gazette*. "*A religious establishment by law is the establishment of a particular mode of worshiping God, with rites and ceremonies peculiar to such mode, from which the people are not suffered to vary.*" That was vastly different from Massachusetts's general assessment for public religion:[42]

> In our laws, which relate to the settlement and support of ministers, I am not able to find any thing that has the appearance of *establishment*. All of the various denominations of Protestants are treated alike. The churches of all denominations are rendered capable of holding estates.[43]

In addition to Backus, opposition to an assessment came from "Mentor," whose arguments championed the idea of separate spheres of civil and religious authority. As members of a civil society, Mentor wrote, people "are accountable for our actions to the community to which we belong," but "as members of the kingdom of Christ, we are accountable only to Him who is the sole fountain of authority." Echoing Locke, Mentor insisted that "the civil magistrate hath authority to bind man only in cases which respect the well-being of civil society, and not in any case as it relates purely to . . . the kingdom of Christ." Turning to the matter of assessments, Mentor asserted that the "civil magistrate can't determine what an orthodox ministry is, without determining what orthodoxy itself is." Also responding to arguments that public worship was intended to ensure the stability of government rather than advance piety, Mentor insisted that if a civil magistrate was authorized to impose assessments "*because the gospel ministry is beneficial to society*, it would follow, by the same rule, that he might adopt *any* of the maxims of the religion . . . which he should judge would be beneficial to society." There was no logical stopping point to such power.[44] The debate over the propriety of an assessment and what constituted a religious establishment continued throughout the drafting of the Massachusetts Constitution and beyond, leading John Adams to remark how a "whole company of earthly hosts hath debated these heavenly things with an hellish intensity."[45]

Adams fully understood the intensity of the debate, as the convention assigned him the task of writing the initial draft of the constitution. As submitted for ratification, it contained several provisions regarding religion. Article II of the Declaration of Rights declared the "right" and "duty" of all men, "publicly," "to worship the SUPREME BEING" but then guaranteed the liberty of "worshipping God in the manner and season most agreeable to the dictates of his own conscience." That strong statement regarding freedom of conscience was juxtaposed with the next article, which addressed the issue of a religious establishments and assessments in particular. Initially, article III asserted that "the good order and preservation of civil government, essentially depend upon piety, religion and morality." That goal was to be accomplished "by the institution of the public worship of God, and of public instructions in piety, religion and morality." Accordingly, the article provided that

> the legislature shall, from time to time, authorize and require, the several towns, parishes, precincts, and other bodies politic, or religious societies, to make suitable provision, at their own expense, for the institution of the public worship of God, and for the support and maintenance of public Protestant teachers of piety, religion and morality, in all cases where such provision shall not be made voluntarily.[46]

An additional provision in article III then instituted a nonexclusive establishment by allowing money assessed to "be uniformly applied to the support of the public teacher of [one's] own religious sect or denomination," provided there was a dissenting church within the parish; otherwise, the tax was to "be paid towards the support of the teacher or teachers of the parish," who were to be elected by the majority of town residents. Article III concluded by guaranteeing that every Christian denomination would have equal "protection of the law" and that "no subordination of any one sect or denomination to another shall ever be established by law." Even though the various provisions appeared to be in tension with each other, the constitution unmistakably formalized Massachusetts's prior general assessment system. It was in some ways a step backward, in that it removed the ability of dissenters to be exempt from paying any assessment, now requiring that the taxes be paid to one's own church or, if not affiliated, to the minister selected by the town. Despite the antisubordination clause, the other provisions erased some of the gains Baptists and other dissenters had made over the previous decades. One historian has asserted that the antisubordination clause and language in article II were included "as sop" to dissenters "in order to assuage the minorities even further."[47]

Thus, despite reauthorizing the assessment system, the constitution revealed the contentious nature of a religious establishment, even a purportedly nonpreferential one. Article III, according to one historian, "was perhaps the most controversial one in the whole constitution." Adams likely realized this, as he wisely declined to draft that article, which was done by a committee. According to another historian, its provisions caused "rancorous debate" among the delegates, and opponents tried valiantly to have the article removed entirely. After another contentious round of newspaper articles and pamphlets over the religious assessment, Massachusetts voters ratified the constitution. Voters considered each article separately, with article III receiving only a 58 percent approval, short of the two-thirds required for ratification. Nonetheless, the constitutional convention declared that the entire constitution had been approved, and it went into effect on October 25, 1780; as Adams remarked at the time, "we might as soon expect a change in the solar system as to expect they would give up on their establishment." Massachusetts had created a religious establishment, though it had not been easy.[48]

Thus, in the ten years since the Continental Congress had declared independence and called upon the united colonies to establish state governments, the new nation had undergone an amazing transformation in church-state arrangements. In that brief decade, the number of states with functioning religious establishments had been reversed, from nine out of thirteen in 1776 to three or four out of fourteen in 1786. It represented a significant reordering of church-state relations in a short period of time, one that would not have occurred without the preceding events that had laid the groundwork for disestablishment.

As can best be determined from the debates over disestablishment in the various states—and the documentary record is far from complete—no proponents called expressly for separation of church and state or used such terminology. The common claims were that religious establishments infringed on liberty of conscience and denied equal standing to all denominations. Religious establishments, even purportedly nonexclusive establishments, afforded privileges to communicants of the dominant denomination at the expense of members of dissenting sects. A related argument against establishments was that they perpetuated a false claim that civil magistrates had authority over religious matters. Establishments perpetuated ecclesiastical tyranny enforced by civil authorities, resulting in the unhallowed perversion of true Christianity. So, Philip Hamburger is correct in maintaining that "the dissenters who campaigned against American establishments, including Baptists, usually revealed little desire for separation of church and state. . . . Instead, these dissenters typically sought constitutional limitations on the power of government, particularly on government's power to legislate an establishment."[49]

Yet that observation may be less significant than it seems. It should not be surprising that popular criticism of establishments concerned more immediate and mundane matters. The various threats dissenters faced—and feared—had arisen under a *union* of church and state, so preventing a reunion was the immediate concern. Also, the enforcement of religious assessments infringed on freedom of conscience in concrete ways that carried significant consequences: imprisonment, eviction, and distraint of property. Being a religious dissenter or operating an unapproved church subjected one to abuse or violence, and dissenters were regularly denied access to legal protections and privileges. And many committed dissenters saw themselves as engaged in a theological battle with the Standing Order over whether establishments corrupted Christianity or ensured public piety. Their concerns, like their rhetoric, were focused on these immediate matters.[50]

Federal Disestablishment

The separationist impulse, though rarely explicit in the events surrounding state disestablishment, nonetheless served as a backdrop in those considerations. The same can be said for the debates surrounding disestablishment at the federal level and in the public discussions about church and state in the succeeding years: separationist ideas were present, though not necessarily front and center. When considering disestablishment at the federal level and the impulse of church-state separation, two events stand out: the adoption of the "No Religious Test Clause" in article VI of the Constitution; and the adoption of the First Amendment's Establishment Clause and Free Exercise Clause two years later.

No Religious Test Clause

Studies on the development of church-state relations at the national level commonly focus on the drafting and ratification of the religion clauses of the First Amendment from 1789 to 1791. While that attention is well deserved, it provides an incomplete account. Disestablishment at the national level began with the drafting of the prohibition on religious tests for federal officeholding contained in article VI, clause 3 of the Constitution. The ensuing debate in the state ratification conventions over that clause demonstrates that contemporaries keenly recognized its impact on church-state relations for the national government. Historians have come to appreciate the significance of the No Religious Test Clause, though they disagree about its relationship to disestablishment and to separation of church and state.[51]

On one level, scholars concur that the federal ban on religious tests for officeholding was "a bold departure from the prevailing practices in Europe, as well as in most of the states." A religious prerequisite for holding any public office or matriculating to a public inurement had long been an important incident of religious establishments. Whig writers, including Richard Price, Joseph Priestly, and James Burgh, had railed against the British Test and Corporation Acts, which had restricted public officeholding and college attendance to Anglicans. Religious tests and oath requirements had been a "favored instrument for preserving the political power of established churches and denying equal political opportunity to adherents of other creeds." Not only did tests reward adherents and disenfranchise dissidents; they also reinforced the ties between the official church and the state, symbolically reaffirming the unity of the two realms. And finally, during a time when many people believed that God held societies collectively accountable, demonstrations of public fealty and virtue were deemed essential for public officials.[52]

That a presumption favoring religious qualifications for officeholding existed in British America is demonstrated by the fact that all of the colonies imposed some form of a religious test, even those without a religious establishment. A majority of new states continued with that practice after 1776 even as most were eliminating or liberalizing their religious establishments. Even tolerant and heretical Rhode Island, which continued operating under its royal charter, retained its 1719 law restricting public offices to Protestants. Only New York and Virginia instituted no religious qualifications, with Jefferson's Statute for Establishing Religious Freedom providing that "all men shall be free to profess, and by argument to maintain, their opinion in matters of religion, and that the same shall in no wise diminish, enlarge, or affect their civil capabilities." But even New York's lack of an express religious test was qualified by constitutional language requiring future immigrants to renounce allegiance to any foreign prince, "ecclesiastical as well as civil," a not-too-subtle reference to the papacy. In 1788, at the urging of John Jay, the legislature enacted a law incorporating that exclusion into the required oath for public officeholders, effectively barring Catholics from positions of public trust.[53]

In that religious tests for public officeholding were the norm, the Constitutional Convention's decision to expressly forbid a religious test at the federal level represented a dramatic break from past and contemporary practices. But how should that deviation be understood? Unfortunately, the legislative record surrounding the drafting of the No Religious Test Clause is sparse, to say the least. Late in the convention's proceedings, Charles Pickney of South Carolina proposed that "[n]o religious test or qualification shall ever be annexed to any oath of office under the authority of the U.S." The only recorded response to the proposal came from Roger Sherman of Connecticut, who "thought it unnecessary," considering "the prevailing liberality being a sufficient security against such tests." The convention then approved the motion, with the North Carolina delegation voting no and the Maryland and Connecticut delegations dividing on the matter.[54] The brevity of the debate over whether to impose a religious test at the federal level apparently surprised some of the delegates. Maryland's Luther Martin, in his report to that state's legislature, wrote that the proposal "was adopted by a great majority of the convention, and without much debate." Evincing a mixture of regret and sarcasm, Martin stated that "there were some members *so unfashionable* as to think that a *belief of the existence of a Deity*, and of a *state of future rewards and punishments* would be some security for the good conduct of our rulers."[55]

The adoption of the No Religious Test Clause in the federal constitution can be interpreted at least two ways. For those who take a more separationist approach to the Constitution's religion clauses, article VI was the first step toward ensuring there would be no religious establishment at the federal level, thus complementing the later Establishment Clause. James E. Wood Jr. argues that the prohibition on religious tests "represented a major achievement for the future course of church-state relations in America" by affirming "the concept of the new Republic as a secular state." According to Wood and others, the ban was an early application of the impulse of church-state separation.[56] This latter view received support from no less a figure than Supreme Court Justice Joseph Story (1812–45)—hardly an enthusiastic separationist—who wrote in his *Commentaries on the Constitution* (1833) that the ban not only appealed to "many respectable persons, who feel an invincible repugnance to any religious test"; it also "had a higher object, to cut off for ever every pretense of any alliance between church and state in the national government."[57]

Other commentators view the significance of the religious test ban as being more ambiguous. They point to the fact that the majority of delegates to the convention hailed from states that had enacted religious tests in their constitutions and that several delegates who advocated on behalf of the federal ban had supported such tests in their home states. This strongly suggests, some argue, that many members of the founding generation did not view a religious test—particularly tests requiring simply a belief in God—as being inconsistent with religious liberty or disestablishment. One way to explain this discontinuity is to view article VI as chiefly a mechanism to protect federalism—that is, that the delegates sought to ensure national unity and state comity by prohibiting the federal government from favoring or interfering with the religious preferences of any state. Pursuant to this interpretation, "the Constitution does not even address the church-state problem, much less solve it, comprehensively or haphazardly." As a result, writes one commentator, it is improper "to coax a 'philosophy' of church and state" out of article VI.[58]

Federalism concerns no doubt played a role in the enactment of article VI. Neither the Second Continental Congress nor the Confederation Congress had imposed a religious test on its members, likely because any restriction would have alienated some states from participating in the body and states would have viewed it as interfering with their sovereign authority over the qualifications of their delegates. So, on one level, the Constitution simply continued that existing practice. This minimalist interpretation of article VI, however, does not adequately explain the body of commentary that suggests that contemporaries viewed the idea of a religious test in broader terms.

Even before the drafting of the US Constitution, people had criticized the inequity of the religious tests being adopted by the states. Influential figures including Benjamin Franklin, Benjamin Rush, Richard Price, and Noah Webster condemned the enactment of test oaths and called on states to liberalize them or abolish them entirely. In a 1787 pamphlet, Webster railed against all religious tests, calling them "a badge of folly, borrowed from the dark ages of bigotry." Webster prayed that a revised test oath in Pennsylvania would be "a prelude to wiser measures; people are just awakening from delusion. The time will come (and may the day be near!) when all test laws . . . will be proscribed from this land of freedom." This suggests that people were reconsidering the fairness and efficacy of religious tests in that decade between the Declaration of Independence and the Constitutional Convention.[59]

The idea that the ban on religious tests initiated a reordering of church-state arrangements is supported by the records of the state ratification debates of the Constitution. Despite the clause being relatively uncontested during the Constitutional Convention, article VI became one of the more contentious items during the ratification debates. Anti-Federalists disagreed with the immediate effect of the test ban and then its implications. A common objection was that the ban was "dangerous and impolitic" because it would allow for "a Papist, a Mohomatan, a Deist, yea an Atheist at the helm of Government." But a religious test did more than ensure the Christian piety and virtue of public officials; it signified something about the nation writ large. The essayist "Samuel," writing in the *Boston Independent Chronicle*, charged that the effect of the oath clause was that "all religion is expressly rejected, from the Constitution." No nation had ever disassociated itself from God and religion. "Was there ever any State or kingdom, that could subsist, without adopting some system of religion?" A contributor to the *Virginia Independent Chronicle* concurred: "[T]he most approved and wisest legislatures in all ages, in order to give efficacy to their civil institutions, have found it necessary to call in the aid of religion." This perspective was pervasive throughout the debates and commentary of the Anti-Federalists.[60]

Federalists responded to these complaints in pamphlets and in the ratification debates, with some readily defending the irreligious character of the

Constitution. Future Supreme Court Chief Justice Oliver Ellsworth, writing as "A Landholder" in the *Connecticut Courant*, responded to criticism that the Constitution lacked a religious foundation. This, he wrote, presented "the true principle by which this question ought to be determined." Highlighting the *civil* nature of the government, Ellsworth asserted that the "business of civil government is to protect the citizen in his rights, to defend the community from hostile powers, and to promote the general welfare." Civil government had no jurisdiction over religious matters and "no business to meddle with the private opinions of the people." Although Ellsworth stopped short of calling for a separation between civil and religious realms, his article emphasized their separate spheres of authority.[61]

What Ellsworth implied about the "civil" nature of the Constitution, New England writer "Elihu" stated expressly. "The time has been when nations could be kept in awe with stories of God's sitting with legislatures and dictating laws. . . . But the light of philosophy has arisen in these latter days. . . . Making the glory of God subservient to the temporal interests of man, is a worn-out trick." He praised the Constitution, writing that "the most brilliant circumstance in honour of the framers [was] their avoiding all appearance of craft" by banning a religious test. "They come to us in the plain language of common sense, and propose to our understanding a system of government, as the invention of mere human wisdom; no deity comes down to dictate it, not even a god appears in a dream to propose any part of it."[62] Other Federalists tied the test ban to preventing a religious establishment. Samuel Spencer, a member of the North Carolina convention, equated test oaths with establishing a particular religion. Religious tests "have been the foundation of persecutions in all countries," Spencer declared. "But, in this case, as there is not a religious test required, it leaves religion on the solid foundation of its own inherent validity, without any connection with temporal authority." And in New Hampshire, Rev. Samuel Langdon told that state's ratifying convention that he "took a general view of religion as unconnected with and detached from the civil power—that [as] it was an obligation between God and his creatures, the civil authority could not interfere without infringing upon the rights of conscience." The principle of separate realms of authority resonated in the defenses of the No Religious Test Clause.[63] The Federalists' vigorous defense of article VI suggests that the purpose of the clause was more than to protect state religious arrangements but represented a guarantee of religious conscience and nonestablishment of religion.

That people came to identify religious tests as instruments of establishment and religious discrimination is substantiated by what happened next. Several states revised their revolutionary constitutions in the 1780s and

1790s, either liberalizing or removing their religious test requirements. The Pennsylvania Constitution of 1790 dropped its requirement to affirm the authority of the Old and New Testament, retaining only a belief in God and in future punishments and rewards. The Vermont Constitution of 1786 removed its requirement for officeholders to be Protestants, while the revised constitutions of Georgia (1789), South Carolina (1790), and Delaware (1792) dropped their religious requirements entirely.[64] Similarly, all of the constitutions of the next generation of states—Kentucky (1792), Tennessee (1796), and Ohio (1802)—expressly prohibited imposing a religious test for officeholding. Article VI and the vigorous debate surrounding its ratification likely influenced this liberalizing trend. Seen in this light, a philosophy of the No Religious Test Clause does emerge, one that reinforced ideas of religious liberty and disestablishment that were expressed in the First Amendment.[65]

Adoption of the First Amendment

Compared to the extensive commentary and debate on article VI, the record surrounding the adoption of the religion clauses is exceedingly sparse. The official record is limited to approximately three pages of debate in the House of Representatives contained in the *Annals of Congress* and then a handful of entries in the *Senate Journal*. As that information is relatively unhelpful in divining a meaning of the religion clauses—let alone a consensus behind them—one must look elsewhere.[66]

During the ratification debates, Anti-Federalists charged that the Constitution would empower the federal government to infringe on state authority and impinge on individual rights. Various Anti-Federalist commentators asserted the need for a federal bill of rights to prevent government overreaching. Pennsylvania writer "An Old Whig" wrote in 1788 that "we have no bill of rights, and every thing therefore is in [Congress'] power and at their discretion."[67] One right that Anti-Federalists believed was at risk was religious liberty. Henry Abbot of the North Carolina convention remarked that people "wish to know if their religious and civil liberties be secured under this system, or whether the general government may not make laws infringing their religious liberties." "[R]especting *liberty of conscience*," wrote Philadelphiensis, "in the new constitution no provision is made for securing to these peaceable citizens their religious liberties."[68] In addition to securing a clause to protect religious exercise and liberty of conscience, Anti-Federalists called for a provision preventing religious preferences through an establishment. Raising the concern that Congress might exercise powers beyond those enumerated, "Deliberator" warned in Philadelphia's *Freeman's Journal* that "Congress may, if they shall think it for the 'general welfare,' establish uniformity in religion throughout the United States. Such establishments have been thought necessary, and have accordingly taken place in almost all the other countries in the world, and will, no doubt, be thought equally necessary in this." Despite responses from Federalists such as Zachariah Johnson that the "multiplicity of sects" would prevent "establishing a uniformity of religion in this country," calls for a guarantee of disestablishment at the federal level persisted.[69]

Madison had opposed a bill of rights on the ground that one would imply the existence of powers the national government did not possess, which would substantiate Anti-Federalists' claims.[70] After lobbying by Jefferson (in Paris at the time), Madison acceded to calls for a Bill of Rights, telling his friend that though he "ha[d] never thought the[ir] omission to be a material defect"—at one point derisively calling them "parchment barriers"—he now saw "the efficacy of a bill of rights in controlling abuses of power" and to protect "the rights of conscience in particular."[71]

On June 8, 1789, Madison introduced two amendments in the House of Representatives that dealt with religion. The first, which would evolve into the First Amendment, was to be inserted into article I, section 9 of the Constitution, which limits powers of Congress. It provided:

> The civil rights of none shall be abridged on account of religious belief or worship, nor shall any national religion be established, nor shall the full and equal rights of conscience be in any manner, or on any pretext, infringed.[72]

Madison's second proposed religious amendment, to be inserted in article I, section 10, which limits the powers of the states, provided that "[n]o State shall violate the equal rights of conscience, or the freedom of the press, or the trial by jury in criminal cases."[73]

The House, acting as a committee of the whole, eventually took up Madison's first proposal on August 15, 1789. (The second proposal, which would have prohibited states from violating equal rights of conscience, was gone.) Madison's proposal had been rewritten to read "[N]o religion shall be established by law, nor shall the equal rights of conscience be infringed." The debate over the amendment was relatively brief, with most comments directed toward stylistic changes to the language. In one substantive proposal, Elbridge Gerry of Massachusetts proposed language to read that "no religious doctrine shall be established by law." This language, if adopted, would have allowed for nonpreferential establishments at the federal level, consistent with the New England practice of multiple establishments. The House did not approve Gerry's proposal; instead, it adopted language proposed by Samuel Livermore of New Hampshire that "congress shall make no laws touching religion, or infringing the rights of conscience." The amendment was then assigned to a committee on style, and five days later the House adopted a motion by Fisher Ames of Massachusetts that read "Congress shall make no law establishing religion, or to prevent the free exercise thereof, or to infringe the rights of conscience." The final language was likely written by Madison, who employed a common technique of having a colleague submit a proposal to garner wider support (as Ames hailed from a state with a religious establishment).[74]

From there, the amendment went to the Senate for consideration. Because records of the Senate debates do not exist, one must draw meaning from the proposals recorded in the *Senate Journal*. Unidentified senators offered a handful of substitutes that would have limited the scope of the amendment, preventing establishing "one religious sect or society in preference to others," "a particular denomination," or "any Religious Sect or Society." All of these proposals would have forbidden only an exclusive establishment, thereby authorizing a multiple religious establishment at the national level. Each of the substitutes failed to garner a majority vote, although the reasons they were rejected are unknown. On September 9, 1789, the Senate finally adopted language providing "Congress shall make no law establishing articles of faith, or a mode of worship, or prohibiting the free exercise of religion," language slightly broader than the other Senate proposals but still directed toward prohibiting an exclusive establishment.[75] The House objected to the Senate's revisions of several amendments, including the religious amendment, and called for a conference committee to resolve the differences. Before the committee met, however, the Senate "recede[d]" from their language for the religion clauses, deferring to the House. The committee then drafted that familiar language that would become the First Amendment: "Congress shall make no law respecting an establishment of religion, or prohibiting the free exercise thereof." Although the exact author of the final language is unknown, two factors suggest that Madison was responsible for the ultimate phrasing. First, the final language closely tracked the House proposal (likely written by Madison) to which the Senate had already acceded. Second, Madison led the House committee delegation and, according to Irving Brant, his fellow members "had shown no interest in the clause on religion." Whether Madison rightly deserves the appellation of "Father of the Constitution," he is entitled to the designation of "Father of the First Amendment."[76]

This limited record surrounding the drafting of the religion clauses reveals little about a philosophy of church and state held by individual members, let alone any consensus understanding. One possible interpretation involves Madison's initial language for the First Amendment that would have prohibited establishing a "national religion." Some have argued that Madison's use of the term *national* indicates that he only opposed creating an official national church, that he thereby accepted forms of government support for religion generally—that is, nonpreferentialism. In the House debate, Madison stated that

> [h]e believed the people feared one sect might obtain a pre-eminence, or two combine together and establish a religion to which they would compel others to conform; he thought the word national was introduced, it would point the amendment directly to the object it was intended to prevent.[77]

If this interpretation of Madison's comments is correct—that he opposed only preferential aid to religion and had no problem with a nonpreferential establishment at the national level—it contradicts his record in securing Virginia's Act for Establishing Religious Freedom and his later writings advocating the "total separation of the Church from the State."[78] At the time, Madison still doubted the efficacy of a bill of rights, and his remarks made clear that he was trying to address the concerns of those who desired a guarantee at the national level: "the word national was inserted . . . [to] satisfy the minds of honorable gentlemen," he explained. He knew that the one point upon which all the legislators agreed was in the inequity of an establishment that preferred one sect over others. But that arrangement did not represent the extent of Madison's views. In the end, the words "national religion" were struck, with the House approving "no law establishing religion" and the ultimate language being "no law respecting an establishment of religion."[79]

A second possible philosophy of church and state that may exist in the drafting of the religion clauses is one of federalism. Similar to the claim about article VI, this interpretation maintains that agreement on the language of the religion clauses reflects a shared concern about preventing federal interference with existing state arrangements; in essence, "no law *respecting* an establishment of religion" barred Congress from legislating about state religious establishments. Proponents of this interpretation point to the variety of opinions regarding establishments and the fact that religious assessments operated in three of the states represented in Congress. As one scholar maintains, the various political actors "simply could not have agreed on a general principle of governing the relationship of religion and government." Rather, "[w]hat united the representatives of all the states . . . was a much more narrow purpose: to make it plain that Congress was not to legislate on the subject of religion, thereby leaving the matter of church-state relations to the individual states." Justice Clarence Thomas has endorsed this interpretation, writing that the "text and history of the Establishment Clause strongly suggest that it is a federalism provision intended to prevent Congress from interfering with state establishments [of religion.]"[80]

While there is merit to the argument that the Bill of Rights was designed to limit federal encroachments on individual and state's rights, there is little support in the debates that the majority of congressmen were concerned about *protecting* state religious establishments through the Establishment Clause.[81] By 1789, people were growing increasingly disillusioned with religious establishments. Physician and historian David Ramsey expressed a common sentiment in declaring that "ecclesiastical establishments . . . promote hypocrisy, and uniformly have been engines of oppression."[82] Officials in New England were defensive about their arrangements and were reluctant to admit to maintaining an establishment due to the negative connotations associated with the term. While New England congressmen would have liked an affirmation that the federal government could not interfere with their assessment systems, it is unlikely that representatives from states without active establishments would have supported the Establishment Clause chiefly to protect the assessment systems in three states. Rather, they likely considered that state religious establishments were simply not a federal matter, a position one could take without endorsing their existence.[83]

During the House debates, only two representatives made comments that can arguably be interpreted as expressing a federalism concern. Benjamin Huntington of Massachusetts voiced concern that the proposed language—"no religion shall be established by law"—could be interpreted to bar federal courts from enforcing financial obligations to "support of ministers, or building of places of worship." A second comment, possibly expressing a federalism concern, came from Peter Sylvester of New York, who said that while he "apprehended that [the proposed language] was liable to a construction different from what had been made by the committee, he feared it might be thought to have a tendency to abolish religion altogether." The term "abolish religion" could refer to abolishing state religious establishments.[84] Of the two statements, only Huntington's mentioned a state establishment and, even then, his comment was narrow in scope—toward ensuring that federal courts give full faith and credit to state legal obligations—not expressing a more general fear that Congress possessed implied authority under the treaty power or the tax and spending clauses that could be used to interfere with state establishments. In that Sylvester hailed from a state without an establishment, his statement about "abolish[ing] religion altogether" probably meant something other than protecting existing state establishments. More likely Sylvester was concerned that the proposed languages could be interpreted to forbid government activities such as thanksgiving resolutions or church incorporations and was therefore "anti-religious." If intended as a defense for state establishments, Sylvester's remark is oblique at best.[85]

In the end, the best that can be derived from the House and Senate deliberations is that the members ultimately rejected proposed language that would have narrowed the scope of the Establishment Clause. Both the House and Senate rejected proposals to define an establishment as favoring one denomination or sect, one "mode of worship," or particular "articles of faith." While it is likely that the various legislators did not agree on the meaning of a "law respecting an establishment of religion"—in either sense of what constituted an "establishment" or a law "respecting" one—it is at least significant that they settled on arguably the broadest language proposed in either the House or Senate. That said, no one used the phrase "separation of church and state" or identified the principle of separationism to explain their understanding of disestablishment. Though the putative author of the First Amendment—James Madison—thought in terms of separationism, there is nothing to indicate that other legislators who voted for his ultimate language shared the Virginian's perspective.

CHAPTER 3

The Early National Period

In the years following the enactment of the Bill of Rights, public attention turned to pressing issues of establishing a national government, developing monetary policy, expanding the frontier, and international intrigue, the last matter involving the French Revolution. Although church-state matters were significantly less visible, a handful of events revealed an ongoing evolution in attitudes about church and state. In 1790, Pennsylvania amended its constitution of 1776. Not only did the legislature liberalize its religious test for officeholding; it also added language to its "no compelled support" clause to prohibit "any religious establishments or modes of worship," thus emphasizing that the constitution excluded all forms of religious establishments. In addition to Pennsylvania, the states of Delaware, South Carolina, and Georgia abandoned their religious tests for officeholding.[1] And although their assessment systems were essentially inoperable, Georgia and Maryland formally abandoned their establishments around the turn of the century, as did Vermont. Finally, the new states of Kentucky (1792) and Tennessee (1796) enacted constitutions that prohibited any religious establishment, with both documents declaring that "no man of right [can] be compelled to attend, erect, or support any place of worship, or to maintain any ministry against his consent." The Kentucky Constitution added language that "no preference shall ever be given by law to any religious societies or modes of worship," while the Tennessee Constitution similarly stated that "no preference shall ever be given by law to any religious establishments or modes of worship." The state of Ohio, which enacted its constitution in 1802, borrowed language verbatim from the Kentucky Constitution. While too much can be read into these transactions, they indicate a hardening of perspectives opposing the government's authority over religious matters.[2]

In New England, the "mild" establishments were increasingly controversial as religious dissenters encountered ongoing difficulties in obtaining exemptions or a share of the assessments. John Leland and Isaac Backus continued their assault against the assessment systems, declaring them unjust in theory and practice. Writing in 1794 after returning to New England from Virginia, Leland condemned "the evils that have heretofore been occasioned in the world by religious establishments," insisting on the need "to keep up the proper distinction between religion and politics." Eight years later, Leland raised similar separationist arguments against the Connecticut establishment: because "religion is a matter between God and individuals, religious opinions of men [were] not . . . the objects of civil government not any ways under its control." Government, Leland maintained, "has no more to do with the religious opinions of men than it had with the principle of mathematics." "The principle of the law," he asserted, is "that civil rulers have nothing to do with religion in their civil capacities."[3]

In the same year that Leland wrote the earlier missive (1794), a different figure mused about church-state relations in the new nation. On July 4, David Ramsey delivered "An Oration . . . in Commemoration of American Independence" to an audience at Charleston's St. Michael's Episcopal Church. Commenting on the freedoms and privileges enjoyed by Americans, Ramsey praised the nation's "exemption from ecclesiastical establishments." Religious establishments had

> transmitted error from one generation to another, and restrained that free spirit of enquiry, which leads to improvement. In this country, no priest can decimate the fruits of our industry, nor is any preference whatever, given to one sect above another. Religious freedom, banished from almost every other corner of the globe, has fixed her standard among us, and kindly invites the distressed from all quarters to repair thither.[4]

Ramsey not only celebrated the absence of ecclesiastical oppression in the new nation; he also commended the model of church-state relations that had emerged from the Revolutionary period. "The experience of eighteen years," Ramsey continued, had proven that "universal [religious] equality is the most effectual method of preserving peace among contending sects. It has also demonstrated, that the church and state are distinct societies, and can very well subsist without any alliance, or dependence on each other."[5]

Religious issues returned to the public spotlight in the closing years of the 1790s, brought about by several interrelated events: the perceived rise of deism in the United States and its connection to the French Revolution, the advent of political partisanship, and the presidential election of 1800, which pitted Thomas Jefferson against John Adams. These events set the stage for Jefferson's famous letter to the Danbury Baptist Association in which he announced the metaphor of a "wall of separation between church and state."

The Election of 1800

The presumed deism of several of the nation's founders—Franklin, Jefferson, Washington—has been discussed extensively in the historical and popular literature; however, their deistic leanings were not widely known at the time. Although deism was not a succinctly defined belief system, it encompassed a rejection of orthodox Christianity doctrines, a belief in a passive and noninterventionist Creator, a denial of the divinity of Jesus, and a skepticism about the veracity of biblical miracles. Many educated Americans of the second half of the eighteenth century held deistic beliefs—particularly enthusiasts of Enlightenment rationalism—though most stopped short of rejecting Christianity and supernaturalism. Gentry generally kept their deistic beliefs to themselves and their close acquaintances; only Benjamin Franklin acknowledged his deistic inclinations, writing in his *Autobiography* (1781) that he became "a thorough Deist" as a young man.[6]

So long as deism remained confined to private parlor discussions of the colonial elite, it raised little concern among the orthodox clergy. However, the religious disruption of the Revolutionary War and encounters with British and French soldiers facilitated the growth of deistic ideas among the common folk. In 1785, Revolutionary War hero Ethan Allen published his deist tract *Reason the Only Oracle of Man*. According to historian Christopher Grasso, Allen's critique of Christian orthodoxy "was read more than its paltry sales might indicate, discussed more than it was read, and treated with clerical contempt more than it was refuted." Allen's book presaged a flood of deistic literature from Europe in the late 1780s, and in 1790 steamship inventor John Fitch organized a deistic club in Philadelphia, called the Universal Society, that attracted merchants and craftspeople. The person most responsible for popularizing deism in the 1790s, however, was the indefatigable writer and organizer Elihu Palmer, who for more than a decade promoted skepticism through a weekly journal, in pamphlets, and by creating deistic clubs in cities along the Eastern Seaboard.[7] And then, in 1794, Thomas Paine published *The Age of Reason*, which was an unrelenting critique of orthodox Christianity: the church fathers were "Christian Mythologists," and the Bible was nothing but "a history of the grossest vices and a collection of the most paltry and contemptable tales." Paine spoke on behalf of the "true Deist"; dedicated to "my fellow citizens of the United States of America," *The Age of Reason* was immensely popular in America, particularly among democratic clubs, deistical societies, and college students, going through seventeen printings by 1796.[8] Confirming the inroads of deism into the nation's colleges, Lyman Beecher wrote that when attending Yale in 1795, "most students were skeptical. . . . That was the day of the infidelity of the Tom Paine school." In the words of historian Gary Nash: "Everywhere Paine was read." This ascent of deism caused considerable consternation among orthodox clergy.[9]

Coinciding with the rise of deism in the 1790s was the French Revolution. Initially Americans of all stripes, including orthodox clergy, celebrated the revolution and the new French Republic as an extension of republican principles to Europe. Writing in a Fourth of July oration in 1793, Congregational minister Enos Hitchcock asserted that Americans should "warmly wish success to the great principles of the French revolution—principles founded on the equal liberty of all men, and the empire of the laws." American support for the French Republic continued even when the violence escalated and became increasingly anticlerical. The "excesses," though worrisome, were explained by French "[i]nexperience in the science of free government, and [being] unprepared for the enjoyment of it by a previous course of [republican] education," Hitchcock insisted. Jedidiah Morse concurred that France's rejection of Christianity "is less to be wondered at, when we consider, in how unamiable and disgusting a point of view it has been there exhibited, under the hierarchy of Rome." Once "peace and a free government shall be established," Morse believed, "the effusions of the Holy Spirit [would bring about] a glorious revival and prevalence of pure, unadulterated Christianity."[10]

By mid-decade, attitudes of Federalists and orthodox clergy toward the French Revolution changed as a result of the ongoing violence and the evolution of French anticlericalism into a generalized attack on Christianity. In 1794, Noah Webster warned that the Jacobins were "atheistical" and waging "an inveterate war on christainity" by seizing churches and abolishing the Sabbath, all in the name of rationalism. Compounding the changing perspective toward France was the concern that Americans were adopting a similar form of militant deism and anticlericalism. Clergy quickly identified France as the source of American deism that was being promoted by the emerging Republican Party led by the Francophile Thomas Jefferson. Clergy feared that the growing influence of deism, fueled by the popularity of Paine's *The Age of Reason*, was contributing the nation's political unrest and social disruption, as represented by the Whiskey Rebellion.[11]

By 1797, the orthodox clergy were in full attack mode. In a sermon widely circulated as a pamphlet, *Duty of Americans, at the Present Crisis*, Yale president Timothy Dwight charged that European infidelity was being imported into America through the secret society of the Bavarian Illuminati, who were reputedly bend on destroying Christianity. The Illuminati, with their deistic and Masonic connections in America, were "inundat[ing] the country with books replete with infidelity, irreligion, immorality, and obscenity." They sought nothing less than "the overthrow of religion, government, and human society civil and domestic."[12] The effects of this rise in infidelity were everywhere. "Has not the worship of God been neglected," asked Connecticut minister John Smalley in an election sermon. "[H]is day and name [have] been prophaned, his laws transgressed, and his gospel despised and rejected, of late years." As for the cause for the rise in irreligion, Smalley asked rhetorically, "Have not infidelity, and all manner of loose principles, and immoral practices, abounded in all parts of the land, since the revolution, and our happy independence[?]" Thus, as the new nation entered the new century, orthodox clergy were attuned to the threat of infidelity.[13]

The obsession among orthodox clergy with deism and infidelity set the stage for the election of 1800 and helps to explain their vociferous reaction to Jefferson's candidacy. The standard account of the conflict paints the clergy as motivated chiefly by partisanship and a fear of losing their privileged status if Republicans prevailed in New England. While it is true that Federalists cultivated orthodox clergy by tying French irreligion and American deism to the Republicans, there is reason to believe that many clergy truly feared that Jefferson's election would mark the ascension, if not victory, of irreligion in America. It was not simply an episode in "political smear," as one author has maintained. At the same time, orthodox clergy sensed that public opinion was shifting in favor of Jefferson's ordering of church-state relations, a position that was to their detriment and that of the New England establishments. In the public debate carried on in newspapers and pamphlets, this latter issue was as prominent as Jefferson's alleged infidelity.[14]

The calumny and vitriol that accompanied the election of 1800 has rarely been matched in American political history. In addition to making gross mischaracterizations about the opposing candidate's political stances, the numerous letters, speeches, and pamphlets by Adams's and Jefferson's surrogates launched scurrilous and vindictive attacks on the other candidate's integrity and virtue.[15] The charges raised by the orthodox clergy about Jefferson's religious heterodoxy rose to another level, with the vice president reportedly being "stigmatized . . . in more than half of the pulpits in New England" throughout 1800. Jefferson was a "deist," an "infidel," and an "atheist" who disputed the scriptures, which invited God's wrath upon the nation. Pamphleteers charged Jefferson was a disciple of Voltaire, Edward Gibbon, Hume, and even Robespierre, eager to impose their form of irreligion on the nation. Jefferson would erect temples for expounding on *The Age of Reason* and "endow colleges and professors for the propagation of deism and anarchy."[16]

Accusers found support in Jefferson's *Notes on Virginia*, where he disputed the authenticity of miracles and wrote that "it does me no injury for my neighbour to say there are twenty gods, or no god." In one pamphlet, *The Voice of Warning to Christians*, Presbyterian minister John Mason insisted that Jefferson's writings insulted the Bible and called for a "civil society as founded on Atheism." Jefferson's indifference to whether there were twenty gods or no god demonstrated his "disregard to the religion of Jesus Christ" and proved him to be "a confirmed infidel" who promoted "the morality of devils." No less incendiary was fellow Presbyterian William Linn's *Serious Considerations on the Election of a President*. Linn charged that Jefferson's "disbelief of the Holy Scriptures, . . . his rejection of the Christian Religion and open profession of Deism" disqualified him from the presidency. He was "a true infidel, . . . being directly opposite to divine revelation." The effect of his election would be "to destroy religion, introduce immorality, and loosen all the bonds of society," while it would invite God's wrath in the new nation.[17] As another pamphlet characterized the perceived threat, there would soon be "chariot wheels . . . rolling around the streets of the federal city, with loads of domestic and imported infidelity." Republicans, asserted Webster, were "a set of unprincipled and abandoned democrats, deists, atheists, adulterers, and profligate men" who would "lead down the people to destruction!"[18]

The Federalist press—the *Gazette of the United States*, the *Commercial Advertiser*, the *Porcupine's Gazette*, among others—also attacked Jefferson's character and integrity with charges of deism and atheism. The "Grand Question" presented with the election, proclaimed the *Gazette of the United States*, was whether voters would choose "GOD—AND A RELIGIOUS PRESIDENT; Or impiously declare for JEFFERSON—AND NO GOD!!!"[19] And the *New-England Palladium* charged,

> Should the infidel Jefferson be elected to the Presidency, the *seal of death* is that moment set on our holy religion, our churches will be

> prostrated, and some infamous prostitute, under the title of the Goddess of Reason, will preside in the Sanctuaries now devoted to the worship of the Most High.[20]

Accusers intertwined charges about on Jefferson's irreligious character with attacks on his stance on church-state matters, with them finding ammunition in his Statute for Establishing Religious Freedom. Mason mocked Jefferson for believing that *"religion has nothing to do with politics!"* Mason charged that due to Jefferson's influence, the Constitution *"makes no acknowledgement of that God who gave us out national existence."* No nation could exist where its government was separated from God. Linn concurred: Jefferson denied "the necessity of religion to government" and wished for a "government in which no religious opinions were held." "Would this not be a nation of Atheists?" Linn asked rhetorically. Although neither Mason nor Linn offered their own understandings of church and state relations, Linn paraphrased Washington's Farewell Address as stating that religion and the state should be "inseparably connected," while he referred to the United States as a "Christian nation." Their attacks suggest they considered Jefferson to be advocating a godless (i.e., secular) state with a high degree of separation between the two institutions and their functions. This, they rejected.[21]

Federalist newspapers concurred that the future of church-state relations hung on the election's outcome. Even before the campaign began, Federalist publishers had raised concerns about Jefferson's stance on church-state matters. Citing to Jefferson's *Notes on Virginia*, Noah Webster's *Commercial Advertiser* charged in 1798 that Jefferson "is very pointed against all establishments in favor of religion." Two years later the *Gazette of the United States* raised the same charge: "Thomas Jefferson . . . is an enemy to all religious establishments. That so very important an assertion should not rest in doubt." In another edition, the *Gazette* elaborated on the threat presented by Jefferson's candidacy. "The condition of Church and State in America is such as to fill every considerate mind with the most unhappy sensations." The problem lay in part with the Constitution, which "preclude[s] any connection [between church and state]. . . . [A] strict and indissoluble alliance of religion to government has been ordained in the nature of things." Implying Jefferson's influence in the constitutional prohibition, the *Gazette* warned voters that "Jacobinism is triumphant, and unless a different tempter shall soon shew itself, it will soon trample underfoot all order, law, property, as it has done [to] religion."[22]

Republican newspapers and pamphleteers fought back, vigorously defending Jefferson's character. They denied Jefferson's deistic leanings, asserting that he was "a *real christian*" and "an excellent christian." One strong defense came from the pen of "Grotius," the pseudonym of future senator and New York governor De Witt Clinton. Not shying away from the charges, Clinton used sections from Jefferson's *Notes on Virginia* and his Statute for Establishing Religious Freedom to demonstrate the latter's religious bona fides. Anyone reading those writings would see that they "abound with just and elevated ideas of the Deity and his attributes," Clinton claimed. Other Republican pamphleteers agreed his *Notes* "not only declare the excellence of a Deity and religion—not only acknowledge the heavenly attributes of the Almighty, but inculcate the belief of a particular superintending providence, tenets which are peculiarly applicable to the serious Christian only."[23] In return, Republicans charged the Federalists and orthodox clergy with hypocrisy for ignoring the deistic inclinations of fellow Federalists, such as their vice presidential candidate, Gen. Charles Cotesworth Pickney. "Mr. Jefferson is at least as good a Christian as Mr. Adams, and in all probability a much better one."[24]

Like their Federalist counterparts, Republicans also understood that the election represented a referendum on the proper ordering of church-state relationships. Whereas Mason and Linn derided Jefferson's stance, Republicans embraced it, again finding support in the Statute for Establishing Religious Freedom. Clinton praised Jefferson for advocating disestablishment and religious freedom. "[T]he boundaries between civil power and liberty in religious matters are clearly marked and determined," Clinton asserted. "For if the magistrate be possessed of a power to restrain and punish any principles relating to religion, . . . [then] religious liberty is entirely at an end." Clinton called for a firm "line" to be drawn between the two entities. Another pamphleteer attacked the privileged status of the orthodox clergy, asserting that "more than half of our present troubles, as a nation, have originated from the religious establishments in the Northern and Eastern States, and want of due obedience to our constitution and laws, as to religious freedom." In contrast, Virginia "has enjoyed peace and liberty without conspiracies of bigotry and spiritual tyranny for twenty years" due to Jefferson's influence. The author called for "put[ting] an end to persecutions, jealousies, rancors and delusions, resulting from the union of church and state, by political establishments."[25]

One strong defense of separation of church and state came from New York lawyer Tunis Wortman. Like his fellow Republicans, Wortman defended Jefferson's religious beliefs, calling him as "a christian" and "a republican" worthy of public office. Wortman also praised the attributes of disestablishment and church-state separation:

> Religion and government are equally necessary, but their interests should be kept separate and distinct. No legitimate connection can ever subsist between them. Upon no plan, no system, can they become united, without endangering the purity and usefulness of both—the church will corrupt the state, and the state pollute the church. Christianity becomes no longer the religion of God—it becomes the religion of temporal craft and expediency and policy.[26]

Wortman urged more than formal political disestablishment. He told his readers it was "your duty, as christians, to maintain the purity and independence of the church, to keep religion separate from politics, to prevent an union between the church and the state, and to preserve your clergy from temptation, corruption, and reproach." For Wortman, "the establishment of Christianity, is incompatible with civil freedom." He called on Christians "to keep things sacred from intermingling with things prophane, to maintain religion separate and apart from the powers of the world." Wortman thus identified separation as an important principle informing church-state matters; moreover, he used the concepts of preventing a "union" between church and state and of church-state separation interchangeably. "The inevitable consequence of an union of the church with the state, will be the mutual destruction of both."[27]

Jefferson, with the assistance of his Republican surrogates, withstood the assault on his character and won the election. Throughout the ordeal he remained silent, telling James Monroe during the campaign that it had "been so impossible to contradict all of their lies, that I have determined to contradict none; for while I should be engaged with one, they would publish twenty new ones." The accusations stung nonetheless, with Jefferson later writing his friend Benjamin Rush how his religious opinions had been "the cause of their printing lying pamphlets against me, forging conversations for me . . . which are absolute falsehoods without a circumstance of truth to rest on." The attacks by the clergy, however, had simply reconfirmed his beliefs, "for I have sworn upon the altar of God, eternal hostility against every form of tyranny over the mind of man." In due time, however, Jefferson had the opportunity to correct the mischaracterizations about his religious positions through his famous letter to the Danbury Baptist Association.[28]

The Letter to the Danbury Baptists

Jefferson's letter to the Danbury Baptist Association is known for its declaration that the purpose of the First Amendment was to "build[] a wall of separation between Church and State," a phrase made famous by its quotation in the Supreme Court decision of *Everson v. Board of Education*. Since the Court's embrace of that metaphor in 1947, the letter has been examined, dissected, praised, and disputed. A comprehensive analysis of the modern debate is beyond the scope of this book; rather, the present focus is on interpreting the letter within its historical context.[29]

Of the four states where religious assessments operated, Connecticut's system was the most intolerant, called by some a "smothering establishment of religion." The Federalist/Congregationalist clergy—led by "Pope" Timothy Dwight of Yale College—held a stranglehold on the state's political establishment. Baptists and other dissenters experienced ongoing difficulties in obtaining exemption certificates so that their assessments could be paid to their own churches.[30] Since the Revolution, however, Baptist membership had grown significantly in Connecticut, becoming that state's largest dissenting religious body by 1800. Baptist frustration with the intransigence of the Congregational Standing Order and their lack of success with a petition drive for an exemption from the assessment led them to write the newly elected president seeking moral support. In October 1801, elders from the Danbury Baptist Association, representing some twenty-six churches, wrote Jefferson congratulating him on his election to "the chief Magistracy of the United States" and commending him for his commitment to religious freedom. Affirming the concept of two separate spheres, the association's letter asserted that "Religion is at all times and place a Matter between God and Individuals" and that "the legitimate Power of civil Government [over religious matters] extends no further than to punish [lawbreakers]." Unfortunately, they continued, in Connecticut "Religion is considered as the first object of Legislation" and that Baptists enjoyed religious privileges only "as favors granted, and not as inalienable rights." They understood that as president, Jefferson had no authority over state religious matters; still, they hoped that "the sentiments of our beloved President" would soon "shine and prevail through all these States . . . till Hierarchy and tyranny [i.e., the Standing Order's power] be destroyed from the Earth."[31]

Several factors likely influenced Jefferson's decision to respond to the Baptists. Beyond the normal presidential courtesy of replying to letters, Jefferson saw an opportunity to make a public statement about his religious opinions—to correct the misrepresentations during the campaign—and to strengthen an alliance with an important political constituency. In a note to his attorney general, Levi Lincoln, that accompanied a draft of his response, Jefferson wrote that while he was generally averse to answering such letters, he saw the opportunity, "by way of answering, of sowing useful truths and principles among the people, which might germinate and become rooted among their political tenets." Jefferson thought his response provided the occasion to explain to his critics why he refused to issue proclamations of fasting and thanksgiving. Jefferson was also still wincing over the attacks on his religious beliefs by the orthodox clergy—some of which were ongoing—so he saw a response as a way to strike back at his detractors. As Jefferson continued to Lincoln, "I know it will give great offense to the New England clergy; but the advocate for religious freedom is to expect neither peace nor forgiveness from them."[32] Finally, Jefferson likely used the letter to signal support to the fledgling Republican Party in Connecticut; it accomplished that goal, as afterward Republican newspapers paid attention to Baptist concerns by endorsing the petition drive and forming a loose coalition to work on eventual disestablishment. Republican newspapers would cite to Jefferson's Statute for Establishing Religious Freedom and Madison's *Memorial and Remonstrance* in those efforts; however, as William McLoughlin notes, even though the Baptists were the beneficiaries of Jefferson's "wall of separation" metaphor, there is no evidence they ever used the phrase or agreed with a strict application of that principle.[33]

Jefferson's letter to the Baptists was brief but gracious:

> Believing with you that religion is a matter which lies solely between man and his God, that he owes account to none other for his faith or his worship, that the legislative powers of government reach actions only, and not opinions, I contemplate with sovereign reverence that act of the whole American people which declared that their legislature should "make no law respecting an establishment of religion, or prohibiting the free exercise thereof," thus building a wall of separation between Church and State. Adhering to this expression of the supreme will of the nation in behalf of the rights of conscience, I shall see with sincere satisfaction the progress of those sentiments which tend to restore to man all his natural rights, convinced he has no natural right in opposition to his social duties.[34]

Jefferson's succinct response made four interrelated points. First, religious convictions were a personal matter between individuals and God, such that people's religious obligations flowed only to God. Second, repeating the assertion in the Baptists' letter, rights of conscience were inalienable, natural rights, not granted by civil government. Third, religious and civil authorities operated in distinct spheres, such that government lacked jurisdiction over religious matters. And finally, all of these principles were affirmed and ensured by the separation of church and state, a protective concept best represented through the symbolism of a wall. As discussed in previous chapters, the phrase "wall of separation between church and state" was not original to Jefferson; likely the metaphor sprung to Jefferson's mind as he drafted his response, based on his reading from a variety of authors including James Burgh and Richard Hooker. Nonetheless, Jefferson's "Letter to the Danbury Baptist Association" has become one of the more famous "thank-you notes" in American history and all but single-handedly turned its iconic phrase into a widely recognized constitutional principle.[35]

Ever since its embrace by the Supreme Court in 1947, advocates and critics alike have sought to expand or minimize Jefferson's meaning of separation of church and state. Supporters of the Court's declaration, including some of its own members, attempted to add rigor to the phrase by applying additional modifiers: "complete and uncompromising," "absolute," "high and impregnable wall." As First Amendment scholar Leonard W. Levy writes about the Danbury letter, Jefferson "had powerful convictions on the subject of establishment and religious freedom, and he approached the discussion of it with solemnity."[36] In contrast, those who have sought to disabuse Jefferson's phrase have adopted several lines of attack. One approach has been to highlight inconsistencies between the letter's declaration and other official actions of Jefferson's that were less separationist: allowing the new Capitol building to be used for religious services and approving a treaty with an Indian tribe that included money for a Catholic mission.[37] Other critiques have focused on Jefferson's specific language in the letter: that in using the word "church" rather than "religion," Jefferson opposed an alliance between ecclesiastical institutions and the government but not a connection between the state and religion per se. Still another critique asserts that Jefferson was making a point about federalism by declaring an interpretation of the First Amendment only. Given his expression of hope to "see with sincere satisfaction the progress of those sentiments" at the state level, "it is not clear that he thought the 'wall' usefully characterized the prudential and constitutional relationship between religion and *all* civil government (both federal and state)," one critic writes. "In short, the 'wall' erected in the Danbury letter, strictly speaking, was between the federal government, on one side, and church authorities and state governments, on the other."[38]

A final critique has focused on Jefferson's motive. It highlights statements in Jefferson's notes to Attorney General Lincoln and Postmaster General Gideon Granger that accompanied drafts for their review, where Jefferson speculated that his response would "give great offense to the New England clergy." These comments, plus language omitted from the initial draft regarding proclamations, have led critics to assert that the Danbury letter was not a statement of principle but "that Jefferson's principal motive in writing the Danbury letter was to mount a political counterattack against his Federalist enemies." Professor Edward S. Corwin made a similar charge shortly following the *Everson* decision, asserting that the Danbury letter "was not improbably motivated by an impish desire to heave a brick at the Congregationalist-Federalist hierarchy of Connecticut, whose leading members had denounced him two years before as an 'infidel' and 'atheist.'" In essence, Corwin insisted that the Danbury letter is less a statement of principle and more an opportunistic broadside on political opponents.[39]

All of these critiques share a common element: that by parsing language or showing inconsistencies, one can demonstrate that Jefferson did not believe in the principle he enunciated in the Danbury letter. These critiques generally ignore evidence that corroborates Jefferson's "wall of separation between church and state" declaration: his numerous letters and writings, such as his *Notes* and Statute for Establishing Religious Freedom, and his refusal to issue religious proclamations as president. As addressed in the introduction, while it is true that Jefferson expressed greater concern about the tyranny of ecclesiastical institutions and of government control over the same, he was likely using common nomenclature—"church and state"—rather than imposing a limitation, and his body of work demonstrates a lifelong concern about the intermixing of religion and government generally.[40]

This is why the federalism critique is also wanting. Deeply committed as he was to the ideal of church-state separation—as demonstrated through his involvement in Virginia's disestablishment battle—there is no reason to believe that he considered the principle enunciated in the Danbury letter should not apply broadly. And while Jefferson clearly had a political axe to grind with the orthodox clergy, it does not detract from principle to possess multiple motives; if that were the case, then the declarations of the nation's political leaders—including George Washington and Abraham Lincoln—would be called into disrepute. According to Robert O'Neil, "the surprise and the exception would be the *absence* of a politically volatile context for a major presidential pronouncement on a matter of state." As Thomas Buckley has written, Jefferson was "expressing his own deeply held convictions about the church-state relationship" while he was "condemn[ing] the Federalist position and welcome[ing] his new-found Baptist allies into the Republican fold." That Jefferson's motives for writing the Danbury letter were intertwined does not make his declaration insincere.[41]

As Jefferson's note to his attorney general indicated, he hoped the Danbury letter would be widely distributed so its contents could "sow[] useful truths and principles among the people." New England newspapers quickly reprinted the letter, so he succeeded in reaching his larger audience. As the Boston *Independent Chronicle* reported, "[t]he Danbury Baptist Association has addressed the President of the United States, and have confirmed from his lips, their favorite truth—that 'religion is a matter which lies solely between a man and his God.'" But as can best be told, following the initial attention given to the letter, it was largely forgotten. Even though the iconic statement in the Danbury letter came to represent Jefferson's expansive views on church-state matters, there is no record of Jefferson ever using the wall metaphor again.[42] A copy of the Danbury letter was included in the 1854 collection of Jefferson's papers commissioned by Congress. That publication possibly served as the source for a reference to the wall of separation metaphor in an 1856 address on "Religious Liberty" given by future attorney general Jeremiah S. Black. Without mentioning either Jefferson or the Danbury letter by name, Black remarked that the founders had intended "to have a *State without religion*, and a *Church without politics*. . . . For that reason they built up a wall of complete and perfect partition between the two." Black's speech, in turn, may have been a source for Chief Justice Morrison R. Waite's use of the Danbury letter two decades later in *Reynolds v. United States*, with its affirmation that the letter was "an authoritative declaration of the scope and effect of the [first] amendment." Although Waite's reference to the Danbury letter did not make it famous, it placed Jefferson's metaphor in the public domain where it became available for future use.[43]

Revivalism

Ironically, at the same time as Jefferson was championing the virtues of church-state separation to the Danbury Baptists, the nation was experiencing the initial pangs of the most transformative religious event in the nation's history: the Second Great Awakening. This is the label given to an ongoing series of evangelical revivals that began in the late 1790s and extended into the 1830s. Later episodes of revivalism occurred in the 1850s, to become all but institutionalized for the remainder of the century. The revivals promoted a personal religious experience, emphasizing religious piety and scriptural authority, while encouraging emotion and enthusiasm over reason. Arising on the frontier, revivals soon swept the Midwest and the South as evangelical enthusiasm took hold of early American culture. Religious affiliation doubled and even tripled as evangelical churches, such as Separate Baptists and New Side Presbyterians, surpassed the more orthodox denominations in membership. New denominations—Methodists, Disciples of Christ, and Cumberland Presbyterians—flourished in the harsh frontier experience that fostered evangelical fervor.[44]

By the 1820s, revivals were springing up in the older northern states. The most famous revivalist of the day was Charles Grandison Finney, whose "New Methods" of enthusiasm and modified Calvinist theology made upstate New York and rural New England fertile grounds for revivals; the former region became known as the "burned over district" for the succession of evangelists who swept through the area.[45] Before long, enthusiasm made inroads into the orthodox churches: Congregational, Old Side Presbyterian, Dutch Reformed, and even some Episcopal churches. Orthodox clergy such as Lyman Beecher and Timothy Dwight were initially suspicious of the "new measures," though they celebrated the revivalists' successes. Witnessing the attraction of the messages and methods within their own churches, orthodox clergy gradually embraced aspects of an evangelical perspective. A Finney-inspired national revival in 1831 led Beecher to declare it "was the greatest work of God, and the greatest revivals of religion, that the world has ever seen." By the middle third of the century, evangelical Protestantism had become the prevailing form of American religion and a dominant force in the nation's culture. In describing this phenomenon, historian Mark Noll notes with irony that "[b]y the early nineteenth century, evangelicalism was the unofficially established religion in a nation that had forsworn religious establishments."[46] This religious transformation led religious commentator Robert Baird to claim in 1844 that while 2,500,000 Americans were in active communion with an evangelical church, another 12,000,000 were under the influence of some evangelical body. Baird's generous tally meant that there were approximately 14,500,000 evangelicals out of a national population of 17,500,000. While Baird's numbers can be questioned, they represented a growing unity among Protestants over basic doctrine, such that all evangelicals could be viewed "as branches of one great body, even (as) the entire visible church of Christ in this land." The evangelical perspective would dominate American culture for the remainder of the century.[47]

New England Disestablishment

The revivals of the Second Awakening only increased the number of religious dissenters in New England, adding to the existing conflict over the state-sanctioned establishments with their assessment systems. In three states—Connecticut, New Hampshire, and Vermont—dissenters, led by Baptists, joined with Republicans to overturn the assessment systems. In Massachusetts, disestablishment arose through a fissure within the established Congregational Church between trinitarian and unitarian factions, ultimately transferring power to the latter group and making traditionalist Congregationalists into dissenters under their own assessment system.

The abolition of Vermont's "unconstitutional" establishment has been discussed, occurring in 1807 after the Republican Party seized power in the state and repealed the 1783 assessment law. A similar coalition of religious dissenters and Republicans in nearby New Hampshire achieved the same result in 1819. Disestablishment took longer in New Hampshire due to several factors: a more entrenched Congregationalist-Federalist alliance, mutual suspicions among Republicans and religious dissenters, and a state constitution that authorized the assessment system. New Hampshire's assessment system had also been sanctioned by the state's courts. In 1803, the Superior Court of Judicature upheld the state's assessment system in a controversy over the assignment of a parish tax. Despite holding for the dissenter, Chief Justice Jeremiah Smith insisted that no one should infer from the ruling "that religion is a thing of no consequence to society." On the contrary:

> It is declared in our Constitution that morality and piety rightly grounded on evangelical principles, that is, on the principles of the Gospel, will give the best and greatest security to government, and . . . that the knowledge of these [principles] is most likely to be propagated through society by the institution of the public worship of the Deity, and by public instruction in morality and religion.[48]

Despite affirming the interdependence of religion and government, Smith denied that the state maintained a religious establishment. "A religious establishment," he insisted, "is where the State prescribes a formulary of faith and worship for the rule of government of all the subjects. . . . Here the state do [sic] neither." The parishes and towns did not "prescribe rules of faith or doctrine for the members of the corporation, but barely [acted] to elect a teacher of religion and morality for the society, who is maintained at the expense of the whole." Because a majority of town voters could select a teacher from any Christian denomination, no church was "superior or inferior to another," Smith declared; nonpreferential support for all denominations was not an establishment.[49]

After reaffirming New Hampshire's assessment system, Smith confused matters by embracing the idea of church-state separation. "Public instruction in religion and morality, within the meaning of our Constitution and laws, is to every purpose a civil, not a spiritual, institution," he asserted. The state constitution "wholly detaches religion, as such, from the civil State. By the mixture of civil and spiritual powers, both become polluted." Nonetheless, Smith professed that "[u]nder our Constitution there is no such union, no such mixture." For Smith, separationism did not prevent the state from providing for the "public instruction in morality and religion."[50]

Chief Justice Smith's denial that New Hampshire maintained an establishment did little to forestall momentum toward disestablishment. The Republicans gained control of the legislature in 1804 and the governor's office in 1805, but they were hesitant to push for disestablishment, preferring to support claims of religious dissenters for exemption certificates. That approach collapsed, however, in 1815 after the New Hampshire Superior Court interpreted state law to authorize tax exemptions only for official town/parish ministers, a decision that dispensed with the veneer of equal treatment of all denominations. In 1817, with the growth of dissenting congregations and a declining Federalist Party, Republicans and their Baptist allies mounted a final drive for disestablishment, proposing a bill to abolish religious assessments, called the Toleration Act. The act passed in 1819, and New Hampshire joined the ranks of disestablished states.[51]

As in New Hampshire, disestablishment occurred in Connecticut after years of agitation by religious dissenters and a political realignment that finally convinced Republicans to support disestablishment. But achieving disestablishment in Connecticut faced additional challenges. As discussed, the state was the center of orthodox Calvinism: home to Yale College (called a "laboratory of church and state" by a Republican critic) and the leaders of the Standing Order, including Timothy Dwight, Samuel Hopkins, Lyman Beecher, and Nathaniel W. Taylor. Connecticut's orthodox Congregationalism stood firm against the unitarian incursions that were taking place in Boston and elsewhere in eastern Massachusetts. As mentioned, the Standing Order was also the largest and most powerful block within Connecticut's Federalist Party, often choosing party candidates.[52] Writing later in his *Autobiography*, Lyman Beecher candidly acknowledged the political power of the Standing Order: "The ministers had always managed [political matters] themselves, for in those days the ministers were all politicians. . . . And, fact is when they got together, they would talk over who should be governor, and who lieutenant-governor and who in the upper house, and their counsels would prevail."[53] Disestablishment in Connecticut would not come easily.

Several developments from 1784 to 1818 contributed to disestablishment in Connecticut. Following the Revolution, the number of dissenting churches and adherents grew dramatically, so that, by 1818, dissenting churches outnumbered Congregational churches. Even though the Connecticut legislature enacted a new certificate system in 1784 that exempted bona fide members of dissenting churches from religious taxes, this privilege frequently depended on whether a church was incorporated or its minister was ordained or serving in a full-time capacity. Baptists still objected to being required to file any certificate with authorities.[54] It was at this time that Baptist leader John Leland wrote his tract *The Connecticut Dissenters' Strong Box*, which condemned the Connecticut establishment. Leland not only called for abolishing the certificate system; he also challenged the Standing Order's claims about the necessity of religious support for civil society. The idea that "the legislature have power to establish a religion. This is false," he wrote. The idea that "they have authority to grant indulgence [i.e., exemption certificates] to non-conformists: this is also false, for religious liberty is a *right* and not a *favor*." Church-state separation was the correct model. "[C]ivil authorities have nothing to do with religion in their civil capacities," Leland insisted; "let us . . . endeavor to divorce them, to dissolve their unnatural connection."[55]

The Standing Order disputed Baptists' charges that Connecticut maintained a religious establishment. In a 1795 treatise, Judge Zephaniah Swift asserted that with the exemption law, "here is a compleat renunciation of the doctrine, that an ecclesiastical establishment is necessary to the support of civil government. No sect is invested with privileges superior to another."[56] Swift renounced "the false principle that government cannot exist without a civil establishment of religion." Borrowing an argument of the dissenters, Swift agreed that where there were no establishments, "religion has become more flourishing, government more energetic, and the people more peaceable. These considerations must demonstrate the important truth, that a religious establishment is not necessary to the support of civil government, and that religion left to itself, will produce the happiest influence on civil society."[57]

As Chief Justice Smith would do in New Hampshire, Judge Swift justified the assessment system on grounds that the "settlement of ministers is merely a civil regulation," one that benefited civil society rather than advanced religion. "The legislature without establishing any religion, has considered christianity to be the religion of the people, and has enacted laws to authorize the people to maintain public worship, in the manner which they deem proper," Swift wrote. The system respected rights of conscience because "[e]very christian may believe, worship, and support in such manner as he things right, and if he does not feel disposed to join public worship, he may stay at home and believe as he pleases, without any inconvenience, but the payment of his tax to support public worship in the located society where he lives." Based on this civil purpose and allowance for conscience rights, Connecticut's system did not constitute an establishment.[58]

It was within this climate that the Danbury Baptist Association wrote Jefferson seeking moral support, resulting in his famous reply. As discussed, Jefferson's letter had little immediate impact on Connecticut's establishment.

For another fifteen years, the Federalist-controlled legislature rejected Baptist petitions, as they did calls for drafting a state constitution. Their ongoing intransigence to religious and political reform helped to unite the Baptists and the Republican Party. Over time, Methodists, Universalists, and liberal Congregationalists (likely unitarian-leaning) also became disaffected from the Standing Order's persistent sectarianism.[59] The Standing Order's insensitivity to the dissenters' complaints only exasperated matters. In an 1814 sermon, Lyman Beecher charged that dissenters had abused the certificate exception law. Even though the purpose of the exemption was "to liberate all conscientious dissenters from supporting a worship which they did not approve," Beecher wrote, its practical effect had been "to liberate a much greater number, without conscience, from paying for the support of the Gospel anywhere."[60] In a second sermon that offended Baptists, Methodists, and other dissenters with lay clergy, Beecher insisted that "[i]lliterate men have never been the chosen instruments of God to build up his cause."[61] The Republican press recirculated Beecher's sermons, criticizing them as confirming "Congregational schemes" to remain in power while keeping down dissenting churches "at any cost and all hazards." As the *American Mercury* wrote in September 1816, the Connecticut government "is and has been for a long time a combination of men of one sect in politics and one sect in religion, firmly bent on their own promotion and relying on the union of Church and state to bear down all opposition."[62]

The turning point came in 1816 when the Episcopalian leadership broke with the Federalists over a funding dispute and, along with religious dissenters, joined with the Republicans to form the Toleration Party with the goals of writing a constitution and abolishing the religious establishment. The Toleration Party captured the legislature in 1818 and called a convention to draft a state constitution to replace the old colonial charter. Included within the bill of rights, article VII provided that "every society or denomination of Christians . . . shall have and enjoy the same equal powers, rights and privileges" and that "no person shall by law be compelled to join or support, nor be classed with, or associated to any congregation, church, or religious association." As home to America's most entrenched religious establishment, it was only fitting that disestablishment was a leading catalyst for constitutional reform in Connecticut rather than simply being a by-product.[63]

Recounting the events later in his *Autobiography*, a forlorn Beecher blamed disestablishment on the Episcopalians, Republicans, religious dissenters, "infidels," and "the rabble." As a result of the revivals, "minor sets had swollen" in membership and had "complained of favoritism" and "of having to get a certificate to pay their tax where they liked," Beecher wrote.[64] Yet all was not lost. Despite the events having caused him "great depression and suffering" at the time, Beecher now believed that disestablishment was "*the best thing that ever happened to the State of Connecticut*. It cut churches loose from dependence on state support [and] threw them wholly on their own resources and on God." Now the "animosity between us and the minor sects was removed," opening the way to "a time of revival as never before in this state." Still, Beecher wanted his readers to appreciate the significance of Connecticut's disestablishment struggle: "[T]his revolution . . . was one of the most desperate battles ever fought in the United States. It was the last struggle of the separation of Church and State."[65]

As mentioned, disestablishment in Massachusetts took a different route. Rather than occurring through the efforts of Baptists and other dissenters, disestablishment came about through internal divisions within Congregationalism between trinitarians and unitarians and the resulting disputes over which faction controlled property, received assessments, and called ministers.

Under article III of the Massachusetts Constitution, religious minorities were required to file certificates of membership in a recognized dissenting church to which their assessment would then be paid. For those who failed to file a certificate or lacked membership in a recognized religious body, their taxes were applied toward the locally settled public teacher of religion, invariably a Congregationalist minister.[66] The formalizing of the assessment system meant that courts were required to decide questions over the requirements for transferring membership to a dissenting church, the procedures for obtaining exemption certificates, and whether eligibility for a certificate depended on the incorporation of that church, the ordination of its minister, or his full-time status. And courts had to decide whether the settled public minister was selected by communicants of the dominant church or residents of the larger town or parish. With courts ultimately resolving this last controversy in favor of parishes/towns over churches, trinitarian Congregationalists increasingly found themselves on the losing end of the assessment system, which led to its eventual demise.[67]

In 1807, the Supreme Judicial Court heard one of the first controversies between unitarian and trinitarian Congregationalists over the selection of settled ministers and the possession of meeting houses. In 1803, the majority of residents of Tyringham voted to dismiss their town minister, Joseph Avery, who was supported by the minority of trinitarian Congregationalists. Avery sued for his salary, prevailing at trial. On appeal, the Supreme Judicial Court held that the constitution distinguished between towns/parishes and church members and that it gave to towns "the exclusive right, *at all times*, of electing their public ministers," but it then held that that authority existed only in instances of a vacancy. Seeking to calm fears that the holding might undermine local establishments, the justices affirmed the importance of the assessment system enshrined in article III:

> In language strong and energetic, the religion of Protestant Christians is *established*. Liberty of conscience is *secured*. Provision is made for the support and maintenance of public Protestant teacher of religion and morality. The exclusive right of electing their public teachers, and of contracting with them for their support and maintenance, is guaranteed to religious societies; and it is made their duty, *at their own expense*, to make suitable provision for the institution of the public worship of God.[68]

Although the high court sided with Avery, it was only a Pyrrhic victory for the trinitarians and for Massachusetts's assessment system. In 1810, the Republicans gained control of the legislature and of the governor's office with the election of Elbridge Gerry. The following year the legislature passed the Religious Freedoms Act to reform the assessment system. The act affirmed the right of every person to have his assessment paid to the church or society of his choice, regardless of its corporate status, by relaxing the filing requirements for exemption certificates. The act also provided that a dissenting minister's eligibility to receive taxes did not depend on his lack of ordination or on the number of churches he served. The cumulative effect of these provisions guaranteed that dissenters would no longer pay religious taxes to support the locally dominant Congregational church.[69]

Then, in 1820, the Supreme Judicial Court heard the case of *Baker v. Fales*, or the "Dedham case," which became the turning point for the Massachusetts establishment. *Baker* involved a dispute between unitarian and trinitarian factions in the town of Dedham over the selection of a new minister. When the former faction, constituting a town majority, chose a new minister from unitarian Harvard College, the trinitarian faction, constituting a majority of church members, withdrew and organized a congregation of their own. They then sued for possession of the church building, claiming to be the rightful "church." The court reaffirmed that town voters possessed the authority to select the settled minister, holding that church members held title to the church property only as trustees for the parish. Thus, "the members of the [trinitarian] church, who withdrew from the parish, ceased to be the first church in Dedham, and that all the rights and duties of that body, relative to property intrusted to it, devolved upon those members who remained with and adhered to the parish." With that holding, trinitarian

Congregationalists who had previously enjoyed the privilege of being the established church found themselves to be religious "dissenters" in those towns with a unitarian majority. Either they had to remain members of a church with a unitarian minister or formally break from the church and organize as a dissenting religious society. Neither alternative was palatable.[70]

Following the Dedham case, some one hundred church buildings changed from trinitarian to unitarian hands from 1820 to 1833, even though unitarians were often a minority of a particular church's membership. Trinitarian Congregationalists accused the unitarians of "plundering" their churches, and they sorely resented their new status as dissenters, which required them to apply for exemption certificates to recover their assessments.[71] The fallout of the *Baker* decision led a growing number of trinitarians to conclude that a religious establishment was no longer sustainable. Witnessing the effects of disestablishment in New Hampshire and Connecticut, Congregational leaders began to embrace the voluntary support of religion as the only path forward for their denomination.[72] At the same time, Baptists, Methodists, Universalists and other dissenters renewed their calls for complete disestablishment. By the late 1820s, only unitarians solidly supported the establishment. In 1829, dissenters initiated a new round of petitions to the legislature calling for the abolition of religious taxes. After three years of political wrangling, the legislature finally submitted an amendment to a plebiscite in 1833. In November, people voted by a ten-to-one margin to dismantle the last remaining religious establishment in the United States.[73]

Throughout these drives toward disestablishment, few people aside from John Leland called for separation of church and state, though a greater number used language that implicated separationism. According to William McLoughlin, "[n]o New England Baptist . . . ever utilized Jefferson's phrase about "the wall of separation" of church and state." The immediate focus for those advocating disestablishment—Baptists, Universalists, Republicans—was to eliminate the assessment systems, equalize the standing of all religious bodies, and curtail the power of the Standing Order. For most proponents of disestablishment, achieving a status of church-state separation was of secondary importance. Yet some may have shared Lyman Beecher's observation that the result of the "last struggle" for disestablishment was "the separation of Church and State."[74]

The Legacy of Jefferson and Madison

Even though the Danbury Letter represents Jefferson's only use of the "wall of separation" metaphor, the Virginian continued to write about religious matters in personal correspondence while serving as president and after leaving office. Jefferson had always attempted to keep his religious views private, and the experience in the 1800 election had only confirmed the wisdom in not writing or speaking publicly about religion. That did not keep him from expressing his views to friends. "What an effort, my dear Sir, of bigotry in politics and religion have we gone through," Jefferson wrote Joseph Priestly shortly after being inaugurated. Commenting to another acquaintance about the just completed election, Jefferson wrote that the "Eastern States will be the last to come over [to disestablishment], on account of the dominion of the clergy, who had got a smell of union between Church and State."[75] The orthodox clergy's treatment of Jefferson during the election reconfirmed his long-standing anticlericalism, and the bulk of his later correspondence about religious matters concentrated on the evils of "priest craft" and sectarianism. Upon retiring from public office, Jefferson wrote, "My opinion is that there never would have been an infidel, if there had never been a priest. The artificial structures they have built on the purest of all moral systems, for the purpose of deriving from it pence and power, revolt those who think for themselves."[76]

In contrast to his extensive ruminations about clergy and theology, much of it taking place through his correspondence with Adams after 1811, Jefferson wrote rarely about church-state relations, at least in the same manner as he did in his Danbury letter.[77] In 1808, shortly before his retirement, Jefferson replied to an inquiry from Presbyterian minister Samuel Miller about his refusal to issue religious proclamations. Citing the First and Tenth Amendments, Jefferson wrote that "no power to prescribe any religious exercise, or to assume authority in religious discipline, has been delegated to the General Government. It must then rest with the States, as far as it can be in any human authority." Daniel Dreisbach argues that this statement demonstrates that Jefferson believed that church-state separation was chiefly a jurisdictional principle that limited the activities of the "general" (i.e., federal) government only. A federalism interpretation is only partially correct; while Jefferson understood that the First Amendment restricted only the powers of the federal government and thus prohibited him from issuing religious proclamations, it does not follow that he viewed separation as solely a jurisdictional constraint. If we read the statement carefully, we see that Jefferson was commenting about different spheres of authority. The First Amendment expressly delineated those spheres at the federal level, so if there could "be in any human authority" to regulate on religious matters (which Jefferson consistently disputed), then such authority would have "to rest with the States" that did not have express prohibitions. Clarifying that view later in the same letter, Jefferson wrote, "I do not believe it is for the interest of religion to invite the civil magistrate to direct its exercises, its discipline, or its doctrines," a more general statement that represented his view about the matter.[78] That Jefferson sometimes raised the issue of federalism when responding to inquiries about "matters of religion" should not be surprising, as it allowed him to avoid detailing his church-state views in public and thus inviting criticism. He used the same technique in his Second Inaugural Address where he wrote that religious matters were "placed by the constitution independent of powers of the general government," which therefore gave him "no occasion, to prescribe the religious exercises suited to it." The federalism defense provided Jefferson a ready response without risking offending people holding less separationist views.[79]

Jefferson commented on church-state matters in a handful of other letters. Many of these comments decried the evils that flowed from intermixing church and state. In an 1808 letter to the Baltimore Baptist Association, Jefferson expressed hope that peoples' "recollection of our former vassalage in religion and civil government" would "unite the zeal of every heart" to "preserve that independence in both" spheres. Reflecting more darkly on the past in an 1815 letter, Jefferson told long-time acquaintance Episcopal rector Charles Clay that religious persecutions have been committed by the "hierarchy of emperors, kings, princes and nobles, as has of popes, cardinals, archbishops, bishops and priests," calling their associations a "loathsome combination of Church and State."[80] Several years later (1822), Jefferson responded to an inquiry by James Smith, a fellow signer of the Declaration of Independence, that commended the superiority of Unitarianism. Using guarded language, Jefferson agreed that by discarding superstitious church doctrines, Unitarianism furthered "the revival of primitive Christianity." A strong case could be made, Jefferson continued, that a restoration of pure Christianity would occur as soon as a nation "vindicates to itself the freedom of religious opinion, and its external divorce from the civil authority."[81]

And finally, in one of his many letters to Adams that touched on religious subjects, Jefferson criticized the ongoing religious establishments in New England and how those states had "made the Bible the common law of their land." This development had "proceeded from your strict alliance of Church and State," he wrote. "In Virginia we have nothing of this," Jefferson continued. "The law for religious freedom, having put down the aristocracy of the clergy [had] restored to the citizen the freedom of the mind." Four years later, in 1817, Jefferson celebrated the political victory of the fusion Republican-Toleration Party in Connecticut. Knowing that it foretold the demise of Connecticut's religious establishment, Jefferson told Adams that "light and liberality" had finally come to that state. They were witnessing "the last retreat of Monkish darkness, bigotry, and abhorrence of those advances of the mind that had carried the other states a century ahead of them" (i.e., disestablishment). Continuing, Jefferson wrote, "I join you therefore in sincere congratulations that this den of the priesthood [i.e., the Standing Order] is at length broken up, and that a protestant popedom [a reference to Timothy Dwight?] is no longer to disgrace the American history and character."[82] Thus, even though Jefferson used the term "separation of church and state" sparingly in his career, in "countless ways," writes Robert M. O'Neil, "the Jeffersonian commitment to separation is remarkably clear and consistent" throughout his life.[83]

In contrast to Jefferson, there is no record that Madison ever used the metaphor of a "wall of separation of church and state." In his later political career and in retirement, however, he wrote extensively about the value of church-state separation, using the term more frequently than did Jefferson. As with Jefferson's Danbury Letter, Madison's numerous writings on church and state have been dissected and disputed. Writers have maintained that Madison was a strong and consistent separationist, a political pragmatist who was willing to sacrifice principle, or someone whose views about church and state evolved over time.[84] Although Madison's perspectives on church and state did evolve, becoming more separationist later in life, there is also a remarkable consistency between the *Memorial and Remonstrance* and his "Detached Memoranda" written approximately forty years later. In all likelihood, Madison was less religiously devout than Jefferson. And unlike his friend who wrote extensively about the true meaning of Christianity, Madison did not ruminate about theological questions. Biographer Lance Banning writes that "Madison's own faith is something of a puzzle. . . . [R]eligious topics simply disappear from his surviving papers after 1776."[85]

Madison's writings throughout his public life reveal a strong commitment to the idea of separationism. As discussed in a previous chapter, the theme runs throughout his *Memorial and Remonstrance*, written in 1785. That document advocates separate jurisdictions and spheres of authority. While it primarily warns about the dangers of government expropriation of religion for political purposes, it also speaks about the threats "ecclesiastical establishments ha[ve] on Civil Society." And even though it addresses ecclesiastical institutions, *Memorial* is not restricted to actions between the *church* and the state; it more commonly uses more general terms "religion" and then "government" and "civil society."[86] Three years later in the *Federalist Papers*, Madison wrote about the political power of religion, warning of the dangers to republican society of a "combination of the majority" of sects. There he did not propose separation as the cure but rather that security would be found in a "multiplicity" of sects and in a system of checks and balances.[87]

As president, Madison undertook actions that were separationist, but not always. In his first Inaugural Address in 1809, he raised the principle of separationism; in listing his duties and obligations as president, he promised "to avoid the slightest interference with the rights of conscience or the functions of religion, so wisely exempted from civil jurisdiction."[88] Consistent with that separationist stance, on two instances in February 1811, Madison vetoed congressional legislation that he believed violated the Establishment Clause. The first involved a bill authorizing the incorporation of an Episcopal church in Alexandria, Virginia, which was then part of the District of Columbia, and the second matter concerned a federal land grant to a Baptist church in the Mississippi Territory. The second veto is more understandable than the first, though both reveal a strict understanding of church-state separation. In the latter, Madison wrote in his veto message that an "appropriation of funds of the United States for the use and support of religious societies" constituted a "law respecting a religious establishment," even though Congress made similar grants to other private entities and there was no evidence that either entity—Congress or the Baptist church—was invading the authoritative sphere of the other. The other veto provides an even greater window into his separationist approach. Madison believed that the incorporation would have given the church certain authority—"a legal force and sanction"—that it could then enforce legally. This, he wrote in his veto message, "would so far be a legal establishment by law." The constitutional transgression was not simply a legal matter; an incorporation would authorize the church to engage in quasi-public functions, including providing "for the support of the poor and the education of poor children," which Madison interpreted as "giving to religious societies as such a legal agency in carrying into effect a public and civil duty." Congress was essentially awarding civil authority to a religious society, which, he wrote, violated "the essential distinction between civil and religious functions." Here was a practical example of a violation of the separate spheres of authority.[89] In contrast to those separationist actions, Madison deviated from that path in issuing four presidential proclamations during the War of 1812 calling for public humiliation and prayer. Years later, Madison defended these actions, while acknowledging they were improper, by explaining he had acted at the request of Congress during a time of war and had only "recommended" for people to respond accordingly.[90]

Upon retiring from public office, Madison referred to church-state separation in a handful of letters. In an 1819 letter to publisher Robert Walsh, Madison wrote at length about his views on church-state matters. He revealed his own anticlericalism by excoriating the "indolence" and "irregular lives of many of the established Clergy" in colonial Virginia. He praised the level of religious pluralism and piety in Virginia, which he attributed to religious disestablishment, while noting that the "Old churches, built under the establishment at public expense, have in many instances gone to ruin." Expounding on the virtues of disestablishment, Madison remarked that "the Universal opinion of the Century preceding the last [was] that Civil Government could not stand without the prop of a Religious establishment, and that the Christian religion itself, would perish if not supported by a legal provision of its Clergy." The experience in Virginia had dispatched both presumptions, Madison declared. Rather, "the number, the industry, and the morality of [clergy] and the devotion of the people have been manifestly increased by the total separation of the Church from the state."[91]

In later correspondence, Madison wrote further about the value of keeping the functions, authority, and jurisdictions of religious and civil entities separate. He used various terms to signify the concept: "mutual independence," "distinct," a "permanent barrier." Writing to Harvard professor Edward Everett in 1823, ten years before disestablishment in Massachusetts, Madison commented that "[t]he settled opinion here [in Virginia] is that religion is essentially distinct from civil government and exempt from its cognizance; that a connection between them is injurious to both." In other letters, Madison elaborated on his views. Responding to a letter from Edward Livingston of Louisiana in 1822, Madison commented that despite the progress toward religious freedom that had taken place over the previous fifty years, there still remained "a strong bias towards the old error, that without some sort of alliance or coalition between Government and Religion neither can be duly supported." Because of "the tendency of such a coalition" to have a "corrupting influence on both parties," that "danger cannot be too carefully guarded against," he warned. Possibly, Madison was making an oblique reference to the rise of evangelical reform societies that advocated behavioral legislation to promote public morality. In place of such coalitions, Madison urged fealty to "a perfect separation between ecclesiastical and civil matters," which he was confident would show "that religion and Government will both exist in greater purity, the less they are mixed together."[92]

Two final writings demonstrate Madison's lifelong commitment to religious freedom and church-state separation. In the spring of 1833, Rev. Jasper Adams, rector of St. Michael's Episcopal Church in Charleston, South Carolina, and nephew and cousin of presidents, sent Madison a printed version of a sermon in which he set out, in great detail, the case that the United States was legally a Christian nation. Had the founders "intended to renounce all connection with the Christian religion?" Adams asked rhetorically, or had they only intended "to disclaim all preference of one sect of Christians over another, as far as civil government was concerned; which they still retained the Christian religion as the foundation-stone of all their social, civil and political institutions?" Adams clearly supported the latter proposition, and his pamphlet provided examples of government recognition of Christianity. This evidence led Adams to declare, in capital letters: "THE PEOPLE OF THE UNITED STATES HAVE RETAINED THE CHRISTIAN RELIGION AS THE FOUNDATION OF THEIR CIVIL, LEGAL AND POLITICAL INSTITUTIONS." Accordingly, Adams insisted, "while all others enjoy full protection in the profession of their opinions and practice, Christianity is the established religion of the nation, its institutions and usages are sustained by legal sanctions, and many of them are incorporated with the fundamental law of the country." Adams's pamphlet, written at a time that evangelical revivals were sweeping the country, was merely one of several revisionist accounts that emerged during the antebellum period that sought to sanctify the nation's founding and its governing documents. Obviously pleased with his work, Adams sent copies of his pamphlet to several leading figures, including Madison.[93]

The reply from Madison, who was now in his eighty-third year, was polite but resolute. Rather than criticizing Adams's account directly, Madison offered his own historical analysis to demonstrate how religious freedom and piety had progressed in the absence of a connection between church and state. History taught that the best system was one where support of religion was "left to the voluntary associations & contributions of individuals." Rights of conscience, Madison insisted, are "more or less invaded by all religious Establishments." The example of Virginia, where "now more than 50 years since the legal support of Religion was withdrawn, sufficiently prove[s] that it does not need the support of Government, and it will scarcely be contended that Government has suffered by the exemption of Religion from its cognizance." Madison acknowledged that "it may not always easy to trace the line of separation between the rights of religion and the Civil authority with such distinctness as to avoid collisions & doubts on unessential points." He insisted, however, that any uncertainty as to those boundaries did not justify intermixing the two entities:

> The tendency to an usurpation on one side or the other, or to a corrupting coalition or alliance between them, will be best guarded against by an entire abstinence of the Government from interference in any way whatever, beyond the necessity of preserving public order and protecting each sect against the trespasses on its rights by others.[94]

Some scholars have highlighted Madison's choice of words, in that he used the phrase "line of separation" rather than employing Jefferson's term "wall." A "line," rather than a "wall," "does not conjure up the image of . . . a clearly defined and impregnable barrier" that separates religion from government, writes historian Sidney Mead. But as has been demonstrated, Madison used multiple terms to describe the concept of church-state separation and would likely have resisted having his views limited to any one metaphor. (Madison did in fact use the term "permanent barrier.") Other language in his reply—decrying "the interference of Government in *any* form" in religion and calling for its "entire abstinence"—indicates that Madison employed several phrases to represent his views on church-state matters.[95]

The other writing that demonstrates Madison's consistent support for church-state separation is his "Essay on Monopolies," better known as his "Detached Memoranda." The manuscript—essentially, a private memoir written from 1817 to 1832—was largely unknown for one hundred years, being first made publicly available in 1946. It contains Madison's most detailed ruminations about church and state aside from his *Memorial*. In places, the "Detached Memoranda" emphasizes the threats to civil society represented by the power and wealth of ecclesiastical institutions. Its discussion begins with a stark warning about "[t]he danger of silent accumulations and encroachments by Ecclesiastical Bodies [that] have not sufficiently engaged attention in the U.S." This concern arose through "the indefinite accumulation of property from the capacity of holding it in perpetuity by ecclesiastical corporations." Madison believed that the "growing wealth acquired by them never fails to be a source of abuses." Here Madison reaffirmed the belief expressed in his 1811 veto of the incorporation of an Episcopal Church that awarding legal power to a church violated the First Amendment: "Strongly guarded as the separation between Religion and Government in the Constitution of the United States [is] the danger of encroachment by Ecclesiastical Bodies."[96] But Madison did not restrict the principle of separationism to incursions by religious institutions. The "Detached Memoranda" speaks more broadly about the value of separating government from religion writ large, decrying "the danger of a direct mixture of Religion and civil Government." Again, Madison raised the example of the Virginia Statute for Religious Freedom, an accomplishment of which he was obviously very proud. The act was "a true standard for Religious liberty; its principle the great barrier against usurpations on the rights of conscience." It ensured "the separation between the authority" of the two spheres.[97]

After announcing those general principles, Madison discussed several actions he believed violated separation of church and state. First, he cited his two vetoes in 1811 when Congress had attempted to grant land and corporate powers to churches; next, he expressed his opposition to a previous attempt by the Kentucky legislature "to exempt Houses of Worship from taxes." Another potential violation involved the failed attempt of Patrick Henry to insert the words "Jesus Christ" after the words "our lord" in the preamble of the Virginia Statute. These demonstrate the extremes to which Madison took the idea of church-state separation. From there, Madison attacked other generally accepted practices. Chaplains in Congress were "a palpable violation of equal rights, as well as of Constitutional principles," Madison charged, which "forbids everything like an establishment of a national religion." Madison even questioned the constitutionality of chaplains for the military, though giving allowance for naval chaplains when ships were at sea. Finally, Madison provided a lengthy discussion about the impropriety of religious proclamations, a practice that he regretted having undertaken. Proclamations "seem to imply and certainly nourish the erroneous idea of a *national* religion." They promote the idea of "a union of all to form one nation under one Government in acts of devotion to God." Madison even backtracked from his earlier justification that he had issued proclamations simply as "recommendations." "An *advisory* Government is a contradiction in terms," he wrote, because it "can in no sense, be regarded as possessing an advisory trust from their Constituents in their religious capacities." Madison believed that even a nonsectarian proclamation "naturally terminates in a conformity to the creed of the majority and a single sect." But the likelihood of a religious preference was not the only concern. For Madison, civil government simply lacked the authority to issue religious statements; religious proclamations "imply a religious agency," which was "no part of the trust delegated to political rulers."[98]

Written as it was after a long public career engaged in thinking about and advocating for religious freedom, Madison's "Detached Memoranda" confirms that he had grown only more certain about the importance of church-state separation for maintaining religious equality and democratic government. It built on his other characterizations of church-state separation: the principle erected a "great barrier" between the two realms, it required the "total" and "perfect" separation, and it ordered the "entire abstinence" of any interference by either entity. Madison's career promoting religious freedom, combined with Jefferson's work on the issue, left a long-standing legacy for future generations.[99]

CHAPTER 4

The Protestant Establishment of the Nineteenth Century

The nineteenth century represents a paradox when one considers the concept of separation of church and state. During this period, church-state separation became a widely accepted principle, not only in the law but in the popular culture as well. As the century unfolded, affirmations of church-state separation appeared in books, journals, speeches, and legal decisions. At the same time, Protestant evangelicalism continued to expand and assert itself as a dominant force in the culture, driving those elements of rationalism and skepticism of the founding period to the margins of society. Despite the political disestablishment of the 1770s, 1780s, and 1790s—culminating with New England disestablishment from 1818 to 1833—the relationship between the nation's civil and religious institutions appeared to grow stronger as the nineteenth century progressed. Religious historian Robert T. Handy once observed that "[i]n many ways, the middle third of the nineteenth century was more of a 'Protestant Age' than was the colonial period with its established churches." Handy was not alone in this assessment; religious historians have long documented how an informal "Protestant establishment" existed in nineteenth-century America, one in which a Protestant ethos held sway over the nation's culture and institutions, including its public schools.[1]

This paradox should not be interpreted as suggesting that people were necessarily divided along religious lines in their support for church-state separation. The real paradox was that practically everyone—except Catholic leadership—professed fealty to the principle. On one side, Baptists, Jews, skeptics, transcendentalists, liberal Christians (Unitarians, now a separate denomination, and Universalists), and members of the emergent Democratic Party perpetuated the Jeffersonian perspective about church-state separation. The more prominent advocates of church-state separationism, however, were evangelicals, who brought their own interpretation to the concept, one that did not bar mutually reinforcing relations between the two entities. At times, they were joined by nativists—some of whom were militant Protestants and some who were not—who vigorously promoted church-state separation as a way of combatting perceived threats of Catholic immigration. Also supporting the principle were public-school educators—some evangelical and some not—and then members of the second Republican Party who frequently embraced separationism for partisan purposes. All of these groups had their own reasons for embracing church-state separation, and their understandings and applications of the concept varied widely. Despite those various interpretations, however, by the end of the century the idea of church-state separation was embedded into the nation's culture and law. Few people would have contested the 1894 declaration of future secretary of state Elihu Root about the necessity of "maintaining the great American principle of eternal separation of church and state."[2]

Foreign visitors to the United States noted Americans' fealty to the idea of church-state separation. The best-known foreign commentator on America's political culture was Alexis de Tocqueville, who traveled the Eastern Seaboard in the early 1830s. Compiling his notes into *Democracy in America* (1835), Tocqueville commented extensively about America's religious situation. A nominal Catholic who had witnessed the religious conflicts in his native France, Tocqueville marveled at "the peaceful dominion of religion in the[] country," which people attributed "to the separation of Church and State." He remarked that he "did not meet with a single individual, of the clergy or of the laity, who was not of the same opinion upon the subject."[3] While Tocqueville likely overstated that degree of consensus, he was not the only foreigner to comment about Americans' commitment to church-state separation, at least as an abstract principle. Hungarian statesman Louis Kossuth wrote in 1852 that while several European countries were endangered by the "direct or indirect amalgamation of Church and State, . . . of this danger, at least, the future of your country is free. [Your] institutions left no power to your government to interfere with the religion of your citizens."[4] Ten years later, another Frenchman, the Count Agénor de Gasparin, declared that the United States had "proclaimed and loyally carried out the glorious principle of religious liberty" while also adopting "another principle, much more contested among [the French], but which I believe destined also to make the tour of the world: the principle of separation of Church and State." Writing around the same time, Polish count Adam G. De Gurowski made a similar observation: "Religious liberty, the absolute separation of Church and State, has become realized in America far beyond the conception, and still more the execution, of a similar separation in any European Protestant country. This separation, and the political equality of all creeds, constitute one of the cardinal and salient traits of the American Community." That European intellectuals praised America's church-state arrangement should not be surprising; at the time, reactionary continental monarchs were supporting Catholic ultramontanism and the church's condemnation of republicanism. Any form of separationism was superior to the religious situation in Europe. Even so, European intellectuals were not simply promoting church-state separation as a counterpoise to the religious arrangements back home but were documenting a pervasive attitude they had observed in the United States.[5]

Nonetheless, nineteenth-century Americans' support for church-state separation can be misleading. As the nation entered the century, at least two overlapping concepts of separationism coexisted in American culture. The first, and narrower, was that older notion of separate spheres of authority and functions of the religious and civil realms. That impulse had long existed within the Protestant and Enlightenment traditions, and the political disestablishment of the founding period had institutionalized that form of separationism. In fact, defenders of New England's assessment systems supported this understanding of separationism, insisting that civil officers should not direct or enforce church doctrine and that clergy should not exercise political power, at least not directly. The second strain of separationism was that broader concept advocated by Jefferson, Madison, and their allies, who viewed church-state separation as a check on ecclesiastical power that threatened religious equality and invited religious divisiveness. In the words of Madison, church-state separation prohibited more than an official relationship but was intended to prevent an "alliance or coalition between government and religion" and the corruptive influence of one entity on the other. The first notion of church-state separation entered the new century with growing support; the second struggled to maintain a following as the century unfolded, though at times it had its vocal advocates.[6]

A salient point in studying church-state relations in the nineteenth century is to understand that matters were neither static nor uniform. The century was a dynamic, transformative period for attitudes about the role of religion in government, the law, and civic institutions. Before the de facto Protestant establishment took hold in the mid-nineteenth century, a lively debate occurred over the proper ordering of church-state relationships. The debate was not binary, between orthodox Protestants and religious freethinkers or between nativists and Catholics, but involved various perspectives about the official and unofficial role of religion in public life. As will be seen, by the 1840s one perspective had emerged largely victorious, but that did not occur without encountering significant resistance.[7]

Moral Reform and Skepticism

Despite the emphasis of the revivals on *personal* salvation, orthodox Calvinists—chiefly Presbyterians and Congregationalists—could not forgo their belief in a collective accountability before God. They agreed with evangelicals about the necessity of creating a godly society, one that—pursuant to postmillennial eschatology—would usher in Jesus's second coming. Yet orthodox Calvinists believed that a Christian "golden age" would not occur simply through individual conversions, particularly in light of the challenges and temptations presented by urbanization and an ever-expanding frontier. Disestablishment had severed the formal bonds between civil and religious authorities, which implied that the former had a limited role in ensuring religious piety. With the new emphasis on religious voluntarism, Protestant leaders realized that they had to adopt affirmative measures to ensure that America would become the Kingdom of God on earth.[8]

As a way of reaching the unchurched, combatting the lingering effects of deism, and addressing the social problems created by demographic displacement, Protestant leaders organized voluntary reform societies and associations to further their goal of Christianizing America. Calls for benevolent reform came chiefly from those Congregationalists and Presbyterians who approached the "new measures" cautiously.[9] The titular leader of the reform movement was Lyman Beecher, who in 1803 made an early plea for moral reform in a sermon titled "The Practicability of Suppressing Vice, by Means of Societies Instituted for that Purpose." Beecher believed America's future depended on maintaining a strong Christian influence over the culture and its institutions. "Our ancestors esteemed religion to be the principal thing," Beecher wrote. "Religion is the corner stone; remove it, and the building falls." Yet, due to "a variety of causes," Beecher continued, "irreligion hath become in all parts of our land, alarmingly prevalent. The name of God is blasphemed; the bible is denounced; the sabbath is profaned; the public worship of God is neglected; intemperance hath destroyed its thousands . . . while luxury, with its diversified evils, with a rapidity unparalleled, is spreading in every direction."[10]

To combat these threats, Beecher urged the "indispensable necessity of executing promptly the laws against immorality. . . . Laws unexecuted are worse than nothing; mere phantoms." But Beecher recognized that with the emphasis on religious voluntarism following disestablishment, government could do only so much to enforce public piety. In order to "secure then, the execution of the laws against immorality, in a time of prevailing moral declension, an influence is needed, distinct from that of the government" but "superior in potency to individual efforts, and competent to enlist and preserve the public opinion on the side of law and order." The solution was to create moral-reform societies that would use persuasion and shame to supplement the law: "in a free government, moral suasion and coercion must be united." Beecher believed that "[t]he suppression of vice by means of societies instituted for the purpose, is the most peaceful, and probably the most effectual method that can be devised." Their role would be "[t]o promote vigilance, to hold up the connection between vice and misery, to give correctness and efficacy to public opinion, and to strengthen the sinews of the law." Benevolent societies would "constitute a sort of moral militia, prepared to act upon every emergency, and repel every encroachment upon the liberties and morals of the State," Beecher proclaimed.[11]

Beecher anticipated criticism that his proposal violated church-state disestablishment. "Those who wish for the preservation of the Sabbath are not bigots; they do not seek a union of church and state; they seek the unextinguished luster of that moral sun, for your sake, who with it will rise."[12] Beecher's sermons and lectures on moral reform laid the foundation for the creation of numerous benevolent societies during the antebellum period, including the American Bible Society (1816), the American Sunday School Union (1824), the American Tract Society (1825), the American Temperance Society (1826), and the American Home Missionary Society (1828), all established with the goal of promoting repentance and morality while encouraging the enforcement of laws promoting social order. Membership in the reform societies included not only orthodox and evangelical clergy but also wealthy Christian businessmen whose political affiliations were overwhelmingly Federalist and then Whig.[13]

Beecher and his allies had reason for concern: despite the phenomenal growth of evangelicalism in the first third of the century, its preeminence was far from certain. In addition to threats from moral declension,

Protestants faced competition from unorthodox forms of religious belief—Shakerism, Mormonism, transcendentalism, and spiritualism—all of which benefited from the same "antebellum spiritual hothouse" that spawned the revivals. Additional challenges came from nonreligious movements such as mesmerism, free thought, and utopian socialism. All of the new movements laid claim to transcendent truths, something that had heretofore been the purview of the established churches, and they competed with evangelicals for adherents. The struggle for evangelical dominance, and the battle for the definition of church-state separation, lay ahead.[14]

The greatest resistance to the Protestant vision of a Christian America came from a variety of groups and interests—skeptics and freethinkers, Jeffersonian Republicans and Jacksonian Democrats, Masons, and radicalized workingmen—that shared an aversion to religious orthodoxy and clerical authority. Of all of these groups, skeptics presented the greatest challenge to the Protestant empire. Some were holdover deists from the 1790s, but most were newly arrived to skepticism.[15] The excesses of the French Revolution and its association with atheism had all but discredited American deism by the early years of the nineteenth century. Despite its decline, Timothy Dwight and other orthodox clergy continued to rail against the evils of infidelity, both French-inspired and homegrown. Picking up where he had left off in 1798, in 1816 Dwight warned that people were again becoming complacent about the "propagators of infidelity and vice." Writing at the same time, Dwight's former student Lyman Beecher urged that unless people adhered to orthodox Christianity, there would be another "brood of infidels, and heretics, and profligates" who would "assail, as they have done [before], our most sacred institutions."[16]

Their fears were soon realized. During the 1820s and 1830s, American skepticism experienced its own revival, spurred on by the notoriety of Frances Wright and the efforts of labor reformer Robert Owen, his son, Robert Dale Owen, George Evans, and others. Wright was a popular lecturer who drew large crowds for her speeches that mixed attacks on religious orthodoxy with advocacy of sexual liberation and workers' rights. This combination found a receptive audience among Jacksonian Democrats, artisans, and workingmen who resented the efforts of the benevolent societies to impose their moral standards on them. Historians have noted that anticlericalism was strong among Jacksonians and their allies, which by the 1830s, had "reached a zenith." These groups believed that Protestant leaders and their Whig business allies were using the reforming techniques of the moral societies to impose forms of social and labor control.[17]

The skeptics' far-reaching agenda caused panic among orthodox Protestants and their Whig allies. Writing in 1836, the *American Monthly Magazine* charged that religious skepticism "marches under the banners of political reform." But, in truth, it "declares a war of extermination upon the established institutions of religion and government. It denominates all religion priestcraft, all property monopoly, and all jurisprudence an organized fraud upon the liberties of mankind."[18] More than any figure, Frances Wright, "both the woman and her philosophy, exemplified the fears and anxieties of her age." Her agenda threatened to undermine Christianity, cause labor unrest, and undo the home and the family. Unsurprisingly, Protestant leaders attacked Wright with unrelenting vitriol. As another journal warned its readers, "[w]ives, once happy in their husbands' arms, seduced by [Wright's] diabolical doctrines, parted from the peaceful and lovely paths of virtue and affection at home" and strayed "into the mazy meanderings of sinful pleasure[,] abandoning themselves to indiscriminate indulgence in libidinous practices."[19] Beecher derisively called Wright "the female apostle of atheistic liberty," while others anointed her the "Red Harlot of Infidelity." Beecher noted aghast that her "lectures were thronged, not only by men, but even by females of respectable standing." Wright's irreligion and feminism represented only part of the threat. She was creating an "invidious distinction between working men and others," Beecher wrote. "[T]his levelling system would destroy the industry of the world."[20]

The number of actual skeptics in antebellum America is impossible to gauge. Although Wright had committed followers, she was also a novelty, and the size of her crowds likely overstated her influence. This did not stop critics from exaggerating the threat infidelity presented to a Christian America as a way of consolidating their position: "the image of Fanny Wright, although it filled the orthodox with anguish, was extraordinarily valuable to their cause."[21] Few people railed against skepticism with the intensity of Lyman Beecher, who delivered a series of public lectures on "Political Atheism, and Kindred Subjects." Beecher asserted that skepticism was an "epidemic" that was "sweep[ing] over the world." The "polluted page of infidelity everywhere" was "an organized effort against our civil and religious institutions." Although Beecher traced skepticism's origins to deism and atheism arising out of the French Revolution, he laid blame for its appeal on the failings of Protestant orthodoxy; skepticism had worked its way into churches that practiced "a lax Calvinism, and Arminianism, and then Arianism, and after that Socinianism," he insisted. "The union of church and state in Protestant nations" had also been "a fruitful cause of skepticism," Beecher declared. He insisted that even though, "[i]n this country, we indeed have no union of church and state," America had "not escaped entirely the amalgamation of the church and the world," by which he meant the corruption of the former by the latter. But Beecher rebuffed charges that reform societies promoted their own union of church and state. "We mean, by the moral influence of Christianity, to save both atheists and ourselves from ruin; and in what better or other way can we do it, than . . . to spread the Bible, and circulate tracts, and multiply ministers and missionaries to preach the Gospel?" Beecher strongly disputed the "allegation of a purpose to unite church and state by one, or by all denominations"; this was "the most foolish, baseless, calumny that was ever uttered." "There will never be a union of church and state in this nation, unless it be one which is sought by infidels in power, to perpetuate their own ascendency, and it will commence in persecution, and end in civil war."[22]

Allegations that orthodox Protestants envisioned a union of church and state gained credibility in 1827 when prominent Presbyterian minister Ezra Stiles Ely called for forming a "Christian party in politics" to unite various evangelical denominations into a political movement. In a widely circulated sermon, Ely declared that "in this christian nation" it was "manifestly the duty of all our Christian fellow-citizens to honour the Lord Jesus Christ and promote christianity by electing and supporting as public officials the friends of our blessed Savior." Ely insisted that he did not recommend imposing a religious test oath or for any state to reestablish "any one religious sect" under law. "[L]et Church and State be forever distinct," he declared, though insisting at the same time that in "this land of religious freedom, what should hinder a civil magistrate from believing in the gospel, and professing faith in Christ?" Thus, Christians should "support no man as a candidate for any office, who is not professedly friendly to Christianity, and a believer in divine Revelation." If the members of various Protestant denominations would vote their conscience, they "could govern every public election in our country."[23]

Based on Ely's close association with benevolent reform societies (and his earlier attacks on skepticism), his sermon invited criticism that he and other reformers were advocating the very union of church and state he disclaimed. The *Universalist Magazine* charged that the Christian party was being organized "*for the express purpose* of obtaining the government of the country and controlling the affairs of the nation." This was but a stark example of an effort "to unite church and state," it charged. Another critic asserted that Ely's Presbyterian Church was "the only denomination which adduces scriptural warrant for the union of church and state, and also for all its infernal persecutions."[24] Ely's proposal fueled anticlerical suspicions about the true goals of the reform societies; Unitarian minister William Ellery Channing led the attack for religious liberals. Writing in 1829, Channing asserted that moral societies were becoming an informal establishment, an "irregular government created within our constitutional government," one that had the "propensity to rule, to tyrannize . . . to make themselves standards for other minds, to be lawgivers, instead of brethren and friends." He charged that their activities were "silencing of free speech, and virtually denying our dearest religious and civil rights."[25] Skeptics also believed that Ely's proposal confirmed their worst fears. George Evans's journal, *Working Man's Advocate*, declared that Ely's Christian party foretold a union of church and state, while Frances Wright warned that it represented a standard "under which all the party-colored ranks of orthodoxy may rally into one phalanx." Though skeptics and religious liberals disagreed on many essential points, they shared a concern that the moral reformers were undermining the promise of disestablishment. This dispute between moral reformers and skeptics set the stage for future debates over the meaning of church-state separation.[26]

The Sunday Mail Delivery Controversy

The most significant antebellum debate over the meaning of church-state separation took place from 1828 to 1830 in a nationwide controversy over mail delivery on Sundays. The episode quickly transcended the specific issue of Sunday mail delivery and became a battle over evangelical efforts to transform public attitudes about Sabbath observance and other church-state matters.[27]

Sabbath observance represented a core concern for orthodox reformers and their evangelical allies. In the early 1800s, every state had laws restricting labor and unnecessary travel on Sundays, with Massachusetts requiring attendance at worship. But as Lyman Beecher had declared in his 1803 litany of reasons for forming reform societies, "the sabbath is profaned; the public worship of God is neglected." For devout Protestants, Sabbath observance represented more than respecting the Lord's Day and protecting Sunday worship from unwelcome disturbances and distractions. Uniform observance of the Sabbath increased public piety, demonstrated a communal respect for religious institutions, and preserved Christian society. For orthodox Calvinists, Sabbath laws also symbolized the nation's covenant with God. Desecration of the Sabbath was therefore "a great national sin."[28]

In 1810, Postmaster General Gideon Granger—the same official who had advised Jefferson on his letter to the Danbury Baptists—had secured a law that required all postmasters to open their offices and distribute mail on every day that mail arrived, Sundays included. This meant that in the twenty-three hundred communities with post offices, people had an alternative place on Sundays to congregate, hear news, and socialize—often accompanied with liquor—rather than attend a local church. Protestant clergy, including Timothy Dwight, Lyman Beecher, and even William Ellery Channing, had objected to the 1810 law, but their petitions had come to no avail, in part because of concerns about inhibiting mail delivery during the War of 1812.[29]

The issue of Sunday mail delivery festered in the minds of moral reformers who viewed it as an impediment to Sabbath observance and an affront their vision of a godly society. As the century progressed, improvements in transportation—post roads, canals, steamships, and then railroads—presented additional challenges to uniform Sabbath observance; with mail traveling on private transport, the Sunday mail law effectively exempted stagecoaches, canal boats, barges, and trains (and their passengers) from complying with local Sabbath laws. Beecher lamented that "the whole nation seems to be on the sabbath in a state of migration . . . the sanctuary empty, and every stage, boat, and tavern full."[30] This worrisome trend led him and his allies to create a new organization in 1828 to spearhead Sabbath observance and seek repeal of the mail delivery law: the General Union for the Promotion of the Christian Sabbath (GUPCS). In December 1828, the GUPCS mounted a new petition drive to Congress seeking repeal of the mail delivery law. Over the course of two years, approximately nine hundred petitions were forwarded to Washington, many of them mass-produced and with signatures running into the hundreds.[31] The memorials argued that Sunday mail delivery violated the "law of God," conflicted with state and local Sabbath laws, and infringed upon the religious rights of Christian postmasters. A handful of petitions asserted that "the Government of the United States was formed under the influence of Christian principles." Other petitions addressed the potential church-state concerns, with petitioners from North Carolina declaring that they "solemnly protest against the union of church and state" and that they "would depreciate such a union as the death-blow to the liberties of their beloved country." Yet "they apprehend[ed] no danger" to that principle through Sabbath enforcement. As a Kentucky petition put it: "Your memorialists protest against States supporting, aiding, or being united to the Church," but "they also protest against the civil power being used to trample down or persecute the Church."[32]

Although the GUPCS and its allies were better organized, they faced significant resistance from a loose coalition of skeptics, workingmen, religious liberals, and Jacksonian Democrats, many of whom believed the move threatened church-state separation. Groups held meetings and rallies in cities and towns across the nation. According to a report from a rally held in New York City's Tammany Hall in January 1829, abolishing the delivery law would "favor [a] . . . peculiar view[] of religious duty" and was "contrary to the letter and spirit of the constitution, which guarantees freedom of opinions to every citizen." The repeal effort was "calculated to prepare the way for the final establishment of a national religion."[33] Other opposition petitions and memorials echoed the same theme. "Your memorialists confess incapable to discover any method of establishing a religion, unless it be by the establishment of its tenets; nor are they able to discover any principle which authorizes your honorable bodies to make one dogma of Christians part and parcel of the law of the land," wrote a group from Vermont in January 1831. The repeal of the delivery law "will result in a union of church and state." A petition from New Jersey agreed, asserting that a repeal would constitute "a direct violation of the principles of the Constitution . . . the object of which would be to sustain their particular tenets or religious creeds to the exclusion of others, thereby uniting ecclesiastical and civil law, and leading ultimately the abhorrent and anti-republican union of church and state." Again and again, the petitions drove home the necessity of "maint[aining] our Constitutional lines of demarcation between the affairs of Church and State." "Against the union of church and state all history rises its warning voice," asserted one petition, while another group of memorialists claimed that "[t]o have proposed an open union of church and state [at the founding] would have been so manifest a violation of republican principle, as must have drawn upon its authors the just resentment of indignant people." For the anti-Sabbatarians, a treasured constitutional principle was at stake, one that transcended the issue of mail delivery.[34]

Such a widespread public debate over the understanding of American church-state relations had not occurred since constitutional ratification. It revealed stark differences of opinion over its meaning—whether it required only an institutional separation that facilitated a Protestant ethos or a Jeffersonian-Madisonian notion that deprived government of all jurisdiction over religious matters. The various petitions, pro and con, were forwarded to the Post Office Committees of the Senate and the House of Representatives, which, after consideration, issued reports that affirmed the 1810 law requiring Sunday mail delivery. Both reports were written by Richard M. Johnson of Kentucky, a leading Democrat and the future vice president under Martin Van Buren. Johnson served in the Senate from 1819 to 1829 and in the House from 1830 to 1837, which allowed him to participate in the considerations about the mail delivery law in both chambers. Johnson reputedly received assistance from Obadiah Brown, pastor of Washington's First Baptist Church, and both reports strongly affirmed the value of church-state separation.[35]

Although the two reports were written some fourteen months apart, they can be viewed as a single exposition about the appropriate bounds of church-state relations. In the reports, Johnson did not confine himself to the issue of Sunday mail delivery; he also responded to the Sabbatarians' broader claims about the religious character of the national government. Because "a variety of sentiment exists . . . on the subject of the Sabbath day," Johnson wrote, "the proper object of government is to protect all persons in the enjoyment of their religious as well as civil rights, and not to determine for any whether they shall esteem one day above another." Not only should Congress avoid choosing sides in a theological disagreement, Johnson declared, but it also lacked all authority to legislate on religious matters. "It is not the legitimate province of the legislature to determine what religion is true, or what false," Johnson wrote in the Senate report. Restating that point with different language in the House report, he added, "The framers of the constitution recognized the eternal principle that man's relation with his God is above human legislation, and his rights of conscience [are] inalienable."[36]

Johnson also responded to the Sabbatarians' assertions about a Christian basis for government and of a corresponding obligation to enact supportive laws. "Our government is a civil, and not a religious, institution," he wrote. Johnson rebuked the moral reformers for their efforts to impose their religious views on society and infuse them into policy. Should Congress bow to their efforts, he continued, "it would establish the principle that the legislature is a proper tribunal to determine what are the laws of God."[37] For Johnson, repealing the mail delivery requirement would impose a religious tenet by law and would be the first step toward a religious establishment:

> If a solemn act of legislation shall, in one point, define the law of God, or point out to the citizen one religious duty, it may, with equal propriety, proceed to define every part of divine revelation, and enforce every religious obligation, even to the forms and ceremonies of worship, the endowment of the church, and the support of the clergy.

For these reasons, he concluded, it "is inevitable that the line cannot be too strongly drawn between church and state."[38]

Coming on the heels of Ezra Stiles Ely's much publicized call for a Christian party, people on both sides of the controversy interpreted Johnson's reports as a repudiation of the growing power of "extensive religious combinations." The reports were widely praised by Democrats, freethinkers, and religious liberals: by "arresting the schemes of an ambitious, irreligious priesthood," asserted a New York Mason in 1833, "Colonel Johnson has done more for liberal principles, for freedom of opinion, and for pure and unadulterated democracy, than any [other] man in our country." In contrast, critics called Johnson's conclusions "most unkind, unfair, and unchristian." "Satan never accomplished a greater temporary victory over this institution . . . than was accomplished by this and the former reports." The reports secured Johnson the loyalty of Democrats and likely facilitated his selection as Van Buren's vice-presidential running mate in 1836.[39]

Sabbatarians and moral reformers were disheartened but not dissuaded by their loss over Sunday mail delivery. They persisted with their campaigns for moral reform while continuing to warn about the threats of irreligion that they believed were fueled by a misguided and antireligious perspective about church-state relations. In 1838, Whig senator Theodore Frelinghuysen wrote a lengthy missive about the dangers of a Jeffersonian view of church-state separation. Frelinghuysen was a devout evangelical, known as "the Christian statesman" and a "man of most preserving religiosity," who was affiliated with several moral-reform societies.[40] In addition to repeating the same litany of immoral behaviors that Beecher had condemned, Frelinghuysen denounced the "false" theory of church-state relations being advanced by Jacksonians and their freethinking allies. The "the danger of formal alliances between church and state, is [a] matter of history and well understood," Frelinghuysen wrote, "but the propriety and merit of *political irreligion*—of carrying on the business of the commonwealth professedly as 'without God in the world' . . . was never openly taught and accredited till very recent times." Frelinghuysen knew who to blame for this trend: "President Jefferson was the first American teacher if this sort of doctrine." The "sophistry of this reasoning" was responsible not only for the rise of immorality but also efforts to restrict Christian influences on society. "The whole land is infected and becoming sick with the notion, that somehow there is that in the nature of our government, that calls not only for caution in regard to religion, but for a distinct jealousy against it." Among "a certain set [i.e., Democrats and freethinkers], it is already fashionable to rail against religion under the very pretext of patriotism or regard for the laws." For Frelinghuysen, the effects of this trend were all too evident: "the majority of the sabbath mails committee, in the most elaborate effort ever made in this country for the political annihilation of christianity, were misled as much by wrong notions in their respect as by ill intentions." He called on people to distinguish the necessary influence of "ethical Christianity" from that of "ecclesiastical Christianity."

"[W]e want the government honestly *administered on christian principles, and with christian ends in view.*" But "Mr. Jefferson's dogma" about church-state separation, Frelinghuysen insisted, represented "a false position."[41]

Frelinghuysen's missive was not unique. As evangelicalism became more entrenched in the culture, calls for a limited understanding of church-state separation grew, fueled in part by revisionist histories that echoed the arguments of Rev. Jasper Adams. Motivated to construct a narrative about the nation's founding that matched their millennial aspirations about America's chosen status, evangelical historians set out to sanctify its origins and to elevate its founders (George Washington in particular) and its governing documents.[42] In his widely read book *Religion in the United States* (1844), Robert Baird wrote that "[a]ll the leading men [at the Constitutional Convention] were believers in Christianity, and Washington, as the world knows, was a Christian." Despite condemning the "union of church and state," Baird asserted the Constitution was based on Christian principles and presumed a close relationship between the two: the "constitution was not intended for a people that had no religion." Rather, "it was for a people already Christian, and whose existing laws . . . gave ample evidence of their being favourable to religion." For Baird, avoiding a "union of church and state" did not require a separation of the two entities.[43]

Other revisionist writers promoted the same narrative. In his 1853 book *The Position of Christianity in the United States*, Stephen Colwell insisted the founders were "Christian men" "of a Christian country" who "acknowledged the revelation of [God's] will contained in the Holy Scriptures" in the Constitution. "[T]hey derived the sanctions of their institutions, and the morality if their legislation and of the whole social system, from the Scriptures."[44] Benjamin Morris concurred in his book *The Christian Life and Character of the Civil Institutions of the United States* (1864) that "the Constitution was formed under Christian influence and is, in its purposes and spirit, a Christian instrument." Like the holy authorship of the Scriptures, a divine hand guided the drafting of the Constitution. "The Christian faith and character of the men who formed the Constitution forbid the idea that they designed not to place the Constitution and its government under the providence and protection of God and the principles of the Christian religion," Morris asserted. In this sanctified understanding of the founding, there was little room for Jeffersonian notions of church-state separation.[45] Both Colwell and Morris envisioned few constraints on the government's ability to advance Christianity. Whereas Baird viewed the Establishment Clause in a negative sense as not barring government aid to religion generally, Colwell and Morris turned the clause into an affirmative obligation to "promote the interest of religion." That religion, of course, was Protestantism. Colwell offered a limited understanding of separation, one that benefited Christianity solely: only "the Christian religion is declared to be out of the reach of Congressional interference," he wrote. "Any other religion inconsistent with Christianity may be prohibited. . . . Legislation may promote the interests of religion by any measures not inconsistent with toleration." Thus, for Colwell, "Christianity has all the authority and control over our legislation, our institutions and their administration." Although these revisionist writers did not attack church-state separation directly, as Frelinghuysen had done, their sanctified interpretations of the founding and of the Constitution left little remaining of the Jeffersonian and Madisonian understanding of separationism. In its place, they promoted a form of separationism that protected Protestant institutions and values. With the growth of evangelicalism and demise of organized free thought after 1840, voices supporting a robust understanding of church-state separation became fewer and fewer.[46]

Church and State in the Courts

During the first half of the nineteenth century, the principle of separation of church and state rarely appeared in judicial decisions. The most likely explanation for this is that judges and attorneys did not perceive it as being a legally operative rule. The idea that litigants could use rights declared in the federal and state constitutions to block a government action was not widely held in the early nineteenth century.[47]

An additional reason for the paucity of judicial acknowledgments of separationism was the prevalence of a competing legal theorem: that Christian principles infused and informed aspects of the common law. The maxim that "Christianity is part of the common law" found its roots in medieval British law and had been promoted by noted British jurists such as Sir Edward Coke and William Blackstone, the latter's *Commentaries on the Common Law* being widely popular among early American lawyers. In addition, two of the nation's more influential jurists, Justice Joseph Story and Chancellor James Kent, embraced the maxim in their writings and legal decisions.[48] What the maxim meant in practical terms was that officials could enforce behavioral laws, such as blasphemy and Sunday observance regulations, according to Christian norms. So, in an 1811 case, *People v. Ruggles*, Kent (then New York chief justice) upheld a blasphemy conviction on the ground that "Christianity, in its enlarged sense, as a religion revealed and taught in the Bible, is not unknown to our law." In a handful of other antebellum blasphemy cases, judges relied on the maxim to turn aside defendants' claims that such prosecutions violated rights of conscience and exceeded the authority of civil officials.[49] The other area in which the maxim found wide application was in prosecutions for Sunday law violations, where the law was seen as originating from the Ten Commandments. Because antebellum judges rarely attempted to reconcile their holdings with notions of church-state separation, it is impossible to determine whether they perceived that any conflict existed.[50]

In one Sabbath case, however, judges were forced to confront that tension. In 1845, a trial judge overturned a fine for a Sunday law violation on the basis that "in a community where there is complete severance between Church and State, and where entire freedom of religious faith and worship is guaranteed to all its citizens alike," matters of religious discipline "in no way pertain to the civil power or legislative authority of the State." Appealing the holding to the South Carolina Supreme Court, the prosecutor argued the fine should be reinstated because "Christianity is part of the common law of the land." Faced with two competing theorems—church-state separation and the maxim—the supreme court chose the latter. "Christianity, general Christianity, is, and always has been, a part of the common law," declared Justice John B. O'Neall. O'Neall perceived no conflict between the legal recognition of Christianity and constitutional principles; on the contrary, it was Christianity that "gave to us this noble safeguard of religious toleration." Although O'Neall acknowledged that under the Constitution, "[t]here could be no union of Church and State [and] no religion established by law," that prohibition "plainly pointed to the evils" that had existed with the "Church of England, as an established State religion." Church-state separation represented nothing more than the abolition of formal religious establishments.[51]

As the century progressed, however, religious justifications for behavioral laws declined in reported cases due to several factors: the professionalization of legal practice, the need for objectivity and predictability in the law, the growing popularity of an amoral legal positivism that served as a counter to natural law theories, and the nation's growing religious diversity.[52] These trends led a handful of judges to side with defendants' religious freedom claims, sometimes disputing the law incorporated Christianity and, at other times, affirming principles of church-state separation. In 1853, the Ohio Supreme Court overturned a Sunday law conviction on the ground that the defendant's activities had not caused a public disturbance. Though leaving the Sunday law in place, Justice Allen Thurman held that it "could not stand for a moment as a law of this state, if its sole foundation was the christian duty of keeping that day holy, and its sole motive to enforce the observance of the day." Under the Ohio Constitution, Thurman wrote, "neither Christianity, nor any other system of religion, is part of the law of the state." "We have no union of church and state, nor has our government ever been vested with authority to enforce any religious observance, simply because it is religious."[53] Five years later the California Supreme Court went a step further, striking down the state's Sunday law for having a religious purpose, the first appellate decision to do so. Chief Justice David Terry wrote that the law conflicted with the state constitution, which guaranteed "not only complete toleration, but religious liberty in its largest sense—a complete separation between Church and State, and a perfect equality without distinction between all religious sects." Church-state separation prevented the government's enforcement of a religious obligation.[54]

Affirmations of separationism occurred in other legal contexts. In 1846, the Virginia Supreme Court struck down the practice of excluding the testimony of witnesses who could not affirm a belief in God and future accountability. Speaking for the court, Justice John Scott observed that the state constitution "wholly and permanently separated 'religion, or the duty which we owe to our Creator,' from our political and civil government" and placed "all religions on a footing of perfect equality; protecting all; imposing neither burdens nor civil incapacities upon any; conferring privileges upon none."[55] Other states were slow to abolish all religious aspects to oath-swearing, with most courts retaining a requirement of some religious obligation to tell the truth. Yet, as the century progressed, a handful of state courts interpreted their constitutions to require the abolition of religious oaths. Writing in 1882, the Kentucky Court of Appeals asserted that the state constitution's no-establishment clause "makes competent as witnesses all persons so far as any religious test is concerned. . . . The object of this provision was to make the divorce between church and state irrevocable, [and] to establish unequivocally that the province of the government is to deal with the temporal relations and affairs of men, and in no case with matters spiritual."[56]

A final area where principles of church-state separation factored prominently involved disputes over church property and the internal decision-making of church bodies. The volatile and competing faith claims inspired by the antebellum revivals, and the impending national conflict over slavery, produced schisms within many congregations, frequently resulting in disputes between factions over the control of church property and assets. Conflicts over property ownership occurred most commonly within denominations where dioceses and synods held title to church buildings. Warring factions often ended up court, requiring judges to adjudicate competing claims involving interpretations of religious doctrine or church polity.[57] Prior to the Civil War, the prevailing rule was based on English precedent—called the "departure from doctrine" rule—which authorized civil courts to examine church doctrines and procedures to determine which faction was in theological error.[58]

As the century progressed, judges began questioning whether civil courts were competent to rule on religious matters. In *Watson v. Jones* (1872), the US Supreme Court considered a dispute involving a Louisville, Kentucky, Presbyterian church whose membership had split over the issue of slavery. There the Court repudiated the departure from doctrine rule, holding that civil courts could not generally adjudicate disputes between members of church congregations over the ownership and use of church property. Writing for the Court, Justice Joseph Miller held that this prohibition applied particularly when disputes involved the interpretation of church doctrine or theology: "the rule of action which should govern the civil courts, founded in a broad and sound view of the relations of church and state under our system of laws . . . is, that, whenever the questions of discipline, or of faith, or ecclesiastical rule, custom, or law have been decided by the highest of these church judicatories . . . the [civil] tribunals must accept such decisions as final, and as binding on them." Justice Miller did not rely expressly on church-state separation, but his opinion presumed distinct spheres of authority that should remain separate. Religious associations had the "unquestioned" right to determine their own doctrines and to control the internal "government of all the individual members, congregations, and officers within the general association," Miller wrote.[59]

Because the *Watson* holding came before incorporation of the First Amendment to the states, it was only advisory and not binding on state courts. Nonetheless, the decision was influential, and state courts shortly adopted its reasoning, with a handful identifying the connection between the rule and church-state separation. The "complete separation of church and state" necessitated the *Watson* rule, wrote one court, while another asserted that "Civil courts in this country have no ecclesiastical jurisdiction. . . . This doctrine inevitably results from that total separation between church and state which . . . is essential to the full enjoyment of the guaranteed rights of American citizenship." Courts should "maintain the boundary between Church and State, and let each revolve in its respective sphere," declared the Illinois Supreme Court. The Nebraska Supreme Court concurred, writing in 1895 that churches "should be free from the interference of the courts where there is nothing drawn into question but the jurisdiction of the church over one of its members or ministers or officers." Not only was this rule "thought to be the best policy, and consistent with good government"; it was also consistent with the principle that "the church and state [should] be completely severed, or as nearly so as may be and can be with due observance of all proper laws." By the late nineteenth century, the idea that church-state separation secured the independence and autonomy of religious institutions over their internal operations was well established.[60]

While the above cases represent only a fraction of the court decisions on oaths, Sunday law enforcement, and church property disputes in which church-state separation was never referenced, they still indicate a degree of familiarity with the concept among nineteenth-century judges and lawyers.

The Church-State "Questions"

Of all of the controversies that impacted the development of church-state relations during the nineteenth century, two stand apart in significance: the controversy over religious instruction in public schools and the funding of parochial schooling, jointly called the "School Question," and the conflict between the federal government and the Church of Jesus Christ of Latter-day Saints (LDS or Mormon Church), known as the "Mormon Question." The School Question captured widespread public attention throughout the century, whereas the Mormon Question did the same for the second half of the century. In both controversies, combatants employed rhetoric of church-state separation to support their positions. More than any other controversy, the School Question unified evangelical Protestants behind church-state separation, with evangelicals finding common ground with religious liberals and freethinkers, though diverging from them over the ultimate meaning of the principle. And with the Mormon Question, both sides justified their competing stances on church-state grounds, with opponents of the LDS Church asserting that the Mormon "theocracy" undermined church-state separation, and LDS leaders responding that the government's efforts to suppress the church violated the same principle. In the debates surrounding both controversies, the rhetoric of church-state separation flowed freely, though not always supplying a coherent message.[61]

The School Question

Public schooling in the United States arose chiefly in the first third of the nineteenth century. Prior to that time, education had taken place in private academies or through private tutors, though in New England a forerunner of public schooling existed in town or "district" grammar schools that commonly operated under a partnership between the town and the locally settled Congregational minister. In addition, most eastern cities had denominationally run "charity schools" that provided rudimentary instruction for poorer children. In all instances, instruction had a strong Protestant orientation, with an emphasis on reading texts such as the Calvinist *New England Primer* and reciting religious catechisms. At the time, all educators concurred that schooling must instill virtues of industry, self-discipline, and morality, and most people believed that those virtues could not be taught without teaching their religious basis.[62]

In the closing years of the eighteenth century, reformers including Benjamin Rush and Noah Webster began calling for a system of common schools that would be under the control of public officials and open to children of all social classes and religions. Though accepting the assumption of a relationship between religion, morality, and education, they criticized the prevailing practice of religious indoctrination. The "frequent repetition . . . of scripture, therefore, which are calculated to strike terror to the mind lose their influence by being too frequently brought into view," wrote Webster. Not only was devotional instruction stultifying and distracting from learning essential subjects; it also encroached on rights of conscience. Yet the same objection did not apply to instruction in "the history and morality of the Bible." Fellow reformer Samuel Knox believed that public schools could identify and teach general principles of Christian morality that were common to all denominations. Knox urged that "a well-digested, concise moral catechism" to "impress on the tender mind a reverence of the Deity," followed by "a short and suitable prayer," was both appropriate and sufficient. Most reformers did not object to using the Bible to instill morality and civic virtue. "My wish," iterated Webster, "is not to see the Bible excluded from schools but to see it is used as a system of religion and morality."[63]

The reformers' idea of a publicly funded and managed system of education gained support, and most early state constitutions included provisions authorizing legislatures to establish schools and create school funding accounts. The idea of nonsectarian education also took root throughout much of the country, though the degree of religious instruction varied greatly, particularly in communities with greater religious homogeneity.[64] In the 1830s, a new generation of education reformers emerged, committed to standardizing public education and refining the understanding of nonsectarianism. These educators were at the forefront of establishing common schools in their states: Horace Mann in Massachusetts, Henry Barnard in Connecticut, Caleb Mills in Indiana, and Samuel Lewis and Calvin Stowe in

Ohio. They sought to change the assumptions and applications of nonsectarian education by eradicating its residual doctrinal character and evangelizing practices. On one hand, reformers believed that religion should remain at the center of public education and that schools had an obligation to teach character and moral virtue that was derived from the scriptures. "[C]orrect moral principles must be inculcated in the common school," wrote Barnard in his *Connecticut Common School Journal* in 1841. Where schools taught a biblical standard for morality, "there will be more order and quietness; the children will be more easily governed, and will make greater proficiency in their studies." At the same time, public schools had to foreswear teaching Protestant doctrines: "Instruction in those points which divide the sects from each other, must be confined to the family and the Sunday school," Calvin Stowe exclaimed. Rather, "[t]he Bible, the whole Bible, and nothing but the Bible, without note or comment, must be taken as the text-book of religious instruction." Teachers should emphasize principles of God's love and sovereignty and those virtues of duty and honesty that all Christians embraced. As Professor Noah Feldman writes, advocates believed nonsectarianism "would keep the state out of bitter inter-denominational disputes, enable the flourishing of diverse voluntary, private churches, and simultaneously enable the state to take a stance in favor of broadly shared, foundational Christian values."[65]

Like his fellow reformers, Horace Mann insisted that the Bible's essential truths were accessible to any person who read the book with an open mind—let the Bible "*speak for itself*," he pleaded. He and other reformers had an unrelenting belief that they could identify and teach moral and religious values that would appeal to all well-meaning Christians, even Catholics. "[T]he points on which different portions of a Christian community differ among themselves are far less numerous than those on which they agree," Mann insisted.[66] This unflinching belief in universality constituted a blind spot for reformers when they encountered complaints from Catholics, Jews, and freethinkers that the "universal" religious truths were not shared by them. "Protestants like Mann sincerely believed that their nonsectarianism was capacious enough to include Catholics, who were Christians like themselves," writes Professor Feldman. Mann did not think his system promoted Protestantism, insisting that common schools "should do all they could to make themselves acceptable to Catholics." In return, Mann hoped that "Catholics ought to participate in the venture of common schools rather than form schools of their own."[67]

In addition to its practical advantages, Mann believed nonsectarianism was consistent with constitutional principles. Writing in his *Twelfth Report* as secretary to the Massachusetts Board of Education, Mann described how all church-state "schemes" fell into two systems. The first system, still prevalent in Europe, held "the regulation and control of the religious belief of the people [is] one of the functions of government." In contrast, under "the other system, religious belief is a matter of individual and parental concern; and, while the government furnishes all practicable facilities for the independent formation of that belief, it exercises no authority to prescribe, or coercion to enforce it." America was the "solitary example" of this latter system. Employing Madison's concept of "jurisdiction," Mann insisted that "there are some things which are within the jurisdiction of government, and other things which are not within it." Rights "which are strictly religious lie out of, and beyond the jurisdiction of civil government." As a result, Mann asserted, there was "a line, dividing the jurisdiction" of each entity. Church and the state operated in separate spheres, with civil government lacking authority over religious matters. Although Mann did not use the exact language of separationism, his report relied on that concept. That notion of separation was not so strict, however, as to prevent the government from using religion to inculcate those important interests of morality and civic virtue necessary for the nation's well-being.[68]

Despite their unflagging belief in the attributes of nonsectarianism, Mann and his fellow reformers could not have been more wrong about its broad appeal, particularly to Catholics. Catholics, evangelicals, and religious liberals assailed his nonsectarian system. "Mann's brand seemed to many evangelical Protestants to be suspiciously 'Unitarian,'" writes historian Sidney Mead, and "what passed as 'nonsectarian' religious teaching seemed to many Unitarians, Roman Catholics, and others to be evangelical Protestantism." Evangelicals accused the Massachusetts schools of being "Godless," while New York Catholic bishop John Hughes charged that nonsectarianism promoted "the sectarianism of infidelity" and Protestantism at the same time.[69]

Mann and his fellow reformers tirelessly promoted nonsectarianism throughout the antebellum period. Gradually evangelical Protestants were won over to the concept, if not necessarily Mann's definition of it. By placing the Bible at the center of nonsectarianism and emphasizing the teaching of Christian morality, reformers were able to convince evangelical doubters that nonsectarianism did not promote infidelity. Although evangelicals lamented the loss of doctrinal rigor, they found comfort in assurances that the emerging public-school system would retain a Protestant character. Congregationalist theologian Horace Bushnell spoke for many evangelicals who resigned themselves to nonsectarian education. Bushnell regretted that many people "have come to look upon the interest of public education as a matter entirely apart from religion." Because Protestantism was "in our civil order and the political fabric of our government," he insisted, "it seems to be quite natural and right . . . that our common schools should remain Protestant." Yet Bushnell recognized that in order to retain religious influences in education, schools had to adapt: "The great point with all Christians must be to secure the bible in its proper place. To this as a sacred duty all sectarian aims must be sacrificed. Nothing is more certain than that no such thing as a sectarian religion is to find a place in our schools."[70]

The reformers' success in winning over evangelicals to nonsectarianism was not replicated with Catholic officials. Whether in a devotional exercise or an unmediated reading, the Bible used was the *Protestant* King James Bible. Catholic leaders objected to the Protestant character of the Bible readings and the Protestant assumption that students could comprehend essential truths through an unmediated reading rather than through one conducted under the guidance of clergy.[71] Adding to the hostile environment for Catholics were the grammar books and popular readers, many produced by the American Tract Society and other benevolent societies, that incorporated material and themes that extolled Protestantism and criticized Catholicism. Protestant cultures were equated with freedom and republican virtues, whereas Catholic societies were said to promote the opposite.[72] As early as 1829, American Catholic bishops circulated a pastoral letter that condemned the frequent "misrepresentation of the tenets, the principles and the practices of our church" in the common schools. In subsequent letters, the bishops' criticisms of the Protestant bias in public schooling intensified, with their 1840 letter remarking that they could "scarcely point out a book in general use in the [common] schools . . . wherein covert and insidious efforts are not made to misrepresent our principles, to distort out tenets, to vilify our practices and to bring contempt upon our Church." So, even if Catholic doctrine had not encouraged a Catholic-centered education, the Protestant character of the common schools would likely have driven Catholic leaders to establish parochial schools.[73]

Conflicts over nonsectarian Bible reading broke out in the 1840s and 1850s with the rise in Catholic immigration and the increased enrollment of Catholic children in the public schools. In places, Catholic and Jewish schoolchildren faced proselytizing by Protestant tract and missionary societies, often with the complicity of school officials. Catholic leaders objected strenuously to the practices, usually to no avail. In 1842, a priest in Upstate New York publicly burned several King James Bibles that tract societies had distributed in Catholic neighborhoods. Protestant and nativist newspapers sensationalized the event, which only reinforced Protestant beliefs about Catholic hostility toward the Bible.[74]

Then, in 1844, a conflict erupted in Philadelphia that demonstrated how Bible reading had become a proxy for anti-Catholicism and fears about economic displacement due to immigration. That summer, the city experienced two rounds of rioting between Protestant craftspeople and Catholic immigrants, ostensibly over the issue of Bible reading in the common schools. The episode, commonly known as the Philadelphia Bible Riots, resulted in approximately thirty deaths and scores wounded. The riots were stoked, in no small part, by the rise of nativist patriotic associations such as the American Republicans and American Protestant Association. Protestant craftspeople and artisans, seeing their economic well-being threatened by an unskilled labor force of immigrants who worked for less money, were drawn to nativist causes.[75]

Nativist writers, including Samuel F. B. Morse and Lyman Beecher, also fueled anti-Catholic sentiments through inflammatory missives that combined stereotypes of ignorant and pliable Irish immigrants with papal designs to undermine America's republican institutions. The Vatican was bent on suppressing republican movements in Europe and exporting its "intolerant and anti-republican tenets" to America through a cadre of foreign-born priests, Beecher charged. In addition to the Catholic threat to republican principles, it was "a union of church and state that we fear," Beecher exclaimed. "No treason against our free institutions would be more fatal than a union of church and state," an arrangement the Catholic Church preferred. "[O]nly keep church and state apart, and there will be no danger."[76] Nativists thus became some of the more vocal supporters of common schooling and church-state separation. As two apologists for the American (Know-Nothing) Party wrote in 1855, "We must maintain our Christian character as a nation. . . . We must continue scrupulously to preserve the Church and State separate from each other. We must again avow and maintain the Christianity of our public education."[77]

In response to a hostile common-school environment, Catholic bishops called for creating parochial schools and then for a pro rata share of funds for their schools.[78] Public-school educators and Protestant leaders vigorously resisted such requests, based in part on anti-Catholic biases and fears that a competing education system would threaten the financial security of the fledgling common schools. Objectors also argued that funding religious education would violate principles of church-state separation.[79] Although separationism was a convenient rationale for masking underlying anti-Catholic sentiments, a ban on public funding of religion had long-standing bona fides. As early as the 1820s, officials of the New York Free School Society—a nonsectarian charity school—had objected to the city's funding of Baptist and Methodist charity schools on the ground that only the society's schools provided a *common* education through its program of nonsectarian instruction. In contrast to its curriculum designed to appeal to children of all faiths, the society argued, the purpose of denominational schools was "to inculcate the particular doctrines and opinions of the sect having the management of them." The public funding of denominational schools "impose[d] a direct tax on our citizens for the support of religion" in violation of rights of conscience, the Society insisted. "[T]he proposition that such a fund should never go into the hands of an ecclesiastical body or religious society, is presumed to be incontrovertible upon any political principle approved or established in this country." In an 1831 report, the city council agreed with the society, declaring that it could not "perceive any marked difference in principle" between the public funding of a church or a religious school; as a result, it would be "a virtual violation of . . . the Constitution to appropriate a fund, purely civil in its character and object, to the support of religious schools." If the public funding of religious schools was allowed, the report maintained, "[t]he unnatural union of Church and State will then be easily accomplished—a union destructive of human happiness and subversion of civil liberty."[80]

Before long, states began enacting laws and constitutional provisions barring the use of public funds for religious education. Massachusetts enacted the first such prohibition as part of its 1827 law requiring nonsectarian public education. In his *Twelfth Report*, Mann relied on this law in asserting that tax support of religious schools "would satisfy, at once, the largest definition of a Religious Establishment." New York enacted a funding ban in 1842, and ten years later the California legislature included a clause in the state's school-fund authorization that restricted the monies to schools "free from all denominational and sectarian bias, control or influence."[81]

Between 1834 and the Civil War, eight states enacted constitutional provisions that prohibited applying public monies for the benefit of any religious school or society. Michigan was the first to enact an express no-funding provision in its 1835 constitution, providing that "no money shall be drawn from the treasury for the benefit of religious societies, or theological or religious seminaries." This provision was in addition to a "no compelled support" of religion clause, a common provision that dated back to the Pennsylvania Constitution of 1776. Over the following decades, Ohio (1851), Indiana (1851), and Massachusetts (1855) added express no-funding provisions to their constitutions, while a handful of new states—Wisconsin (1847), Minnesota

(1857), Oregon (1857), and Kansas (1858)—included no-funding provisions in their initial constitutions.[82] The legislative histories are generally sparse on the rationales behind the adoption of the provisions; at least two of the state conventions—Oregon and Kansas—simply borrowed language from other state constitutions. Yet in Oregon, several delegates spoke about the importance of including a no-funding clause. Delegate George Williams said that he did not

> believe that congress had any right to take the public money, contributed by the people, of all creeds and faith [sic], to pay for religious teachings. It was a violent stretch of power, and an unauthorized one. A man in this country had a right to be a Methodist, Baptist, Roman Catholic, or what else he chose, but no government had the moral right to tax all of these creeds and classes to inculcate directly or indirectly the tenets of any one of them.[83]

Oregon delegate La Fayette Grover concurred, stating that "[t]he late constitutions of the western states have, step by step, tended to a more distinct separation of church and state." It was true, he continued, that "this constitution goes a step further than other constitutions on this subject, but if that step is in the right direction, and consistent with the proper development of our institutions, I see no weight in the objection that it is new. Let us take the step farther, and declare a complete divorce of church and state."[84] While the timing of these constitutional and statutory revisions was likely connected to heightened awareness of Catholic immigration and the creation of competing parochial schools—Massachusetts's 1855 provision arose during a time of Know-Nothing prominence in the state—the development of the no-funding principle also relied on established ideas about church-state separation.[85]

The rule against funding religious schooling went far to solidify evangelical support for church-state separation. At the same time, most people did not see separationism as restricting nonsectarian exercises in public schools, despite their Protestant complexion. That second perception was increasingly challenged in the years following the Civil War, not only by Catholics but also by Jews, freethinkers, liberal Protestants, and professional educators who came to question the efficacy and fairness of nonsectarian Bible reading.

In 1869, the most famous legal case involving nonsectarian Bible reading erupted in Cincinnati after the school board banned the religious exercises in hope of attracting more Catholic children to the public schools. A "Friends of the Bible" committee quickly filed a lawsuit in state court challenging the board's action. After five days of arguments, the Superior Court voted 2–1 to reverse the board's action, with the majority writing that "there never was a State that existed long without the bonds and sanctions of some religion," which, in Ohio, was Christianity. The board's action banning Bible reading could not stand because it "positively prohibit[ed] religious instruction, and thus cut off the instrumentality by which those essentials to good government are cultivated."[86] Judge Alphonso Taft dissented, arguing that Bible reading "was and is sectarian. It is Protestant worship." Taft went on to declare that it was "an entire mistake to assert that the Protestant Christian religion has been so identified with the history and government of our State or country." To hold Protestants were "entitled to have their mode of worship and their Bible used in the common schools is to hold to the union of Church and State, however we may repudiate and reproach the name."[87] After a three-year-long appeal, the Ohio Supreme Court reversed the lower court, reinstating the school board's decision banning Bible reading. Relying on separationist principles, Justice John Welsh declared that religion was "eminently one of those interests, lying outside the true and legitimate province of government." The state "can have no religious opinions," he noted. "United with government, religion never rises above the merest superstition; united with religion, government never rises above the merest despotism; and all history shows us that the more widely and completely they are separated, the better it is for both."[88]

The interrelated issues of nonsectarian exercises in the public schools and the public funding of religious schools came to a head in the mid-1870s in the lead-up to the 1876 presidential election. Challenges to Bible reading continued, stoking concerns among Protestants, while reports emerged that Catholic schools and charitable institutions were receiving public funds despite laws and policies to the contrary. In cities with large Catholic populations, such as New York, Boston, and Baltimore, party bosses regularly granted Catholic requests for public financial assistance in exchange for political support.[89] These controversies fueled concerns among Protestants, educators, and Republican Party officials that the no-funding principle and church-state separation were at risk. As the *New York Tribune* opined in 1875, the School Question was threatening "the very existence of the republic."[90]

Republican leaders, with their Protestant allies, called for a political solution to resolve the School Question. In the fall of 1875, President Ulysses S. Grant, hoping to rehabilitate his tarnished political career, issued a call to "[e]ncourage free schools, and resolve that not one dollar, appropriated for their support, shall be appropriated to the support of any sectarian schools.... Keep the Church and State forever separate." In a later address to Congress, Grant proposed enacting a constitutional amendment to prohibit the "granting of any school funds or taxes . . . for the benefit of or in aid, directly or indirectly, of any religious sect or denomination." Shortly thereafter, Representative James G. Blaine, the front-runner for the 1876 Republican nomination for president, introduced into Congress a proposed amendment to that effect (commonly called the "Blaine Amendment"). Democrats, with their large Catholic constituency, generally opposed the measure, and the School Question quickly became a leading issue in the ensuing election. As the *New York Times* opined, an "appeal to religious passions was worth twenty-five thousand votes to the Republicans."[91]

The twin issues of the Blaine Amendment and nonsectarian instruction ignited another public debate over the relationship between religion and government and the meaning of church-state separation. Parts of the debate were predictable. Catholics and Protestants hurled charges and countercharges at each other, alleging bigotry, political expediency, and hostility to public education. Evangelical Protestants tied the controversy over nonsectarian instruction and Bible reading to Catholic attempts to secure public funding for parochial schools; they believed that Protestants had already conceded too much without placating Catholic opposition to public education. Catholics, in turn, charged Protestants and Republicans with bias and demanded equitable treatment.[92]

The debate was not entirely binary, however. A smattering of educators, liberal Protestants, Jews, and freethinkers argued that separationism prohibited both nonsectarian instruction and the funding of religious education. One leading figure was William Torrey Harris, superintendent of the St. Louis public schools—where he had ended Bible reading—and a future US commissioner of education. In an 1876 article in the *Atlantic Monthly*, Harris called for making public schools "a purely secular institution, without any religious instruction in it whatever." This, he maintained, was required by "wide-spread conviction that church and state should be kept separate." The "incompatibility between religious instruction and secular instruction" necessitated "separating the two for the highest perfection of each." He agreed with Catholic critics that it was "impossible to have any such unsectarian religion that is not regarded as sectarian by the more earnest religious denominations." But the same principle of separationism also prohibited funding of parochial schools. "The step to a church establishment is a very short one from the endowment of church schools." Harris called on all combatants to accept a "slowly, but constantly growing fact in modern history, the separation of church and state."[93]

A host of Protestant ministers and journals joined Harris in proposing an end to Bible reading as the way to defuse the school-funding controversy. Like Harris, many embraced church-state separation as the operative principle. The "secular civil state" required "an entire separation of Church and State," wrote one minister, while another called for "the final and complete severance of church from state." The "association of Church and State . . . is contrary to the principle of republican institutions," charged a Unitarian minister from Iowa, whereas a speaker from Indiana urged erecting "an impassable barrier between the union of Church and State." It was "a fundamental principle, which defines the functions of the civil State" and should guide the State in all its relations to religion. Separation was a "self-evident . . . American doctrine" upon which "all agree."[94] The most prominent minister to add his voice to the debate was Henry Ward Beecher, son of the indefatigable Lyman Beecher. As pastor of Pilgrim Congregational Church in Brooklyn, Beecher was considered to be the nation's foremost preacher, but unlike his father, Beecher was a theological progressive. Authoring a series of articles in his journal, *Christian Union*, Beecher insisted that "compulsory Bible in schools is not in accordance with American doctrines of the liberty of conscience." Like Harris, Beecher argued that the "common school, as supported by the state, is a civil and not a religious institution." As a result, he insisted, it was "too late to adopt the church-state doctrine."[95]

No Protestant leader engaged in the debate more than Presbyterian Samuel T. Spear, editor of *The Independent* and author of a four-hundred-page book titled *Religion and the State*. In his writings, Spear called for a secular education system, an end to Protestant Bible reading under any guise, and a ban on funding parochial schools. "The objection . . . of the Catholic, the Jew, and the Infidel against any Protestant regime in the public school is a valid one," he argued, and should be sustained "unless we abandon the fundamental principles of our republican system." Yet for Spear, while the School Question represented "one of the sharpest issues between" Catholics and Protestants, it "manifestly [did] not cover the whole question in controversy" regarding church and state. The state was "a civil power, existing and acting for temporal purposes." Thus, it had no authority over religion, Spear insisted, and even if it tried, it would always devolve into sectarianism. He asserted that the founders built the nation's political system "upon the principle that religion and civil government were to be kept entirely distinct." People of all faiths stood in equal regard under the Constitution, he maintained, "No class has any monopoly of these rights, whether home or foreign-born, whether of this or that faith." The only way to ensure that equal standing was through the separation of church and state.[96]

Finally, leaders of the Jewish Reform movement also participated in the debate. Rabbis Max Lilienthal and Isaac Mayer Wise called for an end to Bible reading and for restricting public funding to public schools. Rabbi Lilienthal proclaimed Jewish support for "an unsectarian free-school system" and called "separation of church and state . . . the brightest gem of the American diadem." Rabbi Wise went further than Lilienthal, calling for *secular* public schools, commenting that Jews "are opposed to Bible reading in the schools. We want secular schools and nothing else. . . . Having no religion, [the state] cannot impose any religious instruction upon the citizen." Lilienthal's and Wise's support for church-state separation was not surprising considering Jewish disagreement with Sunday law enforcement, but their opposition to Bible reading exposed Jews to criticism from evangelicals. Still, they accepted those risks, and their statements helped solidify Jewish support behind church-state separation, a perspective Jews would carry into the next century.[97]

Back in Congress, the Democratic-controlled House of Representatives passed Blaine's proposal with a proviso that it would "not vest, enlarge, or diminish" Congress's power to legislate on the subject, effectively gutting the amendment. In the Republican-controlled Senate, Republicans introduced a more rigorous version of Blaine's amendment that prohibited the use of any federal, state, or municipal funds for "any school, educational or other institution under the control of any religious or anti-religious sect, organization, or denomination, or wherein the particular creeds or tenets shall be taught." At the last moment, Republicans inserted a clause that the amendment could "not be construed to prohibit the reading of the Bible in any school or institution." Debate in the Senate centered chiefly on issues of state's rights and partisanship; absent one limited exchange, the senators ignored the church-state aspects to the amendment. The Senate voted along party lines, falling just short of the two-thirds majority necessary for a constitutional amendment. Even though the Blaine Amendment failed to be incorporated into the Constitution, twenty-one states would adopt no-funding provisions in their respective constitutions over the ensuing fifty years. While the Blaine Amendment likely inspired some of these state no-funding provisions, states were also affirming a principle against funding religious schooling that had been developing since the 1820s.[98]

While the Blaine Amendment effectively settled questions over funding of religious education, disputes over religious exercises in the public schools persisted for the remainder of the century. Most legal challenges resulted in courts upholding Bible reading as nonsectarian, though a handful of courts struck the practices as sectarian and violating notions of church state separation.[99] At the same time, surveys indicated that an increasing number of school districts were dispensing with nonsectarian Bible reading.[100] Despite whether people advocated for nonsectarian instruction or the secularization of public education, most would have agreed with the 1890 observation of the *Universalist Quarterly and General Review* that the public school was "essential to American institutions" and that it stood "upon the principle of entire separation of church and state." As always, the meaning of that second premise was open to interpretation.[101]

Greater agreement about the meaning of church-state separation existed among Protestants and secularists when the issue turned to funding religious schools. Even Protestant denominations that operated their own religious schools concurred; as the Episcopal bishop of Albany, New York, explained in 1893, religious school funding "would destroy the efficiency of our chosen system of public schools, would foster sectarian rivalries, and deepen the lines of religious division." In addition to those practical considerations, Bishop William Croswell Doane noted that "the fact remains that among the most fundamental principles of this general government is the absolute separation of Church and State." With the School Question controversy, the idea of church-state separation became a firmly established principle.[102]

The Mormon Question

"Separation of church and state" also became a rallying cry in the government's longstanding conflict with the Church of Jesus Christ of Latter-day Saints during the last half of the century. The most familiar aspect of this controversy was the public reaction to the Mormon tenet of polygamy, or "plural marriage," which produced a legal campaign to eradicate it. But conflicts between the government and the Mormon Church, and the church-state disputes they spawned, predated the church's 1852 announcement of the tenet of plural marriage.[103] Many aspects of Mormonism concerned Protestant leaders and public officials: the assertion of a living prophet, a new revealed scripture, a unique cosmology, the separatist and communitarian nature of Mormon communities, and the authoritarian control exercised by church leaders. This last charge led to allegations that that Mormon communities operated as theocracies where the political and religious institutions were melded. Those charges received validation after Mormons established the city of Nauvoo, Illinois, in 1839, where Joseph Smith assumed the mantel of spiritual, political, and military leader, the latter as lieutenant general of the "Nauvoo Legion" militia.[104] In fact, during his 1844 campaign for US president, Smith used the term "Theo-Democracy" to describe his ultimate goal for civil society.[105] Even if Smith had not willingly employed the concept, outside observers and ex-Mormons supplied the charge. Smith's assumption of "all civil and criminal authority" amounted to a "theocracy," asserted the *Southern Literary Messenger* in 1844. Disaffected Mormons raised similar charges, decrying Smith's authoritarian control and announcing that they opposed, "with uncompromising hostility, any union of Church and State" in Nauvoo.[106]

Charges that Mormon society constituted a theocracy persisted after Smith's assassination with Brigham Young's assumption of church leadership and the migration to Utah, or "Deseret," in the late 1840s. Young surpassed the mercurial Smith in his accumulation of power, both temporal and spiritual, serving as president of the church and governor of the Utah territory. The church's announcement of plural marriages then caused a public outrage, and non-Mormons argued that the system was sustained in Utah only through an unholy mixing of church and state. Non-Mormons thus bristled when Mormon leaders defended their right to engage in polygamy on religious freedom grounds. "We are called upon to vindicate the freedom of religious opinion in the face of a theocracy which practically denies it," opined the *New York Times* in 1857. Religion and society in Utah were so "intertwined," wrote another critic, that it demanded "separation" of not only "the government and the Church" but also "of society and religion."[107]

Seeing the widespread opposition to Mormonism and polygamy, Congress responded by enacting a series of increasingly draconian laws to punish polygamists and rein in the civil power of the Mormon Church. The various laws, first enacted in 1862 in the Morrill Act, criminalized bigamy, then polygamy and cohabitation, placed limits on the LDS Church's property rights, and imposed restrictions on the civic and political rights of Mormons, including limitations on officeholding, jury service, and eventually voting.[108] In 1874, church leaders solicited Young's private secretary, George Reynolds, to challenge the constitutionality of the first section of the Morrill Act criminalizing bigamy. Reynolds had two wives, the second of which initially cooperated with the government in testifying as to her husband's polygamous marriages. Found guilty after a second trial, Reynolds appealed his conviction to the Supreme Court, challenging the constitutionality of the Morrill Act, the legality of his second wife's testimony, and the composition of the grand jury, which had excluded Mormon members.[109] After dispatching Reynold's procedural claims, the Court turned to the heart of the appeal: the trial judge's refusal to instruct the jury that Reynolds's second marriage was pursuant to a religious duty and thus protected by the First Amendment. Chief Justice Morrison R. Waite's opinion initially affirmed the importance of religious free exercise: "Religious freedom is guaranteed everywhere throughout the United States." Yet that right was not unlimited, Waite continued:

> Congress was deprived of all legislative power over mere opinion, but was left free to reach actions which were in violation of social duties or subversive of good order. . . . Laws are made for the government of actions, and while they cannot interfere with mere religious belief and opinions, they may with practices.[110]

Because polygamy had "always been odious" among civilized nations, Waite wrote, it was "impossible to believe that the constitutional guarantee of religious freedom was intended to prohibit legislation in respect to this most important feature of social life" (i.e., marriage) that was "from its very nature a sacred obligation. . . . To permit [polygamy] would be to make the professed doctrines of religious belief superior to the law of the land, and in effect to permit every citizen to become a law unto himself."[111]

For support for the proposition that the First Amendment did not prevent the government from punishing "odious" religiously motivated conduct, Waite turned to the history behind the religion clauses, relying on two writings by Thomas Jefferson. The first was the preamble to his Act for Establishing Religious Freedom, which Waite noted prohibited "the civil magistrate to intrude his powers into the field of [religious] opinion." Yet the act acknowledged authority to interfere into religious matters "when principles break out into overt acts against peace and good order." These two principles established "the true distinction between what properly belongs to the church and what to the State." For Waite, Jefferson's act supported the conclusion that the government could prosecute the religious tenet of polygamy.[112] Waite believed a second Jefferson writing reinforced the same distinction between belief and conduct. This was Jefferson's Letter to the Danbury Baptist Association, in which the president had again declared that legislative powers "reach actions only, and not opinions," implying the state could regulate the former. Likely not wanting to edit Jefferson, Waite included a fuller quotation from the letter, repeating the president's famous statement that the purpose of the religion clauses was to "build[] a wall of separation between church and state." These statements, Waite declared, could "be accepted almost as an authoritative declaration of the scope and effect of the [first] amendment." Including the "wall of separation" language from the Danbury letter was not necessary for Waite's holding; yet, ironically, this quotation from *Reynolds* became the most significant part of the decision, serving as an authority for the Supreme Court's holding in *Everson v. Board of Education* some seventy years later.[113]

Despite the *Reynolds* decision, federal officials encountered ongoing resistance to their efforts to suppress polygamy. This led Congress to enact additional legislation in 1882 and 1887 directed at suppressing the Mormon Church by seizing its assets and annulling its corporate status, in addition to depriving Mormons of many civil rights. Congressional proponents of the provisions claimed the steps were necessary to completely undo the Mormon theocracy in Utah—"to cut up by the roots this church establishment." The handful of opponents, in response, countered that Congress was exceeding its authority to outlaw polygamy by suppressing a religion for advocating its tenets. Sen. Wilkinson Call claimed that by dissolving the church, the law effectively declared that "this form of heretical belief, that this false religious establishment, shall be suppressed and destroyed, to the end that true religion, as we conceive it to be, may be maintained." It was Congress's actions, not those of the Mormon-controlled territorial legislature, that constituted a "law respecting an establishment of religion," Call declared.[114]

The new laws, with their enforcement mechanisms, ushered in ten years of aggressive prosecution of Mormon polygamists, commonly referred to as "the Raid," where hundreds of Mormon leaders were imprisoned or driven into hiding.[115] Then, in 1890, the Supreme Court upheld the federal law that dissolved the legal corporation of the LDS Church and seized its assets.[116] Facing an existential crisis, the Mormon Church succumbed to the pressure. Four months after the Supreme Court decision, Mormon president Wilford Woodruff issued a manifesto stating that there was "nothing in my teachings to the Church, or in those of my associates," that was to be construed to "encourage polygamy." Although the language of the manifesto was vague, people interpreted it as a change in church doctrine ending the religious tenet of plural marriage. Non-Mormons greeted the announcement with cautious optimism. For fifty years, wrote *The Independent*, Mormons had "asserted the supremacy of the Church over the State, and openly pronounced the doctrine of polygamy which they already practiced. The union of church and state was a direct violation of the United States Constitution." Happily now, the journal concluded, Mormon leaders "have acted in good faith in annulling the union of Church and State."[117]

An Essential American Value

As the nineteenth century concluded, the idea of church-state separation was firmly embedded into the popular culture and the law. Writers from across the political and religious spectrums either embraced the principle or accepted it as a matter of fact. Understandings of that idea varied widely, however. Congregational minister Josiah Strong, author of the best-selling book *Our Country: Its Possible Future and Its Present Crisis* (1885), spoke for many evangelicals: "Americans are singularly united, *viz.*, the entire separation of Church and State," he declared. None of the "great experiments" of the modern, civilized world was "more distinctively American than the entire separation of Church and State." Yet, as a proponent of evangelical missions and Christian civilization, Strong understood separationism chiefly in institutional terms, rather than as a cultural reality. "When the fathers added to the Constitution, the principle of strict separation of *Church* and State, they did not intend to divorce the State from all *religion*." For Strong, to understand that principle, one needed "to distinguish . . . between *church* and *religion*." Only the former was separated from the state.[118]

The liberal *Universalist Quarterly and General Review* offered a contrasting perspective. The nation's founders strove to ensure the independence of both entities and the equal treatment of all religious bodies, it wrote. To achieve this, they adopted a theory "as new in the history of politics as in the history of religion, i.e., that the Church and State are 'inherently and essentially distinct'; that the functions of the two are entirely separate; [and] that the state is purely a secular organization." The *Universalist Quarterly* also understood separation to mean the state "ought neither to support one form of religious doctrine at the expense of any other, nor even to recognize religion at all." It permitted neither government interference with religious matters nor government support for the same, however beneficial that might be to society. "This is the secular theory of government, held more or less consistently by most Americans today."[119]

Thus, by the close of the century, most people viewed church-state separation as an essential American value. Even a handful of Catholic leaders, such as Cardinal James Gibbons and Archbishop John Ireland, embraced it as the appropriate model for American society.[120] Yet separationism remained an indeterminant concept. Its protean quality invited a variety of interpretations of what separation meant, which allowed people to hold seemingly contradictory notions at the same time. "Ours is a secular nation," declared the *New Englander and Yale Magazine* in 1889, and "separation of Church and State, once declared impossible . . . has been accomplished in the United States." Yet "[o]urs is a Christian nation," continued the next paragraph, and "the same amendment which guarantees religious liberty *ipso facto* adopts the Christian ideal," which "is the ideal of true democracy." It would take another half century for the concept of church-state separation to congeal into its modern, secular form.[121]

Chapter 5

Separation Becomes Constitutional Canon

Conventional wisdom points to the Supreme Court's 1947 holding in *Everson v. Board of Education* as a watershed in church-state jurisprudence. As discussed in the introduction, in *Everson* the justices adopted church-state separation as the touchstone for interpreting the Constitution's religion clauses, effectively making separationism a constitutional rule. That all nine of the justices endorsed separationism as the controlling principle only reinforced the significance of case; in fact, the only disagreement among the justices was over how rigorous the concept should be applied. One could be forgiven for accepting the conventional view that *Everson* represented "a sea change in constitutional law."[1]

A problem with this "watershed" narrative is that it reinforces the impression that the Court's embrace of separationism was novel—that it was a break from the past, as the above statement by Justice Thomas suggests. As this book has demonstrated, the idea of separationism has deep roots in American culture and in popular and legal discourse. Justices Black's and Rutledge's extensive discussions of Jefferson and Madison, respectively, highlighted some of that history, and Black's citation to *Reynolds v. United States* acknowledged the judicial provenance of the term, despite *Reynolds* not being a case about church-state separation. But beyond the nod to *Reynolds*, the justices in *Everson* did not discuss any of the events that had transpired since the founding.[2] This left the impression that little of relevance had occurred since

1802, which again reinforced criticism that the justices had either invented the modern idea of separationism or were resurrecting an outdated concept. What this interpretation obfuscates is how much the justices' attitudes were likely informed by nineteenth-century developments and then events that preceded the *Everson* decision.

Since the end of World War I, clergy, commentators, and legal and religious scholars had been debating the idea of church-state separation in relation to contemporary events. The concept was discussed and promoted in law journals, in the pages of magazines such as the *Christian Century* and *The Nation*, in regional and local newspapers, and then in scurrilous journals such as *The Menace*, an organ of the Ku Klux Klan.[3] The issue figured prominently in the 1928 presidential election and in a series of controversies during the 1930s. This public conversation over whether church-state separation was the appropriate legal standard and cultural norm reached its apex in the years coinciding with the *Everson* and *McCollum* decisions, resulting in the concept becoming more firmly embedded into the law and culture than ever before. Yet, despite an apparent consensus over the concept, the definition of separation remained elusive: did separationism promote a regime of pan-Protestantism, religious pluralism, or secularity? For that reason, separationism's reign of prominence was always tenuous, such that its ultimate dismantling began much earlier than many contemporaries realized.[4]

The New Century

By the turn of the twentieth century, the idea of church-state separation appeared to be firmly embedded in the culture; people holding a variety of ideological perspectives embraced the concept. American Jews, chiefly those within the Reform movement, were among the stronger supporters of church-state separation. In the late nineteenth century, Rabbis Max Lilienthal and Isaac Mayer Wise had been at the forefront of creating the Reform movement and educating American Jews about the importance of church-state separation for protecting the Jewish community and enabling Jews to participate in American society without losing their religious identity. According to Wise, "separation was the only way to establish a republic, and liberty . . . is safe only as long as Church and State remain separate."[5] From 1880 to 1905, however, more than two million Jews immigrated to the United States, chiefly from Eastern Europe. The American Jewish community now faced myriad issues that church-state separation did not address, and the concept was foreign to newer immigrants who chiefly desired the ability to practice their faith without persecution. Still, Jews within the Reform movement and in emerging coordinating agencies remained committed to the principle, with one leader condemning the "unholy alliance between church and state in each and every form."[6] In 1906, Reform's Central Conference of American Rabbis formed a Committee on the Relations of Church and State to promote secular public education and oppose a renewed push for Sunday-law enforcement. The committee prepared and distributed a pamphlet, *Why the Bible Should Not Be Read in the Public Schools*, that advocated church-state separation. Also in 1906, Jewish leaders formed the American Jewish Committee to advocate for Jewish concerns, followed by the Anti-Defamation League in 1913, which focused on combatting anti-Semitism. Both groups, along with the American Jewish Congress, founded in 1922, became strong proponents of church-state separation, with American Jewish Congress taking a leading role in litigating church-state issues after midcentury under the leadership of Leo Pfeffer.[7]

Protestant ministers and seminary professors remained wedded to the principle, despite the growing rift within Protestantism between modernism and orthodoxy, the latter drifting into fundamentalism. Although lingering forms of anti-Catholicism ensured that commitment, many conservative Protestants eschewed the growing secularization of the nation's culture and institutions and viewed separationism as a shield against outside intrusions into church affairs. Baptists, in particular, with their long tradition of supporting church-state separation, "held dogmatically to the ideal of separation of church and state." So, too, did mainstream Protestants, with their leaders reaffirming that "separation of Church and State has been a leading cause of the growth and prosperity of the United States" throughout its history. "We must jealously guard this separation."[8]

At the same time, liberal Protestants struggled to reconcile their faith with the late-century developments of Darwinism and Biblical criticism, the latter disputing scriptural literalism. These "modernists" accepted the idea of human goodness and progress, and many were drawn to the social causes of progressivism. The melding of theological liberalism and social progressivism brought about the Social Gospel movement, which set out to address the many problems associated with urbanization, industrialization, and economic inequality.[9] Notable among those committed to Christian social action were Washington Gladden and Walter Rauschenbusch, the latter becoming the titular leader of the movement. Rauschenbusch, with his German Baptist heritage, had long supported church-state separation. As his commitment to the church's duty to transform society grew, Rauschenbusch refined his understanding of church-state relations, which he explored extensively in his best-selling book *Christianity and the Social Crisis* (1907). Historical experience had "compelled us to separate Church and State because each can accomplish its special task best without the interference of the other," Rauschenbusch wrote. "But they are not unrelated. Our life is not a mechanical duality, built in two air-tight compartments. Church and State both minister to something greater and larger than either, and they find their true relation in this unity and aim of service."[10] Rauschenbusch believed that by employing their "religious impulses toward righteousness," churches could

> cooperate[] with the State by creating the most delicate and valuable elements of social welfare and progress; but if [the church] should enter into politics to get funds from the public treasury or police support for its doctrine and ritual, it would inject a divisive and corrosive force into political life. The machinery of Church and State must be kept separate, but the output of each must mingle with the other to make social life increasingly wholesome and normal.[11]

Rauschenbusch and other Social Gospelers thus believed that "cooperation of the religious and political forces of the community furnishes the positive solution of the problem of Church and State." As the *Harvard Theological Review* asserted, churches could consistently engage in social action while affirming that the "American Republic has carried into practice complete religious toleration and the complete separation of church and state."[12]

Two turn-of-the-century books on church and state written by conservative religious authors promoted narrow understandings of separationism. In the first, Isaac Cornelison acknowledged that it was not the government's "proper function to inculcate, propagate, or even foster religion"; the goal was to prevent a "union of church and state." Still, he insisted that "the civil institutions of this country are necessarily, rightly, and lawfully Christian," which authorized the government's promotion of Christian norms. In the second book, Sanford Cobb also maintained that the nation's "life, custom[s], and institutions" were grounded on Christian principles and that "we may safely declare that, if the American people be not a Christian nation, there is none upon the earth." Yet Cobb viewed nonestablishment in slightly broader terms, asserting that the Constitution guaranteed "the severance of state from Church" by preventing civil authorities from "touching matters of faith, worship, order discipline, or polity" of churches. Conversely, churches had no power "to direct [state] policy or action," other than through their powers of persuasion. In Cobb's mind, this arrangement not only prevented "a union of church and state" but also instituted a "complete separation of state from [the] Church."[13]

Legal commentators also affirmed church-state separation, though usually in measured terms. The leading constitutional scholar of the late nineteenth century, Thomas Cooley, had taken a cautious approach to church-state separation, writing that legislatures were not "at liberty to effect a union of Church and State." That did not mean, however, "that the government should be prohibited from recognizing religion," which permitted public religious acknowledgments and the enforcement of Sunday laws.[14] Subsequent editions of Cooley's influential treatise *Constitutional Limitations* appeared into the 1920s and cast a long shadow over later treatise writers. Law professor Henry Campbell Black, author of the incomparable law dictionary bearing his name, avoided using the term "separation of church and state" in his *Handbook of American Constitutional Law* (1895, 1897), employing instead the phrase "union of church and state." That choice possibly reflected his understanding of the religion clauses as designed chiefly "to prohibit the recognition of any particular form of religion as the established and compulsory religion of the state." Consistent with that approach, Black affirmed that the nation's civil and social institutions were "founded upon the Christian religion," such that the "whole purpose and policy of the law assume that we are a nation of Christians."[15]

The leading church-state scholar of the early twentieth century was Carl Zollmann, a law professor at Marquette University and author of two legal treatises dedicated to church-state relations. Like the above authors, Zollmann had a mixed view about church-state matters. On one hand, he argued that the First Amendment had affected the "[c]omplete religious liberty to all persons, and the absolute separation of the church from the state." On the other, he asserted that the nation's laws and institutions necessarily reflected Christian sentiments. Christianity was "the alpha and omega of our moral law and the power which directs the operation of our judicial system," Zollmann declared. Seeking to reconcile the two statements, Zollmann wrote that the latter view was "not in any manner inconsistent with the great American doctrine concerning the separation of church and state. A distinction must be made by a religion preferred by law and a religion preferred by the people without the coercion of the law, between a legal establishment and a religious creed freely chosen by the people themselves." This distinction allowed Zollmann to accept separationism as a constitutional principle. "The fact that church and state are separated has not done away with the other fact that the Christian religion is and ever has been the religion of the people." For all of these authors, the goal of separation was not to effectuate a secular culture but to protect the autonomy of religious institutions and the religion of the people.[16]

During the prewar years, the Supreme Court heard two Establishment Clause cases that provided the justices with the opportunity to explore the concept of church-state separation. In both instances, the justices interpreted the facts narrowly, which allowed them to avoid addressing the broader constitutional questions. *Bradfield v. Roberts* (1899) involved a taxpayer challenge to a grant from the District of Columbia to a Catholic hospital to build and operate a ward to serve the city's poorer residents. The Court sidestepped the plaintiff's claim that public funds were being paid to a sectarian institution by noting the hospital was separately incorporated from the religious order that operated the hospital (the Sisters of Providence). Relying on this distinction, Justice Rufus W. Peckham asserted that the allegations "do not in the least change the legal character of the hospital, or make a religious corporation out of a purely secular one as constituted by the law." It was "simply the case of a secular corporation being managed by people who hold to the doctrines of the Roman Catholic Church, but who nevertheless are managing the corporation according to the law under which it exists."[17] The Court's facile reasoning allowed the justices to avoid confronting the question of whether the Establishment Clause barred government grants to a religious institution to provide secular services simply because it was religious. That question was squarely before the Court; the Court of Appeals below had upheld the grant despite declaring that the First Amendment secured "complete religious liberty to all persons, and the absolute separation of the Church from the State," going so far as to cite the *Reynolds* quotation about instituting "a wall of separation between Church and State." Yet that principle, the lower court noted, only "prohibit[ed] any preference, by law, in favor of any one religious persuasion or mode of worship." The Supreme Court in *Bradfield* thus had the opportunity to address the meaning of church-separation and whether the Court of Appeals' narrow interpretation was correct, but it declined to do so.[18]

Eight years later the justices heard *Quick Bear v. Leupp*, involving a challenge to a contract between the Bureau of Indian Affairs and the Bureau of Catholic Indian Missions for the latter to operate a school on the Rosebud Sioux Reservation. The challengers claimed that the payments violated the Establishment Clause and an 1897 statute that had ended federal contracts with religious missions on Indian reservations. Once again, the justices sidestepped the constitutional question and the issue of separationism by emphasizing the monies were paid from Indian trust funds and not through a congressional appropriation. "One class of appropriations relates to public monies," wrote Chief Justice Melville W. Fuller, "the other to moneys which belong to the Indians and which is administered for them by the government." Relying on this technical distinction, Fuller declared that the Court could not "concede the proposition that Indians cannot be allowed to use their own money to educate their children in the schools of their own choice because the government is necessarily undenominational, as it cannot make any law respecting an establishment of religion or prohibiting the free exercise thereof." (Fuller's distinction obscured the fact that the complainants were Sioux Indians who alleged that the government had paid their trust funds to the religious mission school without their consent.) This time, lower courts had not broached the subject of church-state separation, so the Court faced no obligation to address the principle. Had the Court in *Bradfield* and *Quick Bear* reconciled those nonseparationist results with the principle and then created precedent, the future course of the Establishment Clause might have turned out quite differently.[19]

The Interwar Years

World War I impacted American Catholicism and Protestantism in vastly different ways. The Catholic Church emerged from the war years united and with a new confidence about its role in transforming American society. Protestantism, in contrast, emerged fractured and questioning its identity and sense of mission in the United States. Both perspectives set the course for church-state conflicts in the interwar years and created the background for the Supreme Court's holdings of the late 1940s.

In 1917, the Catholic bishops had established the National Catholic War Council to coordinate the actions of Catholic fraternal organizations and relief agencies during the war. The War Council worked to unite the various ethnic Catholic communities behind the Allied effort, including encouraging Catholic men to enlist in the armed services. In addition to promoting a sense of patriotism, transforming attitudes of many immigrant Catholics, the war council convinced Catholic leaders about the value of uniting Catholic efforts domestically. Following the Armistice, the war council reorganized as the National Catholic Welfare Council (NCWC), later renamed "National Catholic Welfare Conference," to represent and coordinate Catholic interests nationwide. Church membership also continued to grow, outstripping gains among Protestant denominations. More than ever before, American Catholics were optimistic about participating in the American dream; following the war, writes William Halsey, Catholicism "began a process of culturally and socially defining itself in America." As a result, "American Catholics entered the 1920s with a new feeling of their own Americanism and a new confidence in their ability to contribute to the national welfare."[20]

One source of this new confidence within Catholicism lay in the resurgence of Thomist philosophical thought, which "presented a world of order, balance, and reason capped off with the certitude of faith in an ultimately meaningful human existence." Theologically conservative and comprehensive in scope, Thomism critiqued the perceived strains of materialism, secularism, and relativism in the postwar culture. Thomism unified and invigorated Catholic theology in a way that was lacking within fragmented Protestantism.[21] At the same time, Catholic intellectuals of the 1920s worked to demonstrate that Catholicism was consistent with American democratic values. "There is no discrepancy between the American Constitution and the constitution of the Catholic church," wrote Frederick Joseph Kinsman in his 1924 book *Americanism and Catholicism*. "A loyal upholder of the one may be an equally loyal upholder of the other." Kinsman reprinted excerpts from a 1909 article by Cardinal James Gibbons where the prelate had written that "American Catholics rejoice in our separation of Church and State; I can conceive of no combination of circumstances likely to arise which would make a union desirable for either Church or State." Kinsman insisted that Catholicism was "loyal to the [same] fundamentals of Christianity intended to be the foundations of the American State."[22]

Another Catholic writer who worked to reconcile Catholic theology with church-state separation was Fr. John A. Ryan, a professor of moral theology at Catholic University and a noted progressive on social issues. In his 1922 book *The State and the Church*, Ryan argued that earlier papal encyclicals condemning church-state separation had been misunderstood. "The proposition which affirms that Church and State should be separated, was condemned because of its universal terms," Ryan wrote. Pope Pius IX had "not intend[ed] to declare that separation is always unadvisable, for he had more than once expressed his satisfaction with the arrangement obtaining in the United States. What he condemned was the doctrine that in no country, in no circumstances, should Church and State be united." In other passages, however, Ryan undermined his efforts at allaying Protestant suspicions. Ryan confirmed that Catholic doctrine still taught that the ideal situation was where the "State should officially recognize the Catholic religion as the religion of the commonwealth." The church simply realized that this was not practical in democratic nations like the United States that were not "exclusively, or almost exclusively, made up of Catholics." As much as Ryan attempted to demonstrate that the Catholic Church did not oppose separation of church and state in America, his ideal/practical distinction did little to assuage concerns of critics who interpreted him as stating that Catholic leaders only accepted church-state separation until they could change it through a demographic shift. And whereas a majority of Protestants viewed separation as an inherent constitutional value, Ryan insisted that there was "nothing in the Constitution . . . which declares that the policy of separation is an ideal arrangement, or which forbids any American citizen to hold that it is not ideal."[23]

Catholicism's newfound willingness to identify with American aspirations coincided with a postwar upsurge in xenophobia and nativism. Reacting to immigration and foreign entanglements, Americans and their political leaders embraced isolationism, advocated a "return to normalcy," and promoted "100 percent Americanism." Both phrases contained anti-immigrant, nativist undertones; "normalcy" meant a foregone era without a significant immigrant presence, whereas "100 percent Americanism" meant a nation free from non-Anglo-American traits. In the 1920s, John Higham writes, "100 percent Americanizers opened a frontal assault on foreign influence in American life." The loudest proponent of 100 percent Americanism during the 1920s was the resurgent Ku Klux Klan.[24]

In the 1920s, the American Catholic Church was still largely a community of immigrants, governed by a foreign prelate. This made Catholicism an easy target for the Ku Klux Klan, whose members professed patriotism and Protestantism, frequently of a fundamentalist strain. In rallies, books, and magazines, the Klan spared little in its vitriolic attacks against the Catholic hierarchy. In the process, it became one of the more vocal proponents of church-state separation, insisting on the "absolute separation of church and state." In calling on readers to vote against Catholic political candidates, the Klan journal *The Menace* declared that the "separation of church and state" must be "rigidly observed." Another edition asserted, "We stand firmly by the American principle of absolute separation of church and state and against the appropriation of public funds to sectarian purposes."[25] In 1924, at the height of its political strength, Klan sympathizers successfully blocked Catholic New York governor Al Smith from receiving the Democratic nomination for president. Four years later, with the Klan's influence waning within the Democratic Party, Smith secured the nomination but not before he had to defend himself against charges that his Catholicism disqualified him from being president. A prominent critique in the *Atlantic Monthly* asserted that Smith's Catholicism was "irreconcilable with that Constitution which as President you must support and defend, and with the principles of civil and religious liberty on which American institutions are based."[26] Smith responded,

> I believe in the absolute freedom of conscience for all men and in equality of all churches, all sects, and all beliefs before the law as a matter of right and not as a matter of favor. I believe in the absolute separation of Church and State and in the strict enforcement of the provisions of the Constitution that Congress shall make no law respecting an establishment of religion or prohibiting the free exercise thereof.[27]

Despite his affirmation, Smith went on to lose the election to Herbert Hoover by six million votes. Protestant suspicion of Catholicism was unquestionably a factor, as was Smith's opposition to Prohibition, which was popular among conservative Protestants. As the *Christian Century* reported during the campaign, many people believed that "[o]ur American principle of the absolute separation of church and state is a Protestant principle, conceived and enacted into law by a Protestant-minded democracy." Catholic leaders attributed Smith's defeat to anti-Catholic animus, which reinforced their belief that the Protestant majority was unwilling to accept Catholics on their own terms. For church leaders, this meant that Catholics needed to be more assertive about their legitimate claim on transforming American society.[28]

In contrast to Catholicism, Protestantism emerged from World War I theologically fractured between modernism, evangelicalism, and fundamentalism and with a loss of confidence about its ability to serve as the moral guardian of American culture. For many liberal Protestants, the inhumanity of the war and the horrors perpetrated by technology had shattered their confidence about science and human progress. Mainstream Protestants noted that Protestantism seemed adrift and lacking the ability to address many societal challenges. In an article titled "After Liberalism—What?," theologian John C. Bennett—who would form the neo-orthodoxy movement with Reinhold Niebuhr—declared that the "most important fact about contemporary American theology is the disintegration of [Protestant] liberalism." The self-confidence of the prewar years had vanished. "Now many of us are left with a feeling of theological homelessness." Religious historian Robert Handy aptly describes the situation for mainstream Protestantism in the postwar era as the "American Religious Depression."[29]

Mainstream Protestantism's leading journal, the *Christian Century*, warned of a potential cultural shift. Too many Protestant churches remained complacent about their earlier cultural dominance and did not recognize that divisions within Protestantism rendered it "incapable of united action." "Protestantism, the mother of American culture, must be awakened to the immeasurable value of the treasures in her possession and to the danger that, while she slumbers, there treasures may be lost."[30]

An ascendant Catholic Church was more than happy to fill that void. Emboldened, the Catholic Church began to assert itself publicly in several areas: promoting censorship of immoral movies and magazines, seeking restrictions on the availability of birth control, and expanding its efforts to obtain government financial assistance for its parochial schools. Initially, Protestant groups supported Catholic actions to regulate immoral films and sensationalist pulp fiction, but by the mid-1930s the Catholic Legion of

Decency's influence over the movie industry had grown so strong that Protestants and secularists began to object. A "Catholic campaign for 'decency' inevitably works around to a program of censorship under Catholic control going far beyond the requirements of mere decency," claimed the *Christian Century* in 1936. In an article titled "Vatican over Hollywood," *The Nation* drew parallels to censorship in Nazi Germany, warning against those "over-zealous, cohesive groups which may exert pressure on art and life." The Catholic Church was imposing its values onto American society as never before. But now, with its growing political clout in many cities, the Catholic hierarchy had the patronage of politicians, which many Protestants and secularists believed threatened to undermine the separation of church and state.[31]

The Nation's allusion to fascism reflected larger concerns among Protestants and secularists about the church's apparent support of fascist regimes in Italy and Spain. Catholic officials in Europe and the United States openly admired the governments of Benito Mussolini and Francisco Franco, a fact that reinforced suspicions among Protestants and liberals about the church's ambivalence to democratic values. A 1937 open letter in the *New York Times* signed by 150 Protestant clergy and intellectuals charged that the Spanish hierarchy exhibited "open hostility" to "popular government, freedom of worship, and the separation of church and state." The unwillingness of church officials to condemn the racist, anti-Semitic, and fascist statements of the Detroit "radio priest" Fr. Charles Coughlin only substantiated those concerns.[32]

President Franklin Roosevelt demonstrated his ambivalence to church-state separation through two prewar actions. In 1938, his Advisory Committee on Education proposed federal funding for elementary and secondary schools, including private and parochial schools. The committee's recommendation reflected a trend at the state level where legislatures were approving modest forms of aid for parochial schools, most commonly funds for textbooks and transportation. Educators condemned the committee's recommendation as "a clear violation of the principle of separation of Church and State, therefore vicious and un-American." Public-school educators and their supporters knew that other funding battles lay ahead.[33] Then, in 1939, Roosevelt blindsided Protestant leaders by appointing a personal envoy to the Vatican. The posting, ostensibly for the purpose of securing an ally during the forthcoming war, angered Protestants who interpreted it as an official recognition of the Catholic Church, an affront to church-state separation. Equally troubling, the posting indicated the growing status and political clout of the Catholic Church, a change that came at the expense of Protestantism.

For many Protestants and secularists, the way to resist these "threats" to democratic values was to insist on a legal regime of separation of church and state. None of these contentious issues dissipated during America's involvement in World War II; rather, they simply went on a back burner, where they simmered at a low boil, ready to heat up with the war's end.[34]

The "Watershed" Cases

As it so happened, the modern Supreme Court's initial foray into church-state matters did not involve any of the controversies just discussed. Instead, the justices' first explorations into church-state doctrine concerned state prosecutions of Jehovah's Witnesses for engaging in various activities: street preaching, distributing religious literature, and refusing to pledge allegiance to the flag. From 1937 to 1946, the high court heard thirty-nine cases involving Jehovah's Witnesses litigants, handing down twenty-three opinions on issues related to free expression, freedom of assembly, and religious freedom. The cases required the justices to consider whether neutral, and often salutary, laws should bend to accommodate idiosyncratic religious conduct that many people found offensive.[35] Several justices—Hugo Black, Felix Frankfurter, William O. Douglas, Robert Jackson, and Wiley Rutledge—had secularist inclinations and were suspicious of claims of religious absolutism. The Jehovah's Witnesses cases led them to consider the role of religion in a secular society and whether the government had any duty to facilitate its expression. If the government exempted a religious colporteur from paying a nondiscriminatory licensing fee, was the government effectively subsidizing religious activity? And by excusing Jehovah's Witnesses children from pledging allegiance to the flag during wartime, were the justices "subordinat[ing] the general civil authority of the state to sectarian scruples" in violation of "separation of church and state," Justice Frankfurter asked, a principle "so cardinal . . . for the liberty of our people." By the time the justices considered the meaning and application of the Establishment Clause in 1947, they had been thinking about these issues for a decade.[36]

Questions about whether church-state separation permitted the government to assist religious actors and institutions, even on an evenhanded basis, came to the forefront in the *Everson* and *McCollum* cases. *Everson* involved a New Jersey law, common in approximately one-third of the states, that authorized governments to reimburse the transportation costs of children attending parochial schools. According to a 1941 study, transportation reimbursements and textbook "loans" were the two more prevalent forms of state aid for religious schooling and benefited at least 340 Catholic schools nationwide. States justified such programs on safety grounds and as benefiting schoolchildren, not the parochial schools attended. Indeed, the Supreme Court had used the "child benefit" rationale in 1930 to permit the loan of textbooks to private schools, including religious ones.[37]

That *Everson* would become the vehicle for nationalizing the Establishment Clause and canonizing church-state separation was not foregone conclusion. The challenger to the reimbursement program had not raised an Establishment Clause claim in the New Jersey courts, arguing instead that the program expended public tax money for a private purpose in violation of the Due Process Clause (the claim alleged in the 1930 textbook case). The New Jersey Court of Errors and Appeals disagreed, upholding the program based on the "child benefit" theory.[38] At the US Supreme Court, Arch Everson's lawyer alleged for the first time that a reimbursement for expenses related to religious schooling violated the Establishment Clause, though the argument came secondary to the due process takings claim. Everson's lawyer made only a passing reference to separation of church and state, calling it "the outstanding characteristic of religious liberty." The handful of amicus curiae briefs supporting Everson also emphasized the takings claim while making conclusory statements about the "absolute separation of church and state" without elaborating on its meaning. Only the brief for the ACLU provided a historical argument based on the 1785 Virginia disestablishment struggle and on the writings of Thomas Jefferson and James Madison. That brief alone mentioned Jefferson's Danbury letter with its quotation of "building a wall of separation between church and state." This was likely one source for Justice Black's declarations that would figure so prominently in the Court's jurisprudence.[39]

The ACLU's reference to Virginia's disestablishment and the wall metaphor came close to not happening. Internally, the ACLU was still developing its stance on public funding of religion, and while the case was pending in the New Jersey courts, the ACLU's board of directors had instructed its Committee on Academic Freedom to consider whether the organization should also oppose indirect, auxiliary aid to religious schools. After extended discussion, the committee voted 11–8 to oppose all forms of public aid. One dissenting member of that ACLU committee was theologian Reinhold Niebuhr, who supported providing auxiliary aid related to the health and well-being of schoolchildren. Years earlier Niebuhr had elucidated his understanding of church-state separation. The "American tradition of the separation of church and state represents a delicate balance," Niebuhr wrote in *Christianity and Crisis*, a journal he coedited with John Bennett. "An absolute separation would require . . . that religion be regarded purely a private matter."

Niebuhr rejected that schema, in no small part because it "would mean that the church would not speak on public and social issues." This was anathema for the socially progressive Niebuhr, who believed in the prophetic role of the church. "We have never had that kind of separation of church and state in this country and we certainly do not deserve it." In the end, the ACLU did not adopt Niebuhr's moderate stance on church-state matters; if it had, then its *Everson* brief, with its references to Jefferson, Madison, and the "wall of separation," might have been quite different, as might have the Court's ultimate opinions.[40]

As it so happened, the amicus brief containing the most detailed discussion of church-state separation came from the NCWC, filed under the auspices of the National Council of Catholic Men and the National Council of Catholic Women. The brief was written largely by Catholic theologian and Jesuit priest John Courtney Murray, despite Murray not being a lawyer. Murray argued that "non-profit private schools"—he avoided using the term "parochial schools"—fulfilled a public function by educating children. This meant that "[t]he presence or absence of religious instruction in non-profit private schools could well appear in the eyes of the State as an immaterial element in relation to the State's aim." Turning to the issue of church-state separation, Murray conceded that the "Jeffersonian metaphor of a 'wall of separation' between Church and State has validity." That metaphor, however, should not be taken at face value, Murray insisted, but "must be closely analyzed in order that its true content may be revealed. . . . The essential purpose of the 'wall' of separation between Church and State as erected by the First Amendment is to prevent the invasion of either area, civic or religious by non-competent authority." But the wall should not be transformed into "an illegitimate 'iron curtain' separating areas between which there should be free passage." Thus, rather than rejecting the wall metaphor raised by ACLU, Murray set out to reconstruct it: the wall was to protect religion from the government, not to disadvantage it. In the end, the NCWC brief dedicated more space to discussing the meaning of church-state separation, including the wall metaphor, than any other brief filed in the case.[41]

As commentators on *Everson* noted at the time and have since, the various opinions did more to obfuscate the principle of separationism than to elucidate it.[42] Even though all nine justices agreed that church-state separation represented the constitutional standard, a slim majority upheld the reimbursement program. Justice Black's majority opinion revealed this tension. Without using the term "child benefit," Black wrote that the case involved a "general program . . . which . . . pays the fares of pupils attending public and private schools." Significantly, Black noted, "[t]he State contributes no money to the [parochial] schools. It does not support them." Yet that holding appeared inconsistent with the remainder of the opinion, which embraced no-aid separationism as the controlling principle. His language was emphatic: a state could not "pass laws which aid one religion, aid all religions, or prefer one religion over another. . . . No tax in any amount, large or small, can be levied to support any religious activities or institutions." Still, the reimbursements, though small, indirectly supported the parochial schools, and they set a precedent for more substantial forms of aid. Black apparently thought he could draw a line that would prohibit more robust forms of assistance to religious schools. (After the vote, Black told an acquaintance that he had intended to make his opinion "as tight" as possible so as to forestall larger amounts of aid flowing to parochial schools.) As he wrote, the "wall [of separation] must be kept high and impregnable. We could not approve the slightest breach."[43]

The seeming inconsistency between Black's rhetoric and the holding was more than the dissenters could stomach; Justices Jackson and Rutledge chastised their colleague for not following the constitutional principle he had announced. Rutledge's lead dissent argued that *any* form or amount of aid that assisted religion was unconstitutional. "[T]he object [of the Establishment Clause] was broader than separating church and state in the narrow sense," Rutledge wrote. "It was to create a complete and permanent separation of the spheres of religious activity and civil authority by comprehensively forbidding every form of public aid or support for religion." Justice Jackson concurred, declaring that the nonestablishment principle "was set forth in absolute terms, and its strength is its rigidity." So, despite the justices agreeing on a rigorous view of church-state separation, one that allowed for little or no government support for religion, they could not agree on how that principle applied in practice.[44]

The justices' strong embrace of church-state separation was not preordained; neither was Justice Black's reliance on history and the wall metaphor. In the Court's conference following arguments, the justices had split 6–2 in favor of the program's constitutionality, with Justice Frank Murphy, the Court's only Catholic, abstaining. Only Justices Frankfurter and Rutledge had insisted that the program violated church-state separation, with the former justice stating that "[i]f there is one thing beyond anything else that involves religious freedom, it is the insulation of church and state. . . . The framers wanted *complete and absolute* separation of church and state." Even though the financial benefit provided through the reimbursement was a "little one," Frankfurter acknowledged, "we have rejected that distinction."[45]

Chief Justice Fred Vinson assigned the majority opinion to Justice Black, who circulated a complete draft among the justices two weeks after conference on December 6, 1946. The draft was relatively short—only seven pages—compared to the ultimate opinion, which totals eighteen pages. The initial draft lacked an extensive discussion of history, with Black apparently comfortable that the Court had previously elaborated on "the historical roots of the First Amendment, its meaning and scope, the conditions that prompted its adoption, [and] the evils it was designed forever to suppress." The draft did not discuss Jefferson, Madison, or Virginia's disestablishment, citing only *Reynolds* and *Watson*, the nineteenth-century church property case. It did mention a "wall of separation" but only in the concluding paragraph, less prominently than appeared in the final opinion. The draft stated, "The First Amendment requires a complete and permanent separation between church and state. The wall between the two must be kept high and impregnable if the historic purpose of the First Amendment is to be carried out." Despite calling for the "complete and permanent separation between church and state," the draft used it as a rhetorical flourish rather than making it a central theme. Apparently, at this stage Black did not believe it was necessary to base his understanding of church-state separation on the contributions of Jefferson or Madison and Virginia's disestablishment experience.[46]

Justice Black rewrote his draft, giving more prominence to history and the wall metaphor but only after seeing drafts of Justice Rutledge's dissenting opinion. Rutledge's drafts delved extensively into the historical basis for church-state separation, emphasizing Virginia's disestablishment and the contributions of Madison and Jefferson. Rutledge asserted that the First Amendment was "the direct culmination" of the Virginia struggle based on Madison's leading role in both events. As one of Black's biographers put it, "Rutledge pecked away at Black's arguments; Black tightened them up, revised them, or dropped them completely." The result was that both justices reached similar conclusions about the significance of the Virginia struggle for the meaning of the First Amendment religion clauses, with Black emphasizing Jefferson's Statute for Establishing Religious Freedom and his wall of separation metaphor and Rutledge highlighting Madison's *Memorial and Remonstrance*. Had it not been for the challenge from Rutledge's historicism, the prominence of the Virginia struggle and Jefferson's wall of separation might have been missing in the *Everson* decision.[47]

The public response to the Court's embrace of separation was overwhelmingly positive, though most newspapers criticized the holding. The *St. Louis Post-Dispatch* chastised Black's opinion as superficial while calling

Rutledge's "powerful dissent" "monumental." The *Post-Dispatch* editorialized that despite Black's rhetoric, the holding invited an "abrupt support to an increasing and subtle encroachment to separation of church and state."[48] The *Christian Century* also praised the justices' strong embrace of church-state separation while condemning the holding. Other Protestants agreed: the Baptist Joint Committee on Public Affairs asserted that the holding would "turn[] back the hands of the clock as far as religious liberty and the separation of Church and State are concerned." Understanding that future battles over parochial school funding lay ahead, the Baptists recommitted themselves to "the struggle for religious liberty, in terms of separation of Church and State. Having lost the battle, we have not lost the war."[49]

Catholics alone condemned the Court's embrace of separationism. Despite having prevailed on the merits in *Everson*, Catholic leaders feared that future applications of church-state separation would not go in their favor. Some of the harshest criticism came from Professor James O'Neill, a Catholic member of the ACLU's Committee on Academic Freedom, who would go on to write two books highly critical of the Court's reliance upon church-state separation. O'Neill chastised Justices Black and Rutledge for "relying upon 'history' to show something that the First Amendment means something that it does not say." The "vague, spurious principle of 'complete separation of church and state' is a Protestant" idea, O'Neill declared.[50]

The public reaction to *Everson* had barely subsided when the justices heard their next church-state case. *McCollum v. Board of Education* involved a challenge to the widespread practice of "releasing" public-school children from classes to attend programs of religious instruction conducted by religious groups on school premises (known as "released time"). Local councils on religious education arranged the programs with local schools and enlisted Protestant, Catholic, and (occasionally) Jewish instructors to teach the classes, which schoolchildren attended voluntarily or not at all. Supporters saw released time as a way to accommodate the religious preferences of participating children and believed it was an improvement over school-directed prayer and Bible reading. Opponents charged that schools supported the religious instruction by allowing the classes to take place in school classrooms during the school day; as John Dewey asserted, released time jeopardized "the precious principle of separation of church between state." By the time of the *McCollum* litigation, released-time programs existed in more than twenty-two hundred communities involving two million children.[51]

In a decision that reaffirmed church-state separation, the Supreme Court voted 8–1 that the program violated the Establishment Clause. Justice Black again wrote the majority opinion, this time for six justices. Black held that the released-time program violated the Constitution for two reasons: first, it used "tax supported property for religious instruction," which helped "religious groups to spread their faith," and second, the close cooperation between school authorities and the religious councils, coupled with compulsory attendance requirement, resulted in the state's promotion of religious instruction. Once again, Black affirmed that the purpose of the Establishment Clause was to build a "wall of separation between Church and State." Now, any hesitation over using the phrase was gone; he used it three times in the opinion, leaving no doubt that the justices considered the metaphor to represent the controlling constitutional standard.[52] Justice Frankfurter wrote a separate opinion for himself and the other dissenters from *Everson* so as to emphasize that they still believed *Everson* had been wrongly decided. Frankfurter insisted that public schools must be kept scrupulously secular: "the public school [is] a symbol of our secular unity," he wrote. "Designed to serve as perhaps the most powerful agency for promoting cohesion among a heterogeneous democratic people, the public school must keep scrupulously free from entanglement in the strife of sects." Like Black, Frankfurter affirmed that strict separation of church and state was the correct model, using the wall metaphor five times while employing terms such as "eternal" and "complete" separation. "Separation means separation, not something less," Frankfurter wrote in conclusion. "Jefferson's metaphor . . . of a 'wall of separation' [is] not . . . a fine line easily overstepped."[53]

McCollum's majority and concurring opinions sent a clear message that the Court was committed to church-state separation, but now it seemed to identify separationism with secularism. As a result, public reaction did not break cleanly along Protestant and Catholic lines as before. Evangelical Protestants—the dominant group utilizing released time—overwhelmingly condemned the ruling as being hostile to religion. Many evangelicals who only a year earlier had praised the *Everson* Court's embrace of separationism now asserted that the unyielding rhetoric contained in the various opinions—"eternal separation," "complete separation," a "high and impregnable" wall—went further than was necessary.[54] On the Catholic side, the NCWC decried the decision as a victory for "secularism," while Baltimore archbishop Francis Keough charged that those who supported the *Everson* and *McCollum* decisions were aligned with "secularists in their campaign to drive religion out of public life under the specious pretext of separation of church and state." Later that fall, the Catholic bishops issued an official statement excoriating the *McCollum* holding, writing that "the term 'separation of Church and State' . . . has become the shibboleth of doctrinaire secularism."[55]

On the other side, mainstream Protestants, Jews, and secularists generally praised the holding and the Court's reaffirmation of separationism. The *Christian Century*, whose editors had once endorsed released time as an alternative to school-directed prayer and Bible reading, defended the ruling by emphasizing its limited scope. "The court did one thing only," it opined in a May editorial; "it ruled that the churches may not enter the jurisdiction of the public school and give religious instruction." The magazine recommended that schools adopt "dismissed time" programs so children could be released early once a week to attend religious instruction at local churches. But aside from mitigating the scope of the holding, the *Christian Century* did not retreat from supporting church-state separation or the Court's pronouncements of that principle. Separationism was not the problem, the magazine asserted; instead, Protestants had become complacent by relying on the government to promote religious fealty rather than taking responsibility for doing so themselves. It was "very important to get this matter straight at the outset—that keeping the wall between church and state 'high and impregnable' . . . is not an anti-religious attitude."[56]

This time, a handful of mainstream Protestants expressed concern with the tone of the Court's rhetoric. Following the decision, Reinhold Niebuhr organized a public statement by twenty-four leading Protestant moderates that asserted the Court's view of church-state separation was "unwarranted by the language of the First Amendment." The justices had extended the notion of separation "so that any action by the state that is intended to benefit all religious bodies without discrimination is forbidden." Part of the problem, the signatories contended, was that "Jefferson's oft quoted words, 'wall of separation,' . . . are a misleading metaphor." Following that statement, Niebuhr wrote separately in *Christianity and Crisis* that the Court's "hardening" of the concept of separation "will greatly accelerate the trend toward the secularization of our culture." The constitutional principle of nonestablishment, Niebuhr wrote, "cannot in the long run be tortured to mean such a rigorous separation of church and state that no public-school buildings may be put at the disposal of the churches, if this is done on a fair and equal basis."[57]

Finding common ground with Niebuhr on the issue was Fr. John Courtney Murray. In an article following the *McCollum* decision, Murray reaffirmed that the concept of church-state separation had validity, both historically and practically. The problem, he insisted, was that the justices had defined separation out of context with the nation's traditions and the "accepted habits of our people." The justices had succumbed to a "horror of absolutes" by adopting "absolute separation of church and state, as an absolute principle."

Delving into history, Murray maintained that Madison had identified multiple rationales for "a satisfactory theory of separation of church and state":

> the distinction of the ecclesiastical and civil jurisdictions, the immunity of conscience from coercion by civil authority in the free exercise of religion, the principle of political equality, the legitimate demands of political unity in a religiously divided society, [and] the general requirements of the common good (which include the need of society to be a "good" society).[58]

These, Murray insisted, were "proper and adequate materials from which to fashion an acceptable American philosophy of separation of church and state." In this sense, separationism "appears as instrumental to freedom, therefore as a relative, not an absolute in its own right." For Murray, the Court's version of separation led not only to secularism but the privatization of religion in society. Separationism was "a means, a technique" for "implement[ing] the principle of religious freedom," Murray wrote. "It assumes organic separation but dynamic interaction between church and state; it functions through cooperation without favoritism."[59]

The debate over the meaning of church-state separation continued throughout the years following the *McCollum* decision. The charge that the Court had aligned the principle with secularism persisted, a claim that academics, intellectuals, and magazines such as *The Nation* openly embraced. In contrast, mainstream Protestants, led by the *Christian Century*, insisted that separationism did not mean secularism or necessarily lead to the secularization of the culture. The *Christian Century* and groups such as the Baptist Joint Committee clung to a pan-Protestant understanding of separationism, one that reinforced Protestant values of religious independence and voluntarism. In order to preserve that vision, in 1947, representatives from the Baptist Joint Committee, the *Christian Century*, and other Protestant organizations formed the "action group" Protestants and Other Americans United for Separation of Church and State to provide a stopgap to perceived incursions on church-state separation through lobbying and litigation. During the 1950s, POAU had a meteoric rise, fueled in no small part by its appeals to anti-Catholic sentiments among Protestants and secularists, with the organization taking the lead in challenging many forms of financial aid to religious institutions.[60]

A third understanding of separationism—that its purpose was to promote religious pluralism—arose as an alternative to the other two meanings, and it gained traction in the 1950s. A movement promoting religious pluralism and ecumenism had existed since the creation of the National Conference of Christians and Jews in the 1920s; it now experienced a resurgence in reaction to the anti-Semitic horrors of the war years. Figures such as Reinhold Niebuhr and Will Herzberg, author of the best-selling *Protestant—Catholic—Jew*, promoted the value of religious pluralism, with the latter advocating a form of Judeo-Christian American exceptionalism.[61] This perspective taught that the state should accommodate religious institutions and traditions, and it fit well with the upsurge in religiosity in the 1950s represented by figures such as Billy Graham, Bishop Fulton Sheen, and Norman Vincent Peale. A heightened interest in spirituality and religious belief helped define much of the decade, creating a "culture of religiosity" that existed in tension with the secularity and materialism of society. During the decade, church attendance among all Christian groups—mainline and evangelical Protestants and Catholics—reached its highest levels in US history, and opinion polls indicated 99 percent of Americans believed in God. Finally, a pluralist understanding of church-state separation also conformed with the public reaction to secularism and its equation to godless communism during the Cold War.[62]

It was in this changing climate that the Supreme Court heard a new challenge to the issue of released-time religious instruction. The program in *Zorach v. Clauson* differed from the one in *McCollum* in one important respect: participating children were still released for a designated period during the school day, but the instruction took place *off* school grounds rather than in school classrooms. That distinction was apparently significant for several justices, as the Court voted 6–3 to uphold the off-campus program, this time concentrating on a lack of state coercion and use of state-funded school facilities. Justice Douglas—who had joined in the *McCollum* decision—wrote the opinion, which waxed and waned between approaches. First, he reaffirmed that "[t]here cannot be the slightest doubt that the First Amendment reflects the philosophy that Church and State should be separated," citing *Everson* and *McCollum*. That "separation must be complete and unequivocal," he declared. "[T]he prohibition is absolute." Douglas's tone then shifted to one of government accommodation of religion. "When the state encourages religious instruction or cooperates with religious authorities by adjusting the schedule of public events to sectarian needs, it follows the best of our traditions." This was because "[w]e are a religious people whose institutions presuppose a Supreme Being," Douglas asserted. The government could and should "accommodate [the] spiritual needs" of the people." To hold that the state could not do so "would be to find in the Constitution a requirement that the government show a callous indifference to religious groups."[63]

The three dissenters—Justices Black, Frankfurter, and Jackson—charged that the majority had relied on a trivial factual distinction. They also took Douglas to task for invoking church-state separation. Justice Black asserted that the state was "manipulating its compulsory education laws to help religious sects get pupils. This is not separation but combination of Church and State." Black charged that the majority had succumbed to the public criticism that had followed the *McCollum* holding. The Court's "insistence on 'a wall between Church and State which must be kept high and impregnable'" had been subjected "to a most searching examination throughout the country," Black wrote. "Perhaps few opinions from this Court in recent years have attracted more attention or stirred wider debate." Yet Black reaffirmed his belief that it was the "correct exposition of the philosophy and a true interpretation of the language of the First Amendment to which we should strictly adhere."[64]

Despite Douglas's effort to distinguish *Zorach* from *McCollum* on the facts, most commentators viewed the holding as a retreat from the *McCollum* ruling and its separationist approach. *The Nation* lamented that the holding "represents a clear reversal of [the Court's] position on the *McCollum* case." The Jesuit journal *America* agreed with that analysis but praised the *Zorach* majority for rejecting the "truly revolutionary doctrine of 'separation of Church and State'" announced in *Everson* and *McCollum*. If the Court had not changed course, the journal maintained, it would have secured the "triumph of secularism in our legal system." And the *Christian Century* expressed regret over the holding, writing that it raised "new and grave doubts regarding the extent to which church and state are in fact separate under our constitution." Legal commentators also concurred that the Court had stepped back from its embrace of church-state separation.[65]

Whether a majority of justices had reacted to the public criticism of *McCollum* and reevaluated their understanding of church-state separationism is unclear. In the interim between the two cases, two staunch separationist justices—Rutledge and Murphy—had died and were replaced by Tom C. Clark and Sherman Minton, both of whom were more ideologically moderate. Another justice who had voted with the *McCollum* majority, Harold Burton, had reserved judgment at that time on the constitutionality of off-campus released-time programs, a point he reminded his colleagues in the *Zorach* conference. In that same conference, Chief Justice Vinson agreed that because of the different facts, "*McCollum* does not control this [situation]." The only real surprise was that of Justice Douglas, an otherwise reliable separationist, whose inconsistent opinion revealed his attempt to have it both ways. Nonetheless, the *Zorach* decision suggested that separationism did not presuppose secularism or forbid the government from accommodating people's religious choices, which put a friendlier face on church-state separation that was more in tune with the religious attitudes of the fifties. In so doing, the *Zorach* decision possibly saved separationism as a legal principle. Following *Zorach*, the high court would not consider a case implicating church-state separation for almost a decade.[66]

Chapter 6

Separation's Apex and Decline

The 1960s were in many ways the high point of church-state separation but also the beginning of its decline. During that decade, public attitudes on the left and right began to shift with respect to the value of church-state separation. Those changes, though not felt immediately on the US Supreme Court, came to impact its decision making in the 1970s, initiating the decline of separationism as a legal theorem in the final two decades of the century.

The year 1960 began with the high court granting review in five church-state cases: four cases involved challenges to state Sunday law restrictions and the fifth to a state requirement that officeholders profess a belief in God. In two of the Sunday law challenges, the plaintiffs raised Establishment Clause claims; in the other two, the plaintiffs alleged the restrictions violated their free exercise rights. Chief Justice Earl Warren authored the opinions in all four cases, upholding the closing laws against both claims. Warren readily acknowledged the religious lineage of Sunday laws, but he insisted that their rationales had evolved and had become secular over time as health-welfare regulations. That rationale should have suggested that Sunday laws presented no church-state issue at all; nevertheless, Warren quoted *Everson*'s "no-aid" paragraph with its affirmation of "a wall of separation between Church and State" but noted that the *Everson* majority had distinguished impermissible aid to religion from permissible "general public welfare legislation" that benefited religion indirectly. To prevent states from recognizing Sunday as a "day of rest" would "give a constitutional interpretation of hostility to the public welfare rather than one of mere separation of church and State." Warren's moderate interpretation of *Everson* was likely designed to assuage public concerns that church-state separation barred official accommodations of the nation's religious customs and traditions.[1]

In the remaining case of the 1960 term, *Torcaso v. Watkins*, the Court struck down a state law requiring officeholders to profess a belief in God. In his unanimous opinion, Justice Hugo Black was unclear as to how the religious test violated the Constitution—whether it violated free exercise, nonestablishment, or equal protection, or a combination of all three—simply stating that it violated the applicant's "freedom of belief and religion." (Black referenced, but did not apply article VI's prohibition, which is limited to federal offices.) More significant than the holding was the tone of Black's majority opinion, which was his first on church and state since *McCollum*. Expressing frustration with claims that the Court had retreated from its commitment to church-state separation, Black recounted how people had criticized *Everson*'s separationist language at the time and had called on the justices to repudiate it in *McCollum*. "We declined to do this," Black wrote, "but instead strongly affirmed what had been said in *Everson*." He also asserted that the lower courts had misinterpreted *Zorach* as indicating a retreat from the *Everson-McCollum* holdings. "Nothing decided or written in *Zorach* lends support to [that] idea," Black wrote, putting the best face on Justice William O. Douglas's opinion. Black thus sent a clear message to critics that the high court was not about to abandon its embrace of church-state separation.[2]

In 1960, the issue of church-separation came to the forefront in the political arena. Entering into that year, Massachusetts senator John F. Kennedy was the frontrunner for the Democratic presidential nomination. Besides his youth, good looks, and war-hero record, Kennedy was also a Catholic. Sensing that his religion could be an issue in securing the nomination and election, Kennedy addressed his faith in a 1959 interview in *Look* magazine, affirming his support for church-state separation—calling it a "fundamental" principle—and his opposition to federal aid for parochial schools and to an ambassador to the Vatican. "Whatever one's religion in his private life may be, for the officeholder, nothing takes precedence over his oath to uphold the Constitution and all its parts—including the . . . strict separation of church and state." Announcing his candidacy a year later, Kennedy again affirmed his support for church-state separation.[3] Despite these clear pronouncements, the "religion issue" dogged Kennedy throughout the primaries and general election. Many mainline Protestants, represented through *Christian*

Century, insisted that Kennedy's religion was a legitimate issue because of the Catholic Church's various stances on church-state matters. Evangelical Protestants attacked Kennedy's Catholicism more directly, with *Christianity Today* writing, "We know that Romanists do not accept the separation of the Church and State; we know they oppose a government's treating all churches alike."[4] The Southern Baptist Convention and the National Association of Evangelicals (NAE) adopted resolutions opposing Kennedy's candidacy, while the NAE created a subsidiary organization called Citizens for Religious Freedom (CRF) to work with evangelical ministers and their congregations to organize meetings and distribute literature aimed at defeating Kennedy.[5]

Then, in late summer, prominent Protestant evangelist Billy Graham and the CRF held a secret meeting of evangelical leaders to plan an organized response to Kennedy's candidacy. That meeting led to a larger, publicized gathering of Protestant leaders in Washington, DC, in September. At that gathering, chaired by Protestant minister and author Norman Vincent Peale, attendees heard from various speakers, including the director of POAU, about the risks to church-state separation presented by electing a Catholic president. The organizers issued a prepared public statement at the conclusion that, after asserting that Kennedy's religion was a legitimate election issue, segued into charging that the Catholic Church had "repeatedly attempted to break down the wall of separation of church and state by a continuous campaign to secure public funds" and to impose Catholic social policies on the nation. "It is inconceivable that a Roman Catholic President would not be under extreme pressure by the hierarchy of his church to accede to its policies." The organizers miscalculated, however, as the public response was overwhelmingly negative. Newspapers reported the meeting for what it was: a conspiracy among conservative Protestants to defeat Kennedy simply because he was Catholic.[6] Kennedy then seized the initiative, delivering a masterful speech before a ministerial alliance in Houston, where he declared, "I am not the Catholic candidate for President. I am the Democratic Party's candidate for President who happens to be Catholic." He then reaffirmed his position from his earlier statements:

> I believe in an America where the separation of church and state is absolute—where no Catholic prelate would tell the President (should he be Catholic) how to act and no Protestant minister would tell his parishioners for whom to vote—where no church or church school is granted any public funds or political preference—and where no man is denied public office merely because his religion differs from the President who might appoint him or the people who might elect him.[7]

Kennedy's speech removed all legitimacy from the "religion issue," although the anti-Kennedy campaign continued underground for the remainder of the fall. As is known, Kennedy won one of the narrower elections in history, and many commentators attributed the close results to latent Protestant anti-Catholicism and to concerns about Kennedy's commitment to church-state separation.[8]

The School Prayer Decisions

The most significant and closely followed church-state controversies of the 1960s were the Supreme Court's decisions striking prayer and Bible reading in the nation's public schools. The cases, decided in 1962 and 1963, impacted public attitudes toward church-state separation, both pro and con, in ways not previously matched. The holdings were highly controversial, and they precipitated the unraveling of the Protestant consensus on church-state separation, producing a split between liberals and conservatives. The decisions were the first step in the slow decline of separationism as a legal principle and a cultural construct.

The first school-prayer case, *Engel v. Vitale*, arose out of New York and involved a challenge to what was known as the Regents' Prayer, which was drafted by the New York Board of Regents for use in public schools. Adopted during the Cold War when religiosity was on an upswing, the scripted prayer was designed to be nonsectarian and inclusive: "Almighty God, we acknowledge our dependence upon Thee, and we beg Thy blessings upon us, our parents, our teachers, and our country." School districts were not required to include a prayer in their daily opening exercises, but if they did, it had to be the Regents' Prayer. At the time, the prayer received widespread support for its attempt at inclusiveness; even the separationist-leaning *Christian Century* initially called the prayer "a noble declaration" of the nation's dependence upon God. A group of Long Island parents disagreed with that assessment and challenged the prayer in state court, losing at all levels before securing review at the Supreme Court.[9]

The jurisprudential issue before the Supreme Court was which precedent controlled: the separationist *McCollum* decision or the more accommodationist holding in *Zorach*. The state defended the prayer on grounds it was nonsectarian and permitted under *Zorach*, whereas the plaintiffs insisted the prayer's affirmation of God was sectarian and that the exercise coerced unwilling students to participate in the prayer. Justice Black, writing a 6–1 decision in favor of the plaintiffs, sidestepped the question of which precedent controlled. Appreciating that a decision striking school prayer would be controversial, Justice Black toned down his rhetoric. On the merits, he asserted that there could be "no doubt" that the prayer was religious through its "solemn avowal of divine faith and supplication for the blessings of the Almighty." Black insisted that the prayer was unconstitutional even though it was denominationally neutral and children who objected to the prayer were excused from participating in the exercise. "When the power, prestige and financial support of government is placed behind a particular religious belief, the indirect coercive pressure upon religious minorities to conform to the prevailing officially approved religion is plain."[10]

Turning to the controlling constitutional standard, Justice Black struck a moderate tone. The purpose of the Establishment Clause, Black insisted, was "to stand as a guarantee that neither the power nor prestige of the Federal Government would be used to control, support, or influence the kinds of prayer the American people can say." The founders believed that "a union of government and religion tends to destroy government and to degrade religion," Black wrote. "The Establishment Clause thus stands as an expression of principle on the part of the Founders of our Constitution that religion is too personal, too sacred, too holy, to permit its 'unhallowed perversion' by a civil magistrate."[11] Here Black asserted that one of the chief functions of church-state separation was to protect religion from the government. That was why it was "neither sacrilegious nor antireligious to say that [the government] should stay out of the business of writing or sanctioning official prayers and leave that purely religious function to the people themselves." Black undoubtedly wrote with the Court's critics in mind. Noticeably missing from his opinion was a reaffirmation of a high and impregnable "wall of separation." The closest that Black came was when he repeated the challengers' claim that the prayer "breached the constitutional wall of separation between Church and State." He simply noted that "[w]e agree with that contention." Of the two progenitors of the wall metaphor, only *Everson* received a citation in a footnote, while *McCollum*, which had concerned religious exercises in public schools and was the most relevant precedent, was not discussed or cited at all.[12] Black's effort at assuaging Court critics elicited a different type of criticism, with University of Chicago law professor Philip K. Kurland charging that there was "no consistency" in the Court's church-state decisions. "Such mixed interpretations are part of the judicial record on the issue of separation of church and state," Kurland declared, "which Jefferson saw as a 'wall' but provided no blueprint of it."[13]

Black's failure to rely on either *Everson* or *McCollum* was not an oversight but a conscious decision. In an initial draft of his opinion Black had relied heavily on those cases, repeating *Everson*'s famous "no-aid" paragraph and then asserting that "this interpretation of the Establishment Clause has been repeated, reaffirmed, and relied upon" in *McCollum*, *McGowan*, and *Torcaso*. In handwriting in the margin, Black had added, "We again reiterate the above-quoted statement as the proper interpretation of the Establishment Clause." The reason Black deleted these stronger affirmations of separationism is not clear, but it may have had to do with garnering support from fellow justices. Justice Felix Frankfurter had suffered a disabling stroke following the arguments and soon resigned from the Court, whereas Justice Douglas wanted an even stronger opinion that focused on the use of state-funded school buildings to promote religion. Lacking support from the two reliable separationists, Black had to secure the votes of the moderate justices—Earl Warren, Tom C. Clark, and John Marshall Harlan—and keep the latter two from joining Potter Stewart's dissenting opinion.[14] Black's measured tone did not stop Justice Stewart from charging that the majority had "misapplied a great constitutional principle. I cannot see how an 'official religion' is established by letting those who want to say a prayer say it." And even though Black had not emphasized separationism, Stewart became the first justice to openly question the wall metaphor, writing that "as in all areas of constitutional adjudication, [the Court] is not responsibly aided by the uncritical invocation of metaphors like the 'wall of separation,' a phrase nowhere to be found in the Constitution."[15]

Despite Justice Black's effort at moderation, the public reaction to *Engel* was swift and impassioned. *Christianity Today* reported that the decision produced "a title wave of criticism," while the *New York Times* maintained that the public outcry was "louder than any provoked by the Court since the school segregation decision in 1954." Catholic and Eastern Orthodox churches denounced the decision, as did most evangelical groups. Billy Graham charged the decision was but another step toward secularism: "God pity our country when we can no longer appeal to God for help."[16] Even Reinhold Niebuhr expressed regret over the decision, noting that the prayer was so "innocuous" that it was difficult to see it "being offensive to any religious group." In working so assiduously to achieve the secularization of the public schools, Niebuhr wrote, the Court had countenanced "the suppression of religion and [given] the impression that government must be antireligious." This impression, he insisted, was inconsistent with the desires of the founders and with "our long tradition of separation of church and state, which is based on neutrality and not animosity."[17] Finally, members of Congress, chiefly southern Democrats and conservative Republicans, were apoplectic in their outrage over the holding, with Georgia senator Herman Talmadge calling it "the most tragic [decision] in the history of the United

States." As the *New York Times* reported, in the week following the decision, "all the serious business of the Congress of the United States was put aside while members spent their time denouncing the Supreme Court." Members from both chambers called for a constitutional amendment to overturn the Court's decision.[18]

In contrast, mainline Protestants, Jews, and secularists supported the *Engel* decision, though most commentators emphasized that the Court had struck a *government-drafted* prayer. "Nothing in the June 25 ruling by the Supreme Court prevents teachers or pupils in the public schools from engaging in prayer," wrote *Christian Century*. "Private prayer," it insisted, "remains untouched." But in other articles, *Christian Century* applauded the holding as a victory for church-state separation, asserting that "[i]n our view the Supreme Court has rendered a service of the greatest importance to true religion as well as to the integrity of the democratic state."[19] Surprisingly, *Christianity Today*, the nation's leading evangelical magazine, also endorsed the decision, though cautiously. According to the magazine, the Regents' Prayer suffered from two flaws that should trouble those Christians who valued religious freedom: first, the prayer had been composed by the government, and second, the prayer "promoted a highly-diluted religion-in-general and tended to reduce religion to a mere form." *Christianity Today* also knew that the Court was about to consider the issue of Bible reading in the schools, a matter of greater concern to evangelicals, so it urged restraint among evangelicals and recommended a wait-and-see approach.[20]

Before the dust had settled on *Engel*, the Court granted review in two cases that challenged practices of unmediated Bible reading in public schools, with one of the cases also involving the recitation of the Lord's Prayer. In both instances, teachers or student volunteers read from the King James version, and students were putatively able to excuse themselves from participating in the exercises. The lower courts had split on the constitutionality of the practices, with the Maryland Court of Appeals upholding the exercises by relying on the dicta from the *Zorach* decision while distinguishing *McCollum*. Although that case had received more attention because it was brought by the indefatigable atheist Madalyn Murray, the Court consolidated the two appeals under the name of the other case: *School District of Abington Township v. Schempp*.[21]

Schempp presented the justices with a core church-state issue but one on which the Court had never ruled. Whereas *Engel* had involved the novel situation of a government-comprised prayer, *Schempp* challenged a widespread practice with a long-standing pedigree. Still, as a result of the holding in *Engel* the year before, observers predicted the Court would strike these practices as well.[22] They were correct; by an 8–1 vote, the justices found the practices to be unconstitutional. This time, Justice Clark, a judicial moderate and Presbyterian layman, authored the majority opinion rather than Justice Black, likely a purposeful move by Chief Justice Warren. Justice Clark's opinion sought to assuage the Court's critics, affirming "that religion has been closely identified with our history and government." Not by accident, the first case he cited was *Zorach*, with Clark repeating the phrase that "[w]e are a religious people whose institutions presuppose a Supreme Being." Clark also affirmed that the religion clauses required the government to undertake a "wholesome neutrality" toward religious matters. That meant that "the State may not establish a 'religion of secularism' in the sense of affirmatively opposing or showing hostility to religion." Yet that principle of neutrality did not mean that the Court could ignore instances where the government undertook actions with the "purpose and primary effect" of advancing religion. Bible reading, as conducted in both cases, was religious and sectarian. Thus, according to Clark, the reading of the Bible and the reciting of prayers in public schools violated "the command of the First Amendment that the government maintain strict neutrality, neither aiding nor opposing religion."[23]

As with the opinion in *Engel*, Justice Clark tried to hew to a fine line. As in *Engel*, missing in *Schempp* was an emphasis on the value of church-state separation and any reference to a "wall of separation." At the same time, Clark quoted favorably from the Court's earlier opinions, including Justice Wiley Rutledge's statement from *Everson* where Rutledge had called for "a complete and permanent separation of the spheres of religious activity and civil authority." Still, the absence of any rousing affirmation of the principle of separationism was notable.[24] Justice Stewart again dissented, arguing that the holding interfered with the rights of those children who desired to begin the school day with prayer and Bible readings. Stewart also read more into Clark's opinion than there was, charging the majority with engaging in "a fallacious oversimplification" by "establishing a single constitutional standard of 'separation of church and state'" to "be mechanically applied in every case to delineate the required boundaries between government and religion." Aside from Stewart, however, the majority of justices apparently believed they had disjoined church-state separation from secularism. And they hoped that they had done a better job of explaining it to the American public.[25]

Once again, the justices were unable to satisfy everyone with their decision. Evangelical and Catholic leaders condemned the ruling, again insisting that the decision would lead to the institutionalization of secularism. Conservative politicians raised a similar charge, with South Carolina senator Strom Thurmond calling the decision "another major triumph of secularism and atheism which are bent on throwing God completely out of our national life." As they had done following *Engel*, mainline Protestants and Jews endorsed the decision, as did leading educators. *Christian Century* praised the holding, stating the "decision is a good one, deeply rooted in the spirit of the First Amendment and strongly supported by the Court's previous rulings. . . . The reading of ten verses from the Bible . . . selected by one of the students at random [and] unaccompanied by any comment, degenerates into incantation." Generally, however, the public reaction to *Schempp* was more restrained than it had been following *Engel*. After *Engel*, the ruling was expected; as *Christianity Today* wrote with sense of resignation, "[t]he decision against prayer and Bible reading came as no surprise." The only question had been the tenor of the Court's holding, and the conciliatory nature of Justice Clark's opinion appeared to alleviate some concerns. Summarizing the public reaction later that fall, *Phi Delta Kappan*, a national teachers' journal, observed that "*Engel* was greeted with near hysteria while *Abington* [i.e., *Schempp*] has generally, though sullenly, been accepted."[26]

Following the *Schempp* decision, conservative members of Congress renewed their calls for a constitutional amendment to permit prayer and Bible reading in public schools. In the House, Republican congressman Frank Becker led the charge. By the spring of 1964, he had amassed a sufficient number of cosponsors to force a hearing before the Judiciary Committee. Initially amendment supporters appeared to have the upper hand, and the committee heard from a slew of religious leaders and celebrities, with actors John Wayne and Ronald Reagan endorsing an amendment. Opposition by religious moderates, organized by the National Council of Churches and the Baptist Joint Committee on Public Affairs, helped turn the tide, as did testimony by leading law professors. The bill died in committee that summer.[27] Two years later a second amendment drive took place, this time in the Senate, led by Illinois Republican Everett Dirksen. Once again, after an initial flurry of interest, support for an amendment declined. The hearings on the Dirksen Amendment were poorly attended, and the committee reported the bill for Senate debate without a recommendation but not before Democrats had sufficient votes to defeat it on the floor. Although the Dirksen Amendment proceeded further legislatively than the Becker Amendment, it met the same end. Later efforts to place a "school prayer amendment" in the Constitution would meet a similar fate.[28]

Separationism in Decline

In many ways, the prayer and Bible-reading decisions were the high-water mark of church-state separation, both legally and culturally. This is somewhat ironic, because the justices went out of their way to downplay separation of church and state as the controlling principle or at least to soften its meaning. Still, *Engel* and *Schempp* were separationist holdings, and people viewed them as such. What is additionally ironic is that even though the two cases may represent the apex of separationism, they also precipitated its initial decline. The cases were a turning point in public attitudes toward separationism and a precursor to the gradual weaning of church-state jurisprudence from that principle.[29]

The first factor that led to the gradual dismantling of the cultural and legal consensus behind separationism was the public reaction to *Engel* and *Schempp*. The holdings represented the opening wedge that eventually split the Protestant consensus behind separationism; moderate and liberal churches generally supported the decisions, while evangelical and other conservative Protestants opposed them. The first indication of this rift was in the breakdown of the religious representatives who testified before Congress in the hearings surrounding the Becker and Dirksen Amendments. Testimony in favor of an amendment came largely from evangelical groups, including the NAE—a founding sponsor of POAU—whereas opposition came chiefly from moderate and liberal Protestants, although Southern Baptist and Missouri Synod Lutheran representatives also testified against the amendment. Opposition from these last two conservative bodies indicated that the fissure was not yet complete—based on its long-standing commitment to church-state separation, the Southern Baptist Convention would not abandon its stance until the 1980s. And although critics charged the Court's decisions would lead to cultural secularization, most did not attack church-state separation as the problem. Rev. Daniel Poling, editor of the *Christian Herald*, testified that he supported an amendment to make it "unmistakably clear that separation [of church and state] does not mean exclusion" of religion from public life.[30] Over time, however, conservative Protestants came to see that the problem lay not solely with secularism but with its purported cause, separationism. Anger over the prayer and Bible-reading decisions would fester for years; in the 1970s, it combined with outrage over *Roe v. Wade* and the Internal Revenue Service's revocation of tax exemptions of fundamentalist Christian schools that practiced racial discrimination, leading to the creation of the Religious Right. One leader of that movement, Baptist minister Jerry Falwell Sr., would renounce church-state separation, calling it "bogus," while denying that he had ever supported the principle early in his career.[31]

The second event that helped transform public attitudes about separation of church and state was the public "rehabilitation" of the American Catholic Church, which began in the 1950s. In the 1940s, Protestants and secular liberals had largely succeeded in characterizing the Catholic Church as an authoritarian and antidemocratic institution. Even though this critique was based in part on exaggeration and hyperbole, as represented by Paul Blanshard's best-selling book *American Freedom and Catholic Power*, the church had supplied ammunition for its opponents by supporting fascist regimes in Italy and Spain and working to restrict access to birth control and to censor books, magazines, and motion pictures it regarded as immoral.[32] By the 1950s, however, the long-standing image of Catholicism as an authoritarian and insular immigrant church was quickly changing. Thanks to the booming postwar economy and the GI Bill, rank-and-file Catholics entered the middle class and fled inner-city Catholic enclaves for the suburbs. For many Protestants, their Catholic coworkers and neighbors no longer looked suspiciously foreign but rather familiarly American. The public image of the church also improved due to the new ecumenical spirit and the popular (and widely interfaith) appeal of the avuncular television priest Bishop Fulton Sheen, whose weekly program *Life Is Worth Living* was watched by millions of Protestants and Catholics alike. And finally, the church's long stance against communism—a position that had alienated liberals and intellectuals during the prewar years—appeared very prodemocratic during the Cold War of the 1950s. John F. Kennedy's 1960 embrace of church-state separation went far to dispel suspicions about Catholic loyalties, and his refusal as president to support a federal education bill that included benefits for religious schools solidified perceptions that Catholics could respect American values. Then, from 1962 to 1965, the Catholic Church held its conclave known as Vatican II, which culminated in the adoption of the Declaration on Religious Liberty, written largely by Fr. John Courtney Murray. Also significant for non-Catholic Americans was the church's abandonment of the confessional state model, its preference for state religious establishments, and its insistence on the exclusivity of the Catholic faith. In accepting the legitimacy of other Christian denominations and liberal democratic systems, the Catholic Church ceased to be a threat for many non-Catholic Americans. Church-state separation was no longer necessary to guard against perceived Catholic incursions on democratic America.[33]

The third event of the 1960s that laid the groundwork for the demise of separationism was the rise of federal civil rights legislation and President Lyndon Johnson's Great Society. At risk of oversimplification, comprehensive laws such as the 1964 Civil Rights Act, prohibiting discrimination in areas of public accommodations, employment, and in government-funded programs, introduced a new legal regime: nondiscrimination in access to and receipt of benefits became an important constitutional norm. These laws complemented the rights-oriented approach of the Warren Court of the same period. Coinciding with the "rights revolution" was the expansion of federal social welfare programs under LBJ's Great Society. Two watershed events were the passage of the first significant federal funding programs for education, the Higher Education Facilities Act of 1963 (HEFA) and the Elementary and Secondary Education Act of 1965 (ESEA). Both laws included religious institutions as recipients, with ESEA funding supplemental programs for children in public and private schools, including parochial schools. The Johnson administration was able to overcome opposition to including funding for parochial schoolchildren by recharacterizing the benefits as part of his "war on poverty" agenda. These laws established a presumption that religious institutions were not to be excluded from participating in important social programs simply because of their religious character.[34]

Secular liberals, mainline Protestants, and moderate Jews—constituencies that had been loyal supporters of church-state separation—threw their support behind the civil rights and Great Society legislation. From 1960 to 1963, various mainline denominations and the National Council of Churches (NCC) created offices to train volunteers and organize grassroots support for the civil rights struggle, including sending freedom riders into the South.[35] Then, in 1964, the NCC organized a meeting of twenty-four progressive and mainline religious groups in Cleveland to discuss the relationship between church-state separation and social and economic justice issues. Prior to the meeting, Rev. Dean Kelley, the director of the NCC's religious liberty office, wrote an article in the *Journal of Church and State* titled "Beyond Separation of Church and State." In the article, Kelley condemned the "negativistic, sterile" application of church-state separation on grounds it did not acknowledge the nation's religious pluralism. Too frequently, Kelley insisted, separation was used as a battle cry to oppose the activities of the Catholic Church. Much of the problem lay with the phrase itself, Kelley insisted, in "that it says both too much and too little. It implied that religion has nothing, and should have nothing, to do with men's decisions in matters of state and public policy." Time had come to see church-state separation not as a freestanding value but as how it affected, or impeded, social progress.[36]

Kelley's article set the tenor of the Cleveland meeting. At its conclusion, the attendees issued a statement that revealed a high level of agreement about church-state relations. The statement asserted "the need for rethinking the institutional arrangements between church and state" at "a time of crisis" over the issue. The nation's changing religious demographics revealed that America was no longer "a predominately Protestant society" but a pluralistic one. This "new pluralism and the expansion of government functions require[d] re-examination of the role of the state respecting religion and the churches." As a result, the statement continued, "any attempt to express church-state relations in terms of an absolute and complete separation or of a wall of separation between church and state serves only to obscure the fullness of their relationship rather than offering a fruitful basis for an understanding of the present situation." Based on this "flexible" understanding of church-state separation, the attendees at the Cleveland meeting abandoned their previous opposition to including religious schools and institutions in the Great Society legislation. Thus, by the mid-1960s, religious and secular progressives were increasingly willing to compromise on separationism in order to ensure that government promoted equality and advanced the commonweal.[37]

Criticism of church-separation arose from mainstream academics as well. On the religious-studies side, Franklin Littell of the Chicago Theological Seminary, Thomas Sanders of Brown University, and Philip Wogaman of American University's Wesley Theological Seminary wrote stinging critiques of church-state separation. All three condemned the rhetoric of "absolute" separation and its frequent use to foster Protestant suspicions about Catholicism. Littell argued that an emphasis on separationism interfered with achieving a preferred model of religious pluralism, whereas Sanders and Wogaman argued that by embracing separationism, "Protestantism has often shirked its responsibilities for social change." Rather than accepting separationism at face value, Wogaman wrote, Protestants "should encourage our society to reach deeper into its traditions for grounding in the more basic values and assumptions which gave validity to the doctrine of separation." "Questions of public policy in the area of church relations thus should be made to turn, not on their significance in terms of separation, but on their meaning with respect to the basic values which justified the doctrine in the first place."[38]

A handful of leading legal scholars offered similar critiques. University of Chicago law professor Wilber Katz insisted that church-state separation was "not an independent principle, that the primary principle is that of religious liberty." Separation "ordinarily promotes religious freedom," Katz wrote, but "it is defensible so long as it does, and only so long." In a 1963 book, *The Wall between Church and State*, Katz's colleague Dallin H. Oaks asserted that the "modern popularity of the wall metaphor should not conceal its inappropriateness as an expression of current church-state relationships." Oaks expressed "hope that the wall will soon give way to more accurate, if less conclusive, means of describing the relationship between church and state." And Harvard law professor Mark De Wolfe Howe wrote a 1965 book, *The Garden and the Wilderness*, in which he argued that the true historical basis for separationism was found in Roger Williams's concern for protecting the church, rather than in Jefferson's anticlerical, rationalist approach. The Court's interpretation of church-state separation was "ahistorical," Howe insisted, and was created out of its own "pretense." While these scholarly critiques rarely reached popular audiences, they impacted the thinking of other scholars and members of the judiciary.[39]

Taken together, these various voices and events during the 1960s worked to undermine the legitimacy of church-state separation among members of its core constituency. Those doubts soon made their way into the courts.

Supreme Court in Transition

The transformation in popular attitudes toward church-state separation, at least in its applications, did not immediately impact the justices' perspectives about separationism. Nor did this cultural transition lead directly to the Court's more accommodationist rulings after 1980. As has often been noted about the Court, the justices commonly follow cultural trends rather than direct them. (As an example, one study indicated that by the time of the Court's prayer and Bible-reading decisions, only about 40 percent of school districts conducted such exercises on a regular basis.)[40] Several of the older justices—Black, Douglas, Warren—and newer justices who had practiced law in the 1940s and 1950s—William Brennan, Thurgood Marshall, and John Paul Stevens—remained committed to church-state separation and failed to realize that the ground was slowly shifting beneath their feet.

The first indication of a jurisprudential shift occurred in 1968. In *Board of Education v. Allen* (1968), the Court upheld a New York law modeled on the ESEA that authorized school districts to loan textbooks to parochial schools. Writing for a six-justice majority, Justice Byron White—a Kennedy appointee—found that the beneficiaries of the program were children, not their schools, and he asserted that the Establishment Clause "does not prevent a State from extending the benefits of state laws to all citizens without regard for their religious affiliation." White maintained that *Everson* supported this result. More significant than the outcome, White made three crucial points that extended *Everson*: legislatures were not limited to providing health-welfare assistance to children attending religious schools but could aid in their education as well, religious schools served an important *public* function in addition to a religious function, and those schools' religious and secular functions could be distinguished. In passing, White acknowledged that the "constitutional standard is the 'separation of Church and State'"; however, he emphasized, "like many problems in constitutional law, [it] is one of degree." Most immediately, the *Allen* decision signaled that the federal ESEA was constitutional in principle; challengers would have to satisfy themselves with raising claims about how the law was misapplied.[41] Significantly, three separationist-leaning justices joined Justice White's majority opinion: Warren, Brennan, and the newly appointed Marshall. Dissenting, Justice Black rebuked the majority for turning a blind eye to "powerful sectarian religious propagandists who [were] . . . looking toward complete domination and supremacy of their particular brand of religion," a veiled reference to the Catholic Church. The only way to prevent religious discord and strife among groups, Black asserted, was "to keep the wall of separation between church and state high and impregnable."[42] Commenting on the changed assumptions in the Court's holding, the *New York Times* editorialized that the decision "deepens the already serious inroads that have been made into the vital principle of church-state separation."[43]

Two years later, in a 7–1 decision, with only Justice Douglas dissenting, the Court upheld the constitutionality of property tax exemptions for churches and other houses of worship (*Walz v. Tax Commission*). Even though the state tax exemption was for nonprofit charities generally, the Court acknowledged that the church properties in question were not dedicated to charitable uses. Nonetheless, newly appointed Chief Justice Warren Burger relied on the breadth of the exemption and the historical pedigree of extending tax breaks to houses of worship. Because of the widespread practice of exempting church property, the holding was not unexpected; the only question was what would be the tone of the Court's ruling. Addressing the constitutional standard, Burger remarked that "[n]o perfect or absolute separation is really possible." Because of "the complexities of modern life," where government and private entities interacted on a regular basis, separation "cannot mean absence of all contact." Rather, the touchstone was the notion of "accommodation" of religion, Burger wrote, citing *Zorach*. For Burger, the government had broad authority to accommodate religion, provided it did not involve state "sponsorship, financial support, [or] active involvement . . . in religious activity." Here, a tax exemption limited "the fiscal relationship between church and state," which tended "to complement and reinforce the desired separation" found in the First Amendment.[44] Though the point was subtle, Burger appeared to be saying that the superior value underlying separationism was in the way it insulated religious institutions from government oversight. Also, by restricting the Establishment Clause's scope to prohibiting "sponsorship, financial support, [or] active involvement" of religion, Burger opened the door to other acceptable forms of church-state cooperation. As one church-state commentator observed, Burger's opinion "moved the Court still further away from *Everson* (with its sweeping separationist language and narrow margins for aid), and in the direction indicated in *Allen*."[45]

Together, *Allen* and *Walz* initiated a new approach to aid-to-religion cases and to the way in which a growing number of justices viewed church-state separation.[46] From 1970 to 1985, the Court considered twenty-one Establishment Clause cases, the majority involving public aid to religion. The Court rendered separationist rulings in eleven of those cases, nonseparationist rulings in seven, and mixed rulings in the remaining three cases. More significant than the results, however, was the Court's changed rhetoric, even in those cases where a court majority found an Establishment Clause violation.

In 1971, the Court handed down two consequential holdings that have frequently been considered to be high points of church-state separation: *Lemon v. Kurtzman* and *Tilton v. Richardson*. However, a careful reading of those decisions reveals that they were not ringing endorsements of separationism. *Lemon* involved a challenge to a state statute that provided reimbursements to nonpublic schools for teacher salaries, textbooks, and instructional materials used in secular subjects, whereas *Tilton* concerned HEFA grants to church-related colleges for the construction of academic facilities.[47] The Court split the difference, striking the aid in *Lemon* but upholding the grants in *Tilton* on the condition the funded buildings could not be used for religious instruction or worship. Both decisions were written by Chief Justice Burger, whose opinions were equivocal at best. Burger noted that a teacher in a parochial school was different from a nonideological textbook, such that subsidizing the former raised constitutional issues not presented in funding the latter. In contrast, "religious indoctrination is not a substantial purpose or activity" of most church-related colleges, Burger wrote, and the construction grants were restricted for buildings where secular subjects were to be taught. Although the holdings were arguably separationist, the tone of Burger's opinions belied that intent. "Our prior holdings do not call for total separation between church and state; total separation is not possible in an absolute sense. Some relationship between government and religious organizations is inevitable," Burger wrote. "[T]he line of separation, far from being a 'wall,' is a blurred, indistinct, and variable barrier depending on all the circumstances of a particular relationship." Church-state separation was not a rigid principle but varied depending on the circumstances.[48]

Aside from Burger's rhetoric, the Court in *Lemon* announced a three-part test for scrutinizing Establishment Clause violations. The test examined whether a law or policy had a secular purpose, whether its primary effect advanced or inhibited religion, and whether it resulted in excessive government entanglement with religion. Despite announcing that test, Burger believed that the salary grants did not advance religion, only that the government's oversight of the programs doomed them: "Entanglement is the only problem I see here," Burger declared in conference. The implication was that if the government could adjust its oversight, the aid was constitutional. Justice William Brennan, initially supported by Justices Potter Stewart and Harry Blackmun, maintained that the grants advanced the religious mission of the schools. In the end, the chief justice convinced Stewart and Blackmun to sign on to his narrower approach, leading to a less separationist holding. Following the decisions, a leading commentator concluded that "[t]he 'wall of separation' has had to give way before the realities of the inevitable interaction of church and state, particularly in a complex, highly regulated society."[49]

The conclusion of the Court's term in 1971 marked the retirement of Justice Harlan and, more significantly, that of Justice Black. Those retirements allowed President Richard Nixon to appoint two additional justices to the Court, Lewis Powell and William Rehnquist. At least initially, those appointments, when added to Nixon's earlier appointments of Chief Justice Burger and Justice Blackmun, did not cause a change in church-state jurisprudence. Justice Powell joined Justice Blackmun as a moderate on church-state matters; of the four Nixon appointees, only Justice Rehnquist took a consistent stance opposing separationism.[50]

The next four terms (1972–76) marked what was arguably the busiest period of church-state activity for the Court, with the justices considering eight aid-to-religion cases and two free exercise cases. Commentators have considered the period to be a high-water mark for church-state separation, as the Court struck aid programs in five of the cases, while approving a state's denial of aid in a sixth. The programs found unconstitutional involved both direct aid related to instruction (e.g., tuition and building-maintenance grants) and auxiliary aid (e.g., instructional materials) that the justices believed could be diverted for religious instruction. However, the justices upheld nondivertible assistance (e.g., therapeutic services), textbook loans, and construction grants for college building construction. Many of the decisions resulted in plurality opinions, meaning that a majority of the justices could not agree on a particular rationale. Not only did this produce a patchwork of holdings; it also prevented the authors of the controlling opinions from making firm affirmations of church-state separation, had they been so inclined.[51] Most commentators focused on the outcomes of the cases, interpreting them as creating a line that could not be crossed, without noting the fractured nature of the rulings and the absence of any ringing endorsements of church-state separation. One church-state scholar, Richard E. Morgan, speculated whether the holdings represented the "final installment" on the constitutionality of public aid to religious education. Summarizing the holdings, Morgan concluded that it was clearer than at any previous time "that public funds may not be used in any major amount to relieve the economic distress of church-related schools." Yet the factors that had motivated state legislatures to enact the programs still remained: religious schools, which served a significant number of America's children, were in dire need of assistance, which called for creative solutions rather than adhering to rigid ideologies. As the *New York Times* editorialized in 1973, there "is growing support for the view that the wall of separation between church and state has outlived its usefulness." Particularly in light of "the new ecumenical spirit between the faiths, the old Jeffersonian warning sounds quaint and obsolete to some political pragmatists."[52]

This pattern of fractured holdings in aid-to-religion cases continued throughout the remainder of the 1970s into the 1980s. In *Wolman v. Walter* (1977), for example, the justices considered an Ohio statute that provided auxiliary aid and a host of services to private schools: textbooks, standardized testing, diagnostic and therapeutic services, field trips, and instructional materials and equipment. Justice Blackmun issued an opinion that fluctuated from majority to plurality, upholding the first three categories while striking the latter three. Seven other justices wrote opinions that concurred and dissented in part. Not surprisingly, none of the opinions mentioned separation of church and state. From that point forward, Court majorities rejected most constitutional challenges to programs involving financial aid to religious institutions—the only exception being in two cases in 1985. Increasingly, the justices found no constitutional defect with aid programs that provided in-kind assistance that was ideologically neutral and given to public and private entities alike.[53]

An additional factor leading to constitutionality was when the financial aid flowed directly to parents and children and thus only indirectly to the religious schools. So, in *Mueller v. Allen* (1983), the Court upheld a tax deduction for educational expenses associated with public and private schooling, even though the largest item allowed was school tuition and thus not available for parents of children attending public schools. Three years later the Court upheld an applicant's use of a state college scholarship for disabled students so he could attend a Bible college to train for the ministry. The scholarship was paid directly to the applicant and could be used at various public and private institutions, Justice Marshall noted, such that a religious college benefited only as a result of that applicant's independent "private choice."[54]

The last year that the Court issued a separationist holding in an aid-to-religion case was in 1985 and involved challenges to federal ESEA and state programs that provided supplemental courses in remedial and enrichment subjects for eligible public and private schools. (*Aguilar v. Felton*, *Grand Rapids School District v. Ball*). In the religious schools, the courses were taught by full-time public-school employees. Justice Brennan wrote the opinions in both cases, striking the federal program on entanglement grounds and the state program on the basis that it created a "symbolic union of church and state" and subsidized the educational mission of the religious schools. Brennan favorably cited *Everson* and the aid-to-religion cases of the 1970s but did not refer directly to church-state separation or the wall metaphor.[55] That omission was not lost on Justice Rehnquist. Less than a month earlier, Rehnquist had delivered his missive in the Alabama moment-of-silent-prayer case, *Wallace v. Jaffree*, where he had excoriated the Court's reliance on separation of church and state as the constitutional standard, calling it "useless" and asserting that the "wall of separation between church and State is a metaphor based on bad history" that should "be frankly and explicitly abandoned." Now, in his dissent in *Ball*, Rehnquist chastised the Court majority for "declining to discuss the faulty 'wall' premise upon which [the holding] rest[s]." Uncharacteristically, none of the justices in the majority responded to Rehnquist's broadside. After *Aguilar* and *Ball*, the Court in the future would uphold public aid-to-religion programs, as in *Zelman v. Simmons-Harris* in 2002 with its approval of tuition vouchers for students attending private religious schools and more recently in *Espinoza v. Montana Department of Revenue* in 2020.[56]

In the area of religious activity in public schools, the Court hewed to a more separationist line. In 1980, the Court summarily struck down the posting of the Ten Commandments in public-school classrooms. Five years later, in *Wallace v. Jaffree*, the Court voided an Alabama statute that authorized school prayer and silent meditation. Two years later the justices invalidated a Louisiana law that required that schools provide "equal treatment" of creation science whenever evolution was taught. In 1992, a bare majority struck down a common practice of clergy-led invocations and benedictions at public-school graduation ceremonies. And in 2000, the Court invalidated another common practice of prayers before school athletic events, such as football games. Yet in none of those cases did the majority opinion refer to church-state separation.[57] In fact, in *Wallace*, Justice Stevens's opinion quoted from *Everson*'s no-aid paragraph but then omitted the final sentence about Jefferson's wall of separation.[58]

Not all religion-in-schools cases ended with separationist results. During the same period, the Court upheld a federal law authorizing student-run "Bible clubs" in secondary schools, allowed rentals of public-school auditoriums for religious presentations, and permitted religious groups to use school classrooms at the conclusion of the instructional day to conduct religious clubs for elementary schoolchildren. In that last case, *Good News Club v. Milford Central School*, Justice Clarence Thomas summarily dismissed any similarities to the released-time program in *McCollum*, noting that children's compulsory attendance ended with the closing bell. Again, church-state separation was not mentioned in any of the opinions.[59]

As noted in the introduction, the last majority opinion that affirmed church-state separation as the controlling rule was that of Chief Justice Burger in *Lynch v. Donnelly* in 1984, where he described the concept of a wall of separation as "a useful figure of speech," though not a "wholly accurate description of the practical aspects of the relationship that in fact exists between church and state."[60] Although justices have discussed and debated the importance of church-state separation in subsequent cases, the principle has failed to receive the endorsement of a Court majority.

The issue of church-state separation took on a prominent role in the 2005 case of *Van Orden v. Perry*, involving a challenge to a Ten Commandments monument on the grounds of the Texas state capitol. By a 5–4 vote, the Court upheld the display of the six-foot stone monument, with moderate Justice Stephen Breyer providing the fifth vote. Church-state separation came up in several opinions. In the majority opinion, Chief Justice Rehnquist opined that the Establishment Clause had a Janus-like quality. "One face looks to the past in acknowledgment of our Nation's heritage, while the other looks to the present in demanding a separation between church and state," Rehnquist wrote. "Reconciling these two faces requires that we neither abdicate our responsibility to maintain a division between church and state nor evince a hostility to religion by disabling the government from in some ways recognizing our religious heritage."[61] Rehnquist's acknowledgment was surprising, coming as it did from the same justice who twenty years earlier had excoriated the wall metaphor as being "bad history" and calling for its abandonment. The reference may have been added in response to statements of other justices. In his concurring opinion, Justice Breyer focused on the issue of religious divisiveness, remarking how the religion clauses "seek to maintain that 'separation of church and state' that has long been critical to the 'peaceful dominion that religion exercises in [this] country.'"[62] The most thorough discussion of separationism appeared in Justice Stevens's dissenting opinion. Stevens asserted that the religion clauses "together erect a wall of separation between church and state. This metaphorical wall protects principles long recognized and often recited in this Court's cases." Stevens then responded to the majority's reliance on the historical practice of religious acknowledgments as grounds for upholding the display of the Ten Commandments monument. A reading of the First Amendment dependent on "purported original meanings" would "eviscerate the heart of the Establishment Clause," Stevens wrote.

> It would replace Jefferson's "wall of separation" with a perverse wall of exclusion—Christians inside, non-Christians out. It would permit States to construct walls of their own choosing—Baptists inside, Mormons out; Jewish Orthodox inside, Jewish Reform out. A Clause so understood might be faithful to the expectations of some of our Founders, but it is plainly not worthy of a society whose enviable hallmark over the course of two centuries has been the continuing expansion of religious pluralism and tolerance.[63]

Then, in a footnote, Stevens responded to the scholarly criticism of church-state separation described in this book's introduction. "Whatever one may think of the merits of the historical debate surrounding Jefferson and the 'wall' metaphor," Stevens wrote, "this Court at a minimum has never questioned the concept of the 'separation of church and state' in our First Amendment jurisprudence. The Chief Justice's opinion affirms that principle." Stevens, of course, was attempting to put the best face on the matter. The fact is that several justices had openly criticized the concept, including Chief Justice Rehnquist.[64]

Since then, acknowledgments of the principle of church-state separation have been relegated to concurring and dissenting opinions, usually in the latter. (Justice Thomas has occasionally discussed church-state separation in his concurring opinions, though disparagingly.)[65] References to separationism have commonly taken on the form of a lament that the majority opinions were abandoning an important principle. In his dissent in *Zelman*, for example, Justice Breyer noted how by "drawing fairly clear lines of separation between church and state," the Court had previously diffused religious strife and competition between sects. During his tenure, Justice David Souter also criticized the Court for abandoning "the desired separation insulating church and state."[66] More recently, Justice Sonia Sotomayor has assumed the role of mourning the Court's abandonment of church-state separation, writing in 2017 that the majority's decision allowing a renovation grant to a church had "slight[ed] both our precedents and our history, and its reasoning weakens this country's longstanding commitment to a separation of church and state beneficial to both."[67] Even though the conservative Court majority has abandoned the principle of separationism in most of its applications, more moderate justices have refused to give up on the concept. In 2019, a Court majority upheld the constitutionality of a thirty-two-foot cross on a public thoroughfare based on its status as a war memorial (*American Legion v. American Humanist Association*). In a concurring opinion, Justice Breyer urged that in Establishment Clause challenges the Court should "consider each case in light of the basic purposes that the Religion Clauses were meant to serve: assuring religious liberty and tolerance for all, avoiding religiously based social conflict, and maintaining that separation of church and state that allows each to flourish in its 'separate spher[e].'"[68] Justice Ruth Bader Ginsburg also referenced church-state separation in her dissenting opinion. After quoting Jefferson's Danbury letter about "build[ing] a wall of separation between church and state," she proceeded to comment that "[t]his barrier protect[s] the integrity of individual conscience in religious matters. . . . And while the union of government and religion tends to destroy government and degrade religion, separating the two preserves the legitimacy of each."[69] Unable to resist those references, Justice Thomas responded by again criticizing the "modern myth of separation as an American ideal," calling it "an ahistorical generalization."[70]

In the end, church-state separation's demise as a legal concept was not so much a result of direct attacks but of neglect and changing priorities. Separation of church and state was apparently still alive, though chiefly as a rhetorical device rather than as a concrete legal principle. That transformation elicited a poignant statement from Justice Sandra Day O'Connor in her final opinion in the companion case to *Van Orden v. Perry*: "Those who would renegotiate the boundaries between church and state must therefore answer a difficult question: Why would we trade a system that has served us so well for one that has served others so poorly?"[71]

Conclusion

> Reports of my death have been greatly exaggerated.
>
> —Mark Twain (attributed to)

Despite its evolution and reported decline, the idea of separation of church and state retains a powerful resiliency. This is likely due to several factors. First, the phrase has long been associated with the Constitution and represents a particular cultural ordering that is quintessentially American. The public's familiarity with the phrase may explain its longevity; as one commentator has observed, "[i]f a single metaphor dominates American thinking about church and state it is the metaphor of a wall of separation." And as religious historian Edwin Gaustad once noted, Americans are more familiar with the phrase separation of church and state than with the constitutional language itself. Separation of church and state, it seems, is woven into America's cultural fabric.[1]

A second factor that may explain the resiliency of separation of church and state is the inherent indeterminacy of the concept, if not of the very phrase itself. Does it mean simply a separation of the official functions of the state from an institutional church, or does it imply a greater separation between religious forces and government policies? Does it mean a formal separation, where each entity operates in its own sphere of authority but allows relationships that do not implicate that institutional autonomy? Or does separationism require no interaction between the two spheres? Can the church and state work in tandem to accomplish the common good, or must they relate as strangers? Does separationism require a secular state and public square, or does it allow for religious pluralism? Does separationism prohibit government from acknowledging religious habits and traditions by preventing its use of religion rhetoric and symbolism, or are such acknowledgments not implicated by the concept? And is separationism a freestanding value or only relevant for how it promotes religious freedom in particular? People can embrace any of these positions and still espouse fealty to church-state separation.

Despite its resiliency as an idea, however, church-state separation has declined as a legal rule and cultural construct. As this book has demonstrated, this is due to at least three factors. The first was the modern Supreme Court's initial identification of separationism with secularism rather than as promoting religious pluralism. Despite the justices' later efforts to backtrack on that perception, the association of separationism with secularism stuck, reinforced by controversial decisions such as the school prayer cases. Thus, a principle that had achieved a degree of consensus became a source of division. Separationism became an easy target for political and religious conservatives to demonstrate a hostility toward religion among people with secularist leanings. The second factor is that a rigorous idea of separation failed to keep up with cultural developments that valued religious ecumenism and accepted expanding access to government benefits programs regardless of one's religious identity. Accordingly, the Court's gradual abandonment of separationism had less to do with the appointment of conservative justices after 1980—although they certainly accelerated its decline—and more to do with the justices of the late 1960s and 1970s seeking to reconcile separationism with the times. And, finally, the Court's various—and some would say inconsistent—holdings in this area only invited criticism over the meaning of church-state separation. The inability of the Court to decide on a definition of church-state separation has also added to this sense of indeterminacy. In a sense, the indeterminacy of church-state separation has been both its strength—ensuring the longevity of the idea—and its weakness—by making it more of a rhetorical device rather than a discernable legal rule.

So, what is the legal status of separation of church and state? At the time of writing this book, the legal "health" of the principle depends on the category or subject area. With respect to the category of "church" or religious autonomy, the Court has used separationist principles to impose limits on government regulations of the internal operations of religious bodies, including their employment practices. The more recent holdings of *Our Lady of Guadalupe School v. Morrissey-Berru* and *Hosanna–Tabor Evangelical Lutheran Church*, though decided chiefly on free exercise of religion grounds, have extended this area of church-state jurisprudence that affirms that one function of separation is to protect the autonomy of religious bodies to be free from governmental control. The open question is whether the Court will extend this protective notion of separationism to include religiously affiliated entities that serve the public (e.g., hospitals, social service agencies) or even private businesses operated pursuant to the owner's religious beliefs. It is within this area of religious autonomy that the principle of separationism has been most resilient.[2]

The same cannot be said for other categories of Establishment Clause issues. Separation of church and state technically remains the rule for religion in public education, though the Court has not considered a case since the early 2000s. As discussed, in 1992 and 2000, the Court struck practices of clergy-led prayers at public school graduations and student-led prayers at athletic events, respectively. Even though both holdings were arguably separationist, neither of the majority opinions relied on principles of church-state separation. Justice Anthony Kennedy's narrow opinion in the first case, *Lee v. Weisman*, held that the prayers coerced unwilling students to participate in the exercises. That approach elicited concurring opinions from Justices Harry Blackmun and David Souter that asserted that separationism, rather than coercion, should have controlled the outcome.[3] In contrast, in 2001, the Court held that the free speech interests of outside religious instructors overrode a school's Establishment Clause concerns about keeping schools free from religious indoctrination. Because the school had opened its doors to after-school use by other groups, it had "no valid Establishment Clause interest" in excluding the religious instructors, Justice Clarence Thomas wrote. As the most recent case involving religion in the schools, *Good News Club v. Milford Central School* may indicate that church-state separation no longer represents the dominant constitutional value in this area.[4]

In two remaining Establishment Clause areas—government use of religious rhetoric and symbols and government funding of religious entities—the principle of church-state separation is effectively spent. As noted, the Court has upheld prayers before legislative bodies and government-sponsored nativity scenes, Ten Commandment monuments, and Latin crosses. In all cases a Court majority has spurned separation in favor of a historical-legacy approach.[5] And with respect to government funding of religious institutions, a Court majority has not only held that the Establishment Clause does not bar permissive funding of religion under neutral programs available to secular and religious recipients alike—grants, scholarships, and tuition vouchers; its decisions in 2017 and 2020 have also held that relying on no-aid separationism to deny such funding amounts to discrimination against religion. Under such an interpretation, there is little left of separationism in the funding context, and the Establishment Clause only prohibits religious preferentialism.[6] With the likelihood of a Supreme Court dominated by ideologically conservatives for a generation, church-state separation will play a decreasing role in these last two categories.

In the end, separating church and state has always been an ambitious project, facing resistance at every turn. Disestablishment and the rise of religious voluntarism freed American religion to flourish in the early nineteenth century; as Alexis de Tocqueville observed, a high degree of religiosity existed in the United States alongside a professed allegiance to church-state separation. Despite (or because of) that allegiance, the United States has always had a higher percentage of churchgoing people than most Western democracies.[7] But this has meant that any rigorous form of church-state separation has existed in tension with the preferences of those Americans who decry the separation of religion from American public life. Possibly this dynamic is summed up in the title to a book on American church and state by Professors Ira Lupu and Robert Tuttle: *Secular Government, Religious People*.[8] A cynic might say that true separation of church and state has never existed in this country, that judges and public officials have always been willing to compromise on the concept, resisting taking the principle to its logical conclusion.[9] Perhaps Chief Justice Warren Burger was correct after all when he declared that "the line of separation, far from being a 'wall,' is a blurred, indistinct, and variable barrier depending on all the circumstances of a particular relationship."[10] In the end, this all may explain its resiliency as a concept for many Americans.

Notes

Introduction

1. See Steven K. Green, *The Third Disestablishment: Church, State, and American Culture, 1940–1975* (New York: Oxford University Press, 2019), 249–300.

2. Richard John Neuhaus, *The Naked Public Square: Religion and Democracy in America* (Grand Rapids, MI: William B. Eerdmans, 1984); Stephen L. Carter, *The Culture of Disbelief: How American Law and Politics Trivialize Religious Devotion* (New York: Basic Books, 1993).

3. Jones v. Wolf, 443 U.S. 595 (1979); Hosanna-Tabor Evangelical Lutheran Church v. EEOC, 565 U.S. 171, 189 (2012) ("the power to determine which individuals will minister to the faithful also violates the Establishment Clause, which prohibits government involvement in such ecclesiastical decisions").

4. See Steven K. Green, "Religious Liberty as a Positive and Negative Right," *Albany Law Review* 70 (2007): 1453–72; Suzanna Sherry, "Enlightening the Religion Clauses," *Journal of Contemporary Legal Issues* 7 (1996): 473.

5. A fourth decision, Trump v. Pennsylvania, involved a church-state issue indirectly: whether the Donald J. Trump administration followed appropriate procedures in expanding a religious exemption to the contraceptive-coverage compliance requirements under the Affordable Care Act. 140 S. Ct. 2367 (2020).

6. Our Lady of Guadalupe School v. Morrissey-Berru, 140 S. Ct. 2049 (2020).

7. Hosanna-Tabor Evangelical Lutheran Church, 565 U.S., 181.

8. Our Lady of Guadalupe School, 140 S. Ct., 2065–66.

9. Bostock v. Clayton County, 140 S. Ct. 1731 (2020).

10. Espinoza v. Montana Department of Revenue, 140 S. Ct. 2246, 2260–61 (2020).

11. Espinoza, 2266 (Thomas, J., concurring).

12. Espinoza, 2292 (Sotomayor, J., dissenting).

13. Trinity Lutheran Church v. Comer, 137 S. Ct. 2012 (2017). In her dissent in that case, Justice Sotomayor offered an extensive defense of church-state separation: "If . . . separation means anything, it means that the government cannot, or at least need not, tax its citizens and turn that money over to houses of worship." Espinoza, 2027.

14. Erwin Chemerinsky, "*Symposium: The Crumbling Wall Separating Church and State,*" SCOTUSblog, June 27, 2017, 10:18 a.m., http://www.scotusblog.com/2017/06/symposium-crumbling-wall-separating-church-state/; "Why Trinity Lutheran Is the Most Important Case of the 2016 Term," *Liberty and Law*, June 26, 2017; David French, "Legal Radicals Don't Want the 'Separation of Church and State,'" *National Review*, June 28, 2017, https://www.nationalreview.com/2017/06/separation-church-state-legal-radicals-want-more-state-less-church/.

15. Bowen v. Kendrick, 487 U.S. 589 (1988); Mitchell v. Helms, 530 U.S. 793 (2000); Zelman v. Simmons-Harris, 536 U.S. 639 (2002); Trinity Lutheran Church (2017); Greece v. Galloway, 572 U.S. 565 (2014); Van Orden v. Perry, 454 U.S. 677 (2005); American Legion v. American Humanist Association, 139 S. Ct. 2067 (2019).

16. Santa Fe Indep. School District v. Doe, 530 U.S. 290 (2000); Board of Education v. Mergens, 496 U.S. 226 (1990); Good News Club v. Milford Central School District, 533 U.S. 98 (2001).

17. Everson v. Board of Education, 330 U.S. 1, 15–16 (1947).

18. Everson, 19 (Jackson, J., dissenting); Everson, 21–22 (Rutledge, J., dissenting); McCollum v. Board of Education, 333 U.S. 203, 212 (1948); McCollum, 213, 231 (Frankfurter, J.).

19. "High Court Backs State Right to Run Parochial Buses," *New York Times*, February 11, 1947, 1, 31; "The New Jersey School Transportation Case," *New York Times*, February 11, 1947, 26; "Public Funds for Sectarian Schools," *Harvard Law Review* (1947): 793–800.

20. "3 Faiths File Brief for Released Time," *New York Times*, June 17, 1948, 27; *Christianity and Crisis*, 8 (1948): 90; "Cushing Stresses Parents' Rights," *New York Times*, April 10, 1947, 18; J. M. O'Neill, "Church, Schools, and the Constitution," *Commentary* (June 1947): 562–70; Milton R. Konvitz, "Separation of Church and State: The First Freedom," *Law and Contemporary Problems* 14 (1949): 44–60.

21. E. Bruce Thompson, "The Development in History of the Principle of Separation of Church and State," in *Church and State in Scripture, History, and American Law*, ed. James E. Wood Jr. (Waco, TX: Baylor University Press, 1958), 57; Dallin H. Oaks, *The Wall between Church and State* (Chicago: University of Chicago Press, 1963), 2; Philip E. Hammond, "The Shifting Meaning of a 'Wall of Separation,'" *Sociological Analysis* 42 (Autumn 1981): 227–34; Harold D. Hammett, "Separation of Church and State: By One Wall or Two?," *Journal of Church and State* 7 (1965): 190–206.

22. Wheaton College Special Collections, collection 113, National Association of Evangelicals, box 1, file Temporary Committee for Evangelical Action; Axel R. Schafer, *Piety and Public Funding: Evangelicals and the State in Modern America* (Philadelphia: University of Pennsylvania Press, 2012), 62–65, 111–12; Mark S. Massa, "A Catholic for President? John F. Kennedy and the 'Secular' Theology of the Houston Speech, 1960," *Journal of Church and State* 39 (1997): 297–317.

23. Engel v. Vitale, 370 U.S. 421 (1962); School District of Abington Township v. Schempp, 374 U.S. 203 (1963); Lemon v. Kurtzman, 403 U.S. 602 (1971); Tilton v. Richardson, 403 U.S. 672 (1971); Levitt v. PEARL, 413 U.S. 472 (1973); Sloan v. Lemon, 413 U.S. 825 (1973); PEARL v. Nyquist, 413 U.S. 756 (1973); Meek v. Pittenger, 421 U.S. 349 (1975).

24. Leo Pfeffer, *God, Caesar, and the Constitution: The Court as Referee of Church-State Confronation* (Boston: Beacon Press, 1975), 346.

25. Robert S. Alley, *School Prayer: The Court, the Congress, and the First Amendment* (Buffalo, NY: Prometheus Books, 1994), 163–205; Joan DelFattore, *The Fourth R: Conflicts over Religion in America's Public Schools* (New Haven, CT: Yale University Press, 2004), 178–98; Ronald Reagan, "Remarks to the National Association of Evangelicals," March 8, 1983, American Presidency Project, https://www.presidency.ucsb.edu/documents/remarks-the-annual-convention-the-national-association-evangelicals-orlando-florida.

26. Robert L. Cord, *Separation of Church and State: Historical Fact and Current Fiction* (Grand Rapids, MI: Baker Book House, 1982, 1988); Neuhaus, *Naked Public Square*; Stephen L. Carter, *God's Name in Vain* (New York: Basic Books, 2000), 78, 72.

27. McCollum, 333 U.S., 247 (Reed., J, dissenting).

28. Lemon, 403 U.S., 612–13, 614.

29. Wallace v. Jaffree, 472 U.S. 38, 107 (1985) (Rehnquist, J., dissenting); Derek Davis, *Original Intent: Chief Justice Rehnquist and the Course of American Church/State Relations* (Buffalo: Prometheus Books, 1991), 94–97.

30. Lamb's Chapel v. Center Moriches Union Free School District, 508 U.S. 384, 398 (Scalia, J., concurring in the judgment). Justice Thomas charged that the Court's separationist jurisprudence was "in hopeless disarray," in part because of "extreme notions of separation of church and state." Rosenberger v. University of Virginia, 515 U.S. 819, 861, 855 (1995) (Thomas, J., concurring).

31. Ira C. Lupu, "The Lingering Death of Separationism, *George Washington University Law Review* 62 (1994): 230–79.

32. Lynch v. Donnelly, 465 U.S. 668, 673 (1984). In Van Orden v. Perry, 545 U.S., 683–84, Chief Justice Rehnquist made an oblique acknowledgment of church-state separation in noting two aspects to the Establishment Clause: "One face looks to the past in acknowledgment of our Nation's heritage, while the other looks to the present in demanding a separation between church and state. Reconciling these two faces requires that we neither abdicate our responsibility to maintain a division between church and state nor evince a hostility to religion by disabling the government from in some ways recognizing our religious heritage."

33. Witters v. Washington Department of Services for the Blind, 474 U.S. 481 (1986); Zobrest v. Catalina Foothills School District, 509 U.S. 1 (1993); Capitol Square Review and Advisory Board v. Pinnette, 515 U.S. 753 (1995); Rosenberger, 515 U.S. 819; Agostini v. Felton, 521 U.S. 203 (1997); Mitchell v. Helms, 530 U.S. 793; Good News Club, 533 U.S. 98; Zelman v. Simmons-Harris, 536 U.S. 639; Van Orden v. Perry, 545 U.S. 677; Greece v. Galloway, 572 U.S. 565. In Mitchell v. Helms, Justice David Souter penned a strongly separationist dissent that quoted Justice Black's "wall of separation" declaration from Everson. 530 U.S., 873. See also Van Orden v. Perry, 545 U.S., 709 (Stevens, J., dissenting) (stating that the Establishment and Free Exercise Clauses together "erect a wall of separation between church and state").

34. Robert Boston, *The Most Dangerous Man in America? Pat Robertson and the Rise of the Christian Coalition* (Amherst, NY: Prometheus Books, 1996), 69–76; Frederick Clarkson, *Eternal Hostility: The Struggle between Theocracy and Democracy* (Monroe, ME: Common Courage Press, 1997), 16–18.

35. "Cause for Concern," Focus on the Family, 2008, https://www.focusonthefamily.com/socialissues/religious-freedom/separation-of-church-and-state/separation-of-church-and-state-cause-for-concern.

36. John Witte Jr., "Facts and Fictions about the History of Separation of Church and State," *Journal of Church and State* 48 (2006): 15–45. See David Barton, *The Myth of Separation* (Aledo, TX: WallBuilder Press, 1992); David Barton, *Original Intent: The Courts, the Constitution, and Religion*, 5th ed. (Aledo, TX: WallBuilder Press, 2011); Peter A. Lillbacj, *Wall of Misconception: Does the Separation of Church and State Mean the Separation of God and Government?* (West Conshohocken, PA: Providence Forum

Press, 2007); and John W. Whitehead, *The Separation Illusion: A Lawyer Examines the First Amendment* (Milford, MI: Mott Media, 1977).

37. Wallace, 472 U.S., 107.

38. Philip Hamburger, *Separation of Church and State* (Cambridge, MA: Harvard University Press, 2002), 29, 481. This critique was raised following the *Everson* and *McCollum* decisions by James M. O'Neill, Edwin Corwin, and Wilfrid Parsons. See J. M. O'Neill, *Religion and Education under the Constitution* (New York: Harper & Bros., 1949); Edwin Corwin, "The Supreme Court as a National School Board," *Law and Contemporary Problems* 14 (1949): 3–22; and Wilfrid Parsons, SJ, *The First Freedom: Considerations on Church and State in the United States* (New York: Declan X. McMullen, 1948).

39. Daniel Dreisbach, *Thomas Jefferson and the Wall of Separation between Church and State* (New York: New York University Press, 2002), 25–54; Cord, *Separation of Church and State*, 17–47.

40. Schempp, 374 U.S., 306 (Goldberg, J., concurring); Neuhaus, *Naked Public Square*; Parsons, *First Freedom*, ix; J. Judd Owen, *Religion and the Demise of Liberal Rationalism: The Foundational Crisis of the Separation of Church and State* (Chicago: University of Chicago Press, 2001); Philip Hamburger, "Separation and Interpretation," *Journal of Law and Politics* 7 (2002): 7–64, 63–64.

41. Hamburger, *Separation of Church and State*, 492, 399; Thomas C. Berg, "Anti-Catholicism and Modern Church-State Relations," *Loyola University of Chicago Law Review* 33 (Fall 2001): 121–72, 123; Stephen L. Carter, *The Dissent of the Governed: A Meditation on Law, Religion, and Loyalty* (Cambridge, MA: Harvard University Press, 1998), 128; Mitchell, 530 U.S., 829.

42. See Nicholas P. Miller, *The Religious Roots of the First Amendment: Dissenting Protestants and the Separation of Church and State* (New York: Oxford University Press, 2012).

43. Green, *Third Disestablishment*, 128–33.

44. Steven D. Smith, "The Establishment Clause and the 'Problem of the Church,'" in *Challenges to Religious Liberty in the Twenty-First Century*, ed. Gerard V. Bradley (New York: Cambridge University Press, 2012), 3–24. Mark McGarvie offers a different take on the issue of institutional separation. He argues convincingly that disestablishment effectively stripped churches of their public functions, turning them into private entities. This, according to McGarvie, brought about a separation of church and state. Mark Douglas McGarvie, *One Nation under Law: America's Early National Struggles to Separate Church and State* (DeKalb: Northern Illinois University Press, 2004).

45. McCollum, 333 U.S., 244, 255–56 (Reed, J., dissenting); Everson, 330 U.S., 31–32 (Rutledge, J., dissenting).

46. Sidney E. Mead, "Neither Church nor State: Reflections on James Madison's Line of Separation," *Journal of Church and State* 10 (1968): 349–63, 350; James Madison to Jasper Adams, September 1833, in *The Sacred Rights of Conscience*, ed. Daniel L. Dreisbach and Mark David Hall (Indianapolis: Liberty Fund, 2009), 612–14; Hamburger, *Separation of Church and State*, 28.

47. Douglas Laycock, "The Many Meanings of Separation," *University of Chicago Law Review* 70 (Autumn 2003): 1667–701, 1669–70.

48. See Howard Gillman and Erwin Chemerinsky, *The Religion Clauses: The Case for Separating Church and State* (New York: Oxford University Press, 2020), 18.

49. Zorach v. Clauson, 343 U.S. 306, 313–14 (1952); Robert C. Harnett, "Religious Education and the Constitution," *America*, May 17, 1952, 195–97. Jackson's letter is reprinted in J. Woodford Howard Jr., "The Robe and the Cloth: The Supreme Court and Religion in the United States," *Journal of Law and Politics* 7 (1991): 481–524, 496–97.

50. Schempp, 374 U.S., 217.

51. "State of the First Amendment, 2011," First Amendment Center, 6, https://www.freedomforuminstitute.org/wp-content/uploads/2014/09/FAC_sofa_2011report.pdf.

52. "State of the First Amendment, 2008," First Amendment Center, https://www.freedomforuminstitute.org/wp; James Lankford and Russell Moore, "The Real Meaning of the Separation of Church and State," *Time*, January 16, 2018, http://time.com/5103677/church-state-separation-religious-freedom/.

53. Hamburger, "Separation and Interpretation," 30.

54. James David Hunter, "The Williamsburg Charter Survey: Methodology and Findings," *Journal of Law and Religion* 8 (1990): 257–71, 262; Ted G. Jelen and Clyde Wilcox, *Public Attitudes toward Church and State* (Armonk, NY: M. E. Sharpe, 1995), 76, 109.

55. Recent books advocating for church-state separation include Gillam and Chemerinsky, *Religion Clauses*; Jack N. Rakove, *Beyond Belief, Beyond Conscience: The Radical Significance of the Free Exercise of Religion* (New York: Oxford University Press, 2020); and Randall Balmer, *Solemn Reverence: Separation of Church and State in American Life* (Hanover, NH: Steerforth, 2021).

56. See William O. Douglas, *The Bible and the Schools* (Boston: Little, Brown, 1966), 16; Hugo LaFayette Black, *A Constitutional Faith* (New York: Alfred A. Knopf, 1968), 44.

57. Laycock, "The Many Meanings of Separation"; Frank Lambert, *Separation of Church and State: Founding Principle of Religious Liberty* (Macon, GA: Mercer University Press, 2014).

58. T. Jeremy Gunn and John Witte Jr., eds., *No Establishment of Religion: America's Original Contribution to Religious Liberty* (New York: Oxford University Press, 2012).

59. Witte, "Facts and Fictions," 15–45.

60. Robert T. Handy, *A Christian America: Protestant Hopes and Historical Realities* (New York: Oxford University Press, 1984); David Sehat, *The Myth of American Religious Freedom* (New York: Oxford University Press, 2011).

1. Historical Antecedents of Separationism

1. E. Bruce Thompson, "The Development in History of the Principle of Separation of Church and State," in *Church and State in Scripture, History, and American Law*, ed. James E. Wood Jr., (Waco, TX: Baylor University Press, 1958), 57; John Witte Jr., "Facts and Fictions about the History of Separation of Church and State," *Journal of Church and State* 48 (2006): 16.

2. Witte, "Facts and Fictions," 16–28; Nicholas P. Miller, *The Religious Roots of the First Amendment: Dissenting Protestants and the Separation of Church and State* (New York: Oxford University Press, 2012), 63–88, 157–65; James M. Byrne, *Religion and the Enlightenment* (Louisville, KY: Westminster John Knox Press, 1996).

3. Roland H. Bainton, *Christendom* (New York: Harper Torchbooks, 1966), 1:139–51.

4. Augustine, "City of God," in Dreisbach and Hall, *Sacred Rights of Conscience*, 16; Bainton, *Christendom*, 121–31; Thompson, "Development in History," 59–61; Witte, "Facts and Fictions," 18–19.

5. Harold J. Berman, *Law and Revolution: The Formation of the Western Legal Tradition* (Cambridge, MA: Harvard University Press, 1983), 92–99.

6. Thompson, "Development in History," 61–64; Witte, "Facts and Fictions," 19–21; Nicholas Cheetham, *Keepers of the Keys: A History of the Popes* (New York: Charles Scribner's Sons, 1982), 30.

7. John Witte Jr., "That Serpentine Wall of Separation," *Michigan Law Review* 101 (2003): 1869–905, 1881.

8. Witte, "That Serpentine Wall of Separation," 1883–84; Heinrich Bornkamm, *Luther's Doctrine of the Two Kingdoms in the Context of His Theology* (Philadelphia: Fortress Press, 1966); John Witte Jr., *Law and Protestantism: The Legal Teachings of the Lutheran Reformation* (New York: Cambridge University Press, 2002), 87–117; Miller, *Religious Roots of the First Amendment*, 20–25.

9. John Calvin, *Institutes of the Civil Religion*, in Dreisbach and Hall, *Sacred Rights of Conscience*, 24–27; Witte, "That Serpentine Wall of Separation," 1884–85; Thompson, "Development in History," 68.

10. Witte, "Facts and Fictions," 21–22; Dreisbach, *Thomas Jefferson and the Wall of Separation*, 73.

11. Philip Hamburger, *Separation of Church and State* (Cambridge: Harvard University Press, 2002), 28.

12. Edmund S. Morgan, *Roger Williams: The Church and the State* (New York: W. W. Norton, 1967), 11–27; William G. McLoughlin, *Soul Liberty: The Baptists' Struggle in New England, 1630–1833* (Hanover, NH: University Press of New England, 1991), 18–20; Thomas S. Kidd and Barry Hankins, *Baptists in America: A History* (New York: Oxford University Press, 2015), 5.

13. Richard Hooker, "Of Laws and Ecclesiastical Polity," in Dreisbach and Hall, *Sacred Rights of Conscience*, 30–33.

14. Hamburger, *Separation of Church and State*, 29–38; Dreisbach, *Thomas Jefferson and the Wall of Separation*, 76.

15. Morgan, *Roger Williams*, 66–67; Edmund S. Morgan, *The Puritan Dilemma: The Story of John Winthrop* (Boston: Little, Brown, 1958), 163.

16. Roger Williams, "Mr. Cottons Letter Lately Printed, Examined and Answered," (1644), in Dreisbach and Hall, *Sacred Rights of Conscience*, 523–24; Edwin S. Gaustad, *Liberty of Conscience: Roger Williams in America* (Grand Rapids, MI: Eerdmans, 1991), 38–43, 72–85, 203, 206–7; Timothy L. Hall, *Separating Church and State: Roger Williams and Religious Liberty* (Urbana: University of Illinois Press, 1998), 24–26; Mark De Wolf Howe, *The Garden and the Wilderness* (Chicago: University of Chicago Press, 1965), 6; David Little, "Roger Williams and the Puritan Background to the

Establishment Clause," in Gunn and Witte, *No Establishment of Religion*, 112; James Calvin Davis, *On Religious Liberty: Selections for the Works of Roger Williams* (Cambridge, MA: Belknap Press of Harvard University Press, 2008), 21–22, 38–40.

17. Miller, *Religious Roots of the First Amendment*, 56–63; William Penn, *The Great Cause of Liberty of Conscience* (1670), in Dreisbach and Hall, *Sacred Rights of Conscience*, 42–46.

18. *Frame of Government of Pennsylvania* (1682) and "Laws Agreed Upon in England" (1682), in Dreisbach and Hall, *Sacred Rights of Conscience*, 116–19; J. William Frost, *A Perfect Freedom: Religious Liberty in Pennsylvania* (New York: Cambridge University Press, 1990), 13–18, 33.

19. Ethan H. Shagan, *The Birth of Modern Belief* (Princeton, NJ: Princeton University Press, 2018), 207–49; James MacGregor Burns, *Fire and Light: How the Enlightenment Transformed Our World* (New York: St. Martin's, 2013), 3–4.

20. Burns, *Fire and Light*, 3–4; Carolina Robbins, *The Eighteenth-Century Commonwealthman* (Cambridge, MA: Harvard University Press, 1961), 70–72; Miller, *Religious Roots of the First Amendment*, 41.

21. Donald S. Lutz, *The Origins of American Constitutionalism* (Baton Rouge: Louisiana State University Press, 1988), 143. Locke was the most commonly cited secular authority in writings during the 1760s and 1770s.

22. John Marshall, *John Locke, Toleration and Early Enlightenment Culture* (Cambridge: Cambridge University Press, 2006), 17–193; Sanford Kessler, "John Locke's Legacy of Religious Freedom," *Polity* 17 (1985): 484–503.

23. John Locke, *A Letter on Toleration*, ed. Raymond Klibansky (Oxford: Clarendon Press, 1968), 65–71, 77, 85.

24. Locke, *Letter on Toleration*, 145.

25. Locke, 71–73, 131, 133; Kessler, "John Locke's Legacy of Religious Freedom," 493–99, 503; Robert P. Kraynak, "John Locke: From Absolutism to Toleration," *American Political Science Review* 74 (March 1980): 53–68; George Windstrup, "Freedom and Authority: The Ancient Faith of Locke's Letter on Toleration," *Review of Politics* 44 (1982): 242–65.

26. David McCabe, "John Locke and the Argument against Strict Separation," *Review of Politics* 59 (1997): 233–58; Hamburger, *Separation of Church and State*, 53–55.

27. Lutz, *Origins of American Constitutionalism*, 142–45.

28. Roger B. Oake, "Montesquieu's Religious Ideas," *Journal of the History of Ideas* 14 (1953): 548–60; Montesquieu, *Spirit of the Laws*, bks. 12 and 25, in *The Founders' Constitution*, vol. 5, amendment I (Religion), doc. 12, http://press-pubs.uchicago.edu/founders/documents/amendI_religions12.html.

29. Douglass Adair, "That Politics May Be Reduced to Science: David Hume, James Madison, and the Tenth Amendment," *Huntington Library Quarterly* 20 (1957): 343–59.

30. David Hume, "Of Parties in General," in *Essays Moral, Political and Literary*, ed. Eugene F. Miller (Indianapolis: Liberty Fund, 1987), 61–62; David Hume, "The Idea of a Perfect Commonwealth," in Miller, *Essays Moral, Political and Literary*, 520, 526; David Hume, *A History of England*, ed. William B. Todd (Indianapolis: Liberty Fund, 1983), 134–36.

31. James Madison, "Federalist 10 and 51," in *The Federalist Papers*, ed. Clinton Rossiter (New York: New American Library, 1961), 79, 324; Mark M. Arkin, "'The Intractable Principle': David Hume, James Madison, Religion, and the Tenth Federalist," *American Journal of Legal History* 39 (1995): 148–76; Mark G. Spencer, "Hume and Madison on Faction," *William and Mary Quarterly* 59 (2002): 869–96.

32. Bernard Bailyn, *The Ideological Origins of the American Revolution* (Cambridge, MA: Belknap Press of Harvard University Press, 1967), 35–36; Robbins, *Eighteenth-Century Commonwealthman*, 9–13.

33. Bailyn, *Ideological Origins*, 36; Robbins, *Eighteenth-Century Commonwealthman*, 115–20; Patricia U. Bonomi, *Under the Cope of Heaven: Religion, Society, and Politics in Colonial America* (New York: Oxford University Press, 1986), 193–95.

34. Richard Price, *Observations on the Nature of Civil Liberty, the Principles of Government, and the Justice and Policy of War with America* (New York: S. Loudon, 1776), 3; Gregory I. Molivas, "Richard Price, the Debate on Free Will, and Natural Rights," *Journal of the History of Ideas* 58 (1997): 105–23; Robbins, *Eighteenth-Century Commonwealthman*, 335–47.

35. Joseph Priestley, *Essay on the First Principles of Government; and on the Nature of Political, Civil, and Religious Liberty*, 2nd ed. (London: Printed for J. Johnson, 1771), 53–55, 65, 77–78, 82; Ira V. Brown, "The Religion of Joseph Priestley," *Pennsylvania History* 24 (April 1957): 85–100; Isaac Kramnick, "Eighteenth-Century Science and Radical Social Theory: The Case of Joseph Priestley's Scientific Liberalism," *Journal of British Studies* 25 (January 1986): 1–30; Robbins, *Eighteenth-Century Commonwealthman*, 347–54.

36. Isaac Kramnick, "Republicanism Revisited: The Case of James Burgh," in *The Republican Synthesis Revisited*, ed. Milton M. Klein (Worcester, MA: American Antiquarian Society, 1992), 19–36; Carla H. Hay, *James Burgh, Spokesman for Reform in Hanoverian England* (Washington, DC: University Press of America, 1979), 42–43, 50–52; Carla Hay, "The Making of a Radical: The Case of James Burgh," *Journal of British Studies* 18 (1979): 90–117; Robbins, *Eighteenth-Century Commonwealthman*, 363–68; Oscar Handlin and Mary Handlin, "James Burgh and American Revolutionary Theory," *Proceedings of the Massachusetts Historical Society* 73 (1961): 38–57; *Crito, or Essays on Various Subjects*, in Dreisbach and Hall, *Sacred Rights of Conscience*, 524–25.

37. Edwin Scott Gaustad, *The Great Awakening in New England* (New York: Harper & Brothers, 1957); Alan Heimert, *Religion and the American Mind from the Great Awakening to the Revolution* (Cambridge, MA: Harvard University Press, 1966); Frank Lambert, *Inventing the "Great Awakening"* (Princeton, NJ: Princeton University Press, 1999); Thomas S. Kidd, *The Great Awakening: The Roots of Evangelical Christianity in Colonial America* (New Haven, CT: Yale University Press, 2007).

38. Kidd, *Great Awakening*; Gordon Wood, "Religion and the American Revolution," in *New Directions in American Religious History*, ed. Harry S. Stout and D. G. Hart (New York: Oxford University Press, 1997), 182–87.

39. Kidd, *Great Awakening*; Curry, *First Freedoms*, 96–104.

40. Stephen A. Marini, "Religion, Politics, and Ratification," in *Religion in a Revolutionary Age*, ed. Ronald Hoffman and Peter J. Albert (Charlottesville: University Press of Virginia, 1994), 188–93.

41. Thomas J. Curry, *The First Freedoms: Church and State in America to the Passage of the First Amendment* (New York: Oxford University Press, 1986), 99–100; Rhys Isaac, *The Transformation of Virginia, 1740–1790* (Chapel Hill: University of North Carolina Press, 1982), 148–51.

42. Lewis Peyton Little, *Imprisoned Preachers and Religious Liberty in Virginia* (Lynchburg, VA: J. P. Bell, 1938), 24–25; Isaac, *Transformation of Virginia*, 149.

43. Little, *Imprisoned Preachers and Religious Liberty*, 496; Isaac, *Transformation of Virginia*, 149–54; Curry, *First Freedoms*, 99–100.

44. Isaac, *Transformation of Virginia*, 163–77; Rhys Isaac, "Evangelical Revolt: The Nature of the Baptists' Challenge to the Traditional Order in Virginia, 1765 to 1775," *William and Mary Quarterly* (1974): 345–68; Robert B. Semple, *A History of the Rise and Progress of the Baptists in Virginia*, rev. ed. (Philadelphia: 1810; repr. American Baptist Publishing Society, 1894), 11–28.

45. Little, *Imprisoned Preachers and Religious Liberty*, 229–31, 265–73; Semple, *History of the Rise and Progress of the Baptists*, 27, 29–30; John A. Ragosta, *Wellspring of Liberty: How Virginia's Religious Dissenters Helped Win the Revolution and Secured Religious Liberty* (New York: Oxford University Press, 2010), 29–36.

46. Semple, *History of the Rise and Progress of the Baptists*, 29–54; Isaac, *Transformation of Virginia*, 162–63.

47. James Madison to William Bradford, January 24, 1774, in *The Papers of James Madison*, ed. William T. Hutchinson and William M. E. Rachel (Chicago: University of Chicago Press, 1962), 104–6; Ralph Ketcham, *James Madison: A Biography* (Charlottesville: University of Virginia Press, 1996), 56–59.

48. William Bradford to James Madison, March 4, 1774, and James Madison to William Bradford, April 1, 1774, in Hutchinson and Rachel, *Papers of James Madison*, 108–9, 111–13.

49. William Lee Miller, *The First Liberty: Religion and the American Public* (New York: Alfred A. Knopf, 1986), 87–96; Madison, "Autobiographical Draft" (1832), 1:107.

50. James Madison to William Bradford, December 1, 1773, in Hutchinson and Rachel, *Papers of James Madison*, 100–101; Ketcham, *James Madison*, 55–56; Spencer, "Hume and Madison on Faction," 889–91.

51. C.C. Goen, *Revivalism and Separatism in New England, 1740–1800* (Middletown, CT: Wesleyan University Press, 1987), 236, 273–79.

52. William G. McLoughlin, *New England Dissent, 1630–1830* (Cambridge, MA: Harvard University Press, 1971), 454–88.

53. Hamburger, *Separation of Church and State*, 77; William G. McLoughlin, "Isaac Backus and the Separation of Church and State in America," *American Historical Review* 73 (1968): 1392–413; McLoughlin, *New England Dissent*, 466–67.

54. McLoughlin, *New England Dissent*, 466–67; McLoughlin, "Isaac Backus and the Separation of Church and State," 1400, 1405–6.

55. McLoughlin, "Isaac Backus and the Separation of Church and State," 1406; Isaac Backus, "An Appeal to the Public for Religious Liberty" (1773), in *Political Sermons of the American Founding Era, 1730–1805*, ed. Ellis Sandoz (Indianapolis: Liberty Fund, 1991): 331–68.

56. McLoughlin, "Isaac Backus and the Separation of Church and State," 1406; J. Judd Owen, "The Struggle between 'Religion and Nonreligion': Jefferson, Backus, and the Dissonance of America's Founding Principles," *American Political Science Review* 101 (August 2007): 493–503.

57. Carl Bridenbaugh, *Mitre and Sceptre: Transatlantic Faiths, Ideas, Personalities, and Politics, 1689–1775* (New York: Oxford University Press, 1962), 25–32; Arthur Lyon Cross, *Anglican Episcopate and the American Colonies* (Hamden, CT: Archon Books, 1964); William M. Hogue, "The Religious Conspiracy Theory of the American Revolution: Anglican Motive," *Church History* 45 (1976): 277–92.

58. Bridenbaugh, *Mitre and Sceptre*, 92–115; Cross, *Anglican Episcopate*, 88–112.

59. Jonathan Mayhew, "A Discourse Concerning Unlimited Submission and Non-Resistance to the Higher Powers" (1750), in *Religion and the Coming of the American Revolution*, ed. Peter N. Carroll (Waltham, MA: Ginn-Blaisdell, 1970), 30–52.

60. John Adams to Hezekiah Niles, February 13, 1818, in John Adams, *Works*, ed. Charles Francis Adams (Boston: Little & Brown, 1850–61), 10:288; John Adams to William Tudor, April 15, 1818, in Adams, *Works*, 10:301; Chris Beneke, "The Critical Turn: Jonathan Mayhew, the British Empire, and the Idea of Resistance in Mid-Eighteenth-Century Boston," *Massachusetts Historical Review* 10 (2008): 23–56.

61. John Webb Pratt, *Religion, Politics, and Diversity, The Church-State Theme in New York History* (Ithaca, NY: Cornell University Press, 1967), 67–74.

62. William Livingston, "The Independent Reflector, No. 22," April 26, 1753, in Carroll, *Religion and the Coming of the American Revolution*, 52–60; Bridenbaugh, *Mitre and Sceptre*, 138–68.

63. William Livingston, "The Absurdity of the Civil Magistrate Interfering in Matters of Religion," *Independent Reflector*, no. 36, August 2, 1753, in Carroll, *Religion and the Coming of the American Revolution*, 60–63.

64. *New York Mercury*, July 9, 1753, reprinted in Bridenbaugh, *Mitre and Sceptre*, 152.

65. Bridenbaugh, *Mitre and Sceptre*, 153–65; Pratt, *Religion, Politics, and Diversity*, 67–74.

66. Bridenbaugh, *Mitre and Sceptre*, 86–87, 178, 268–69.

67. Theodore Draper, *A Struggle for Power: The American Revolution* (New York: Random House, 1996), 183–275; Arthur M. Schlesinger, *Prelude to Independence* (New York: Vintage Books, 1965); Hogue, "Religious Conspiracy Theory," 290.

68. Cross, *Anglican Episcopate*, 146–49; Hogue, "Religious Conspiracy Theory," 287–89; Richard James Hooker, "The Mayhew Controversy," *Church History* 5 (1936): 239–55.

69. Charles Chauncy, "A Letter to a Friend Containing Remarks on . . . the Incorporated Society for the Propagation of the Gospel in Foreign Parts" (1767), in Carroll, *Religion and the Coming of the American Revolution*, 95–101.

70. Thomas Chandler, "An Appeal to the Public on Behalf of the Church of England in America," in Bridenbaugh, *Mitre and Sceptre*, 289–96; Cross, *Anglican Episcopate*, 161–74.

71. Cross, *Anglican Episcopate*, 173–77; McLoughlin, *New England Dissent*, 597–98.

72. Cross, *Anglican Episcopate*, 174–75.

73. John Adams, *A Dissertation on the Canon and Feudal Law* (1765).

74. John Adams to J. Morse, December 2, 1815, in Adams, *Works*, 10:185; Adams to H. Niles, Feb. 13, 1818, in Adams, 10:288; Bonomi, *Under the Cope of Heaven*, 199.

2. Disestablishment and Separationism

1. Arthur Lyon Cross, *The Anglican Episcopate and the American Colonies* (Hamden, CT: Archon Books, 1902, 1964).

2. Thomas J. Curry, *The First Freedoms: Church and State in American to the Passage of the First Amendment* (New York: Oxford University Press, 1986), 104–33; Carl H. Esbeck, "Dissent and Disestablishment: The Church-State Settlement in the Early American Republic," *Brigham Young University Law Review* (2004): 1385–584.

3. Curry, *First Freedoms*, 29–62; Rhys Isaac, *The Transformation of Virginia, 1740–1790* (Chapel Hill: University of North Carolina Press, 1982), 65, 146–57; Edward L. Bond, *Damned Souls in a Tobacco Colony: Religion in Seventeenth-Century Virginia* (Macon, GA: Mercer University Press, 2000).

4. Curry, *First Freedoms*, 31–53; John D. Kruger, "'With Promise of Liberty in Religion': The Catholic Lords Baltimore and Toleration in Maryland, 1634–1692," *Maryland Historical Magazine* 79 (1984): 21–43; Richard A. Gleissner, "Religious Causes of the Glorious Revolution in Maryland," *Maryland Historical Magazine* 64 (1969): 327–41; "An Act Concerning Religion," in *Sacred Rights of Conscience*, ed. Dreisbach and Hall (Indianapolis: Liberty Fund, 2009), 104–7.

5. Frank Lambert, *Inventing the "Great Awakening"* (Princeton, NJ: Princeton University Press, 1999).

6. Curry, *First Freedoms*, 1–28, 106–8.

7. William G. McLoughlin, *New England Dissent, 1630–1883: The Baptists and the Separation of Church and State* (Cambridge, MA: Harvard University Press, 1971), 1:113–27, 200–43, 263–77; Curry, *First Freedoms*, 106–12.

8. John Webb Pratt, *Religion, Politics, and Diversity: The Church-State Theme in New York History* (Ithaca, NY: Cornell University Press, 1967), 3–25; Paul Finkelman, "Toleration and Diversity in New Netherland and the Duke's Colony: The Roots of America's First Disestablishment," in *No Establishment of Religion*, ed. Gunn and Witte (New York: Oxford University Press, 2012), 125–57; "Dutch West India Company Instructions," in Dreisbach and Hall, *Sacred Rights of Conscience*, 108.

9. Pratt, *Religion, Politics, and Diversity*, 26–67; Finkelman, "Toleration and Diversity," 147–48.

10. Gaustad, *Liberty of Conscience: Roger Williams in America*; Morgan, *Roger Williams: The Church and the State* (New York: W.W. Norton, 1967); "Charter of Rhode Island and Providence Plantations" (1663), in Dreisbach and Hall, *Sacred Rights of Conscience*, 114–16; R. E. E. Harkness, "Principles Established in Rhode Island," *Church History* 5 (September 1936): 216–26; Theodore Dwight Bozeman, "Religious Liberty and the Problem of Social Disorder in Early Rhode Island," *New England Quarterly* 45 (March 1972): 44–64.

11. William Penn, *The Great Cause of Liberty of Conscience* (1670), in Dreisbach and Hall, *Sacred Rights of Conscience*, 42–46; "Frame of Government" (1682), in *The Federal and State Constitutions, Colonial Charters, and Other Organic Laws of the States, Territories, and Colonies Now or Heretofore Forming the United States of America*, ed. Francis Newton Thorpe (Washington, DC: Government Printing Office, 1909), 5:3052–63; Frost, *Perfect Freedom*, 12–15; Edwin B. Bronner, *William Penn's "Holy Experiment"* (New York: Temple University Publications, 1962), 6–8; Evarts B. Greene, *Religion and the State* (New York: New York University Press, 1941), 56.

12. Frost, *Perfect Freedom*, 21–28; Curry, *First Freedoms*, 74–76.

13. Curry, *First Freedoms*, 72–73, 76–77; Frost, *Perfect Freedom*, 17–18; Thorpe, *Federal and State Constitutions*, 5:2579–80, 1:558.

14. Green, *Second Disestablishment*, 26–27; Chris Beneke, *Beyond Toleration: The Religious Origins of Religious Pluralism* (New York: Oxford University Press, 2006), 15–48.

15. Lutz, *Origins of American Constitutionalism*, 104–6; John K. Wilson, "Religion under the State Constitutions, 1776–1800," *Journal of Church and State* 32 (1990): 753–73.

A state-by-state account of disestablishment is related in *Disestablishment and Religious Dissent: Church-State Relations in the New American States, 1776–1833*, ed. Carl H. Esbeck and Jonathan J. Den Hartig (Columbia: University of Missouri Press, 2019).

16. New Hampshire Constitution of 1784, art. VI, Thorpe, *Federal and State Constitutions*, 2454; Curry, *First Freedoms*, 185–88.

17. New York Constitution of 1777, arts. 38 and 35, Thorpe, *Federal and State Constitutions*, 2636–37; Pratt, *Religion, Politics, and Diversity*, 82–93.

18. North Carolina Constitution of 1776, art. 34, Thorpe, *Federal and State Constitutions*, 2793; Curry, *First Freedoms*, 151–52; Nicholas P. Miller, "North Carolina: Early Toleration and Disestablishment," in Esbeck and Den Hartog, *Disestablishment and Religious Dissent*, 97–114.

19. Georgia Constitution of 1777, art. LVI; Georgia Constitution of 1789, art. IV, sec. 5; and Georgia Constitution of 1798, art. IV, sec. 10, Thorpe, *Federal and State Constitutions*, 784, 789, 800–801; Nichols, "Religious Liberty in the Thirteenth Colony," 1723–1727; Curry, *First Freedoms*, 152–53.

20. South Carolina Constitution of 1778, Thorpe, *Federal and State Constitutions*, 3255–56; Miles Smith IV, "South Carolina," in Esbeck and Den Hartog, *Disestablishment and Religious Dissent*, 181–201.

21. South Carolina Constitution of 1778, 3256–57; McGarvie, *One Nation under Law*, 141–44; Curry, *First Freedoms*, 150.

22. Maryland Constitution of 1776, Thorpe, *Federal and State Constitutions*, 1689–90; Curry, *First Freedoms*, 153–58; Michael D. Breidenbach, "Church and State in Maryland," in Esbeck and Den Hartog, *Disestablishment and Religious Dissent*, 302–26.

23. Thorpe, *Federal and State Constitutions*, 3752; Curry, *First Freedoms*, 188–89; McLoughlin, *New England Dissent*, 2:795–812; Shelby M. Balik, "In the Interests of True Religion: Disestablishment in Vermont," in Esbeck and Den Hartog, *Disestablishment and Religious Dissent*, 293–308.

24. William Tennent, *Speech on the Dissenting Petition* (Charles-Town, SC: Peter Timothy, 1777), 15–16.

25. Pennsylvania Constitution of 1776, Thorpe, *Federal and State Constitutions*, 3082; Pennsylvania Constitution of 1790, Thorpe, 3100; Curry, *First Freedoms*, 160–61; Frost, *Perfect Freedom*, 74–78.

26. Delaware Constitution of 1776, Thorpe, *Federal and State Constitutions*, 567; Delaware Constitution of 1792, Thorpe, 568, New Jersey Constitution of 1776, Thorpe, 2597; Curry, *First Freedoms*, 159–60; John Fea, "Disestablishment in New Jersey," in Esbeck and Den Hartog, *Disestablishment and Religious Dissent*, 25–36.

27. See Chester James Antieau, Arthur L. Downey, and Edward C. Roberts, *Freedom from Federal Establishment: Formation and Early History of the First Amendment Religion Clauses* (Milwaukee: Bruce, 1964), 134.

28. James Madison, June 12, 1788, in *The Debates in the Several State Conventions, on the Adoption of the Federal Constitution*, ed. Jonathan Elliot (New York: Burt Franklin, 1827; repr. 1888), 3:330; Curry, *First Freedoms*, 146–48, 160.

29. Thomas E. Buckley, *Church and State in Revolutionary Virginia, 1776–1787* (Charlottesville: University Press of Virginia, 1977), 17–70; Irving Brant, "Madison: On the Separation of Church and State," *William and Mary Quarterly* 8 (1951): 3–24; John A. Ragosta, *Religious Freedom: Jefferson's Legacy, America's Creed* (Charlottesville: University of Virginia Press, 2013), 60–65.

30. "Act for Establishing Religious Freedom," in *Founders Constitution*, 5, doc. 44; Thomas Jefferson, *Autobiography*, in *Founders Constitution*, 5, doc. 45; Buckley, *Church and State*, 46–47.

31. Buckley, *Church and State*, 50–62.

32. Curry, *First Freedoms*, 139–40; Buckley, *Church and State*, 108, 188–89; Brant, "Madison," 7–9; *Papers of James Madison*, 8:195–96; Lance Banning, *The Sacred Fire of Liberty: James Madison and the Founding of the Federal Republic* (Ithaca, NY: Cornell University Press, 1995), 88–97.

33. Irving Brant, *James Madison, the Nationalist, 1780–1787* (Indianapolis: Bobbs-Merrill, 1948), 343.

34. Thomas Jefferson, *Memorial and Remonstrance* (published in the *Virginia Journal* on November 17, 1785), in *Founders Constitution*, 5, doc. 43; Curry, *First Freedoms*, 134–48; Buckley, *Church and State*, 131–36; Donald L. Drakeman, "Religion and the Republic: James Madison and the First Amendment," *Journal of Church and State* 25 (1983): 427–45, 435; Brant, "Madison," 9–11; Lance Banning, "James Madison, The Statute for Religious Freedom, and the Crisis of Republican Convictions," in *The Virginia Statute for Religious Freedom*, ed. Merrill D. Peterson and Robert C. Vaughn (New York: Cambridge University Press, 1988), 109–38.

35. Madison, *Memorial and Remonstrance*; Curry, *First Freedoms*, 134–48; Buckley, *Church and State*, 137–43; Ketcham, *James Madison*, 162–66; James Madison to Thomas Jefferson, August 20, 1785, and James Madison to Thomas Jefferson, January 22, 1786, in *The Republic of Letters: The Correspondence between Thomas Jefferson and James Madison*, ed. James Morton Smith (New York: W. W. Norton, 1995), 1:373–75, 401–2.

36. Oscar and Mary Handlin, eds., *The Popular Sources of Political Authority: Documents on the Massachusetts Constitution of 1780* (Cambridge, MA: Belknap Press of Harvard University Press, 1966), 190–201, 202–323; Ronald M. Peters Jr., *The Massachusetts Constitution of 1780: A Social Compact* (Amherst: University of Massachusetts Press, 1978), 31.

37. Phillips Payson, "Election Sermon," in *American Political Writing*, ed. Hyman and Lutz (Indianapolis: Liberty Fund, 1983), 529–30.

38. Isaac Backus, *Government and Liberty Described and Ecclesiastical Tyranny Exposed* (Boston: Powars & Willis, 1778), 4, 13, 11.

39. Backus, *Government and Liberty*, 12–13.

40. Peters, *Massachusetts Constitution of 1780*, 33.

41. *Boston Gazette*, October 23, 1780, 1.

42. *Boston Gazette*, November 2, 1778, 1.

43. *Boston Gazette*, December 28, 1778, 1.

44. Mentor, *Boston Gazette*, January 26, 1778, 1.

45. Adams, *Works*, 8:55.

46. Thorpe, *Federal and State Constitutions*, 1889–90; Handlin, *Popular Sources*, 442–43.

47. Samuel Eliot Morison, "The Struggle over the Adoption of the Constitution of Massachusetts, 1780," *Massachusetts Historical Society Proceedings* 50 (1916–17): 353, 371; Peters, *Massachusetts Constitution of 1780*, 33, 50–54; Jacob C. Meyer, *Church and State in Massachusetts from 1740 to 1833* (New York: Russell & Russell, 1968), 107–8.

48. Robert J. Taylor, "Construction of the Massachusetts Constitution," *Proceedings of the American Antiquarian Society* 90 (1980): 331–32; Handlin, *Popular Sources*,

443; Morison, "Struggle over Adoption," 411; McLoughlin, *New England Dissent*, 560, 601–12, 617–35.

49. Hamburger, *Separation of Church and State*, 107.

50. McLoughlin, *New England Dissent*, 591–635; Buckley, *Church and State*, 178–82.

51. Gillman and Chemerinsky, *Religion Clauses*, 34 (through article VI, "the Constitution incorporated a separation of church and state"); Gerard V. Bradley, "The No Religious Test Clause and the Constitution of Religious Liberty: A Machine That Has Gone of Itself," *Case Western Reserve Law Review* 37 (1986): 674–747; Daniel L. Dreisbach, "The Constitution's Forgotten Religion Clause: Reflections on the Article VI Religious Test Ban," *Journal of Church and State* 38 (1996): 261–95; James E. Wood Jr., "'No Religious Test Shall Ever Be Required': Reflections on the Bicentennial of the Constitution," *Journal of Church and State* 29 (1987): 199–208; Wilson, "Religion under the State Constitutions," 761–62, 764–66; Miller, *First Liberty*, 108–9; Kramnick and Moore, *Godless Constitution*, 26–45.

52. Dreisbach, "Constitution's Forgotten Religion Clause," 262–63.

53. Dreisbach, 265–68; Bradley, "No Religious Test Clause," 681–84; Pratt, *Religion, Politics and Diversity*, 93–97, 107–8; Curry, *First Freedoms*, 161–62.

54. Max Farrand, *The Records of the Federal Constitution of 1787* (New Haven, CT: Yale University Press, 1911), 3:599; James Madison, *Notes of Debates in the Federal Constitution of 1787* (Athens: Ohio University Press, 1984), 486, 561.

55. Elliot, *Debates*, 1:385–86; *Founders' Constitution*, vol. 4, art. 6, clause 3, doc. 18.

56. Wood, "No Religious Test Shall Ever Be Required," 206; Kramnick and Moore, *Godless Constitution*, 26–45; Gillman and Chemerinsky, *Religion Clauses*, 34.

57. Joseph Story, *Commentaries on the Constitution of the United States*, 4th ed. (Boston: Little, Brown: 1873), 2: 590, sec. 1847.

58. Bradley, "No Religious Test Clause," 690, 693–94; Dreisbach, "Constitution's Forgotten Religion Clause," 285–89.

59. Benjamin Franklin to Richard Price, October 9, 1780, *Founders' Constitution*, 4:5; Benjamin Rush to Richard Price, October 15, 1785, April 22, 1786, *Founders' Constitution*, 4:8; Noah Webster, *On Test Laws, Oaths of Allegiance and Abjuration, and Partial Exclusions from Office* (March 1787), in Dreisbach and Hall, *Sacred Rights of Conscience*, 368–70.

60. *Freeman's Oracle*, February 8, 1788, in Herbert J. Storing, *The Compete Anti-Federalist* (Chicago: University of Chicago Press, 1981), 4:242; "Essay by Samuel," in Storing, *Compete Anti-Federalist*, 4:195–96; *Virginia Independent Chronicle*, October 31, 1787, in Storing, 5:126.

61. "A Landholder," *Connecticut Courant*, December 17, 1787, in *Debate on the Constitution*, ed. Bernard Bailyn (New York: Library of America, 1993), 1:521–25.

62. Elihu, in Storing, *Compete Anti-Federalist*, 4:248–49.

63. Elliot, *Debates*, 4:200 (Spencer); Elliot, 2:148 (Backus); Kramnick and Moore, *Godless Constitution*, 38–39.

64. Thorpe, *Federal and State Constitutions*, 568 (Delaware), 786 (Georgia), 3100 (Pennsylvania), 3263 (South Carolina), 3752 (Vermont).

65. Thorpe, 1247 (Kentucky), 3422 (Tennessee), 2910 (Ohio).

66. *The Annals of Congress: The Debates and Proceedings in the Congress of the United States* (Washington, DC: Gales & Seaton, 1834), 1:757–59.

67. Storing, *Complete Anti-Federalist*, 3:37.

68. Elliot *Debates*, 4:191 (Abbot); Storing, *Complete Anti-Federalist*, 3:107.

69. "Essay by Deliberator," *Freeman's Journal*, February 20, 1788, Storing, *Complete Anti-Federalist*, 3:179; Zachariah Johnston, "Virginia Convention, June 1788," in Bailyn, *Debate on the Constitution*, 2:752–53.

70. James Madison, "Virginia Ratifying Convention, June 12, 1788" (expressing doubt that "a bill of rights [provides] security for religion"), in *Founders' Constitution*, 5:88.

71. Madison to Jefferson, October 17, 1788, Jefferson to Madison, November 8, 1788, in Smith, *Republic of Letters*, 1:562–66, 566–67; Richard Labunski, *James Madison and the Struggle for the Bill of Rights* (New York: Oxford University Press, 2006), 159–77; Paul Finkelman, "James Madison and the Bill of Rights: A Reluctant Paternity," *Supreme Court Review* (1990): 301–47.

72. *Annals*, 1:451.

73. *Annals*, 1:452.

74. *Annals*, 1:757–759 (August 15, 1789); *Annals*, 1:796 (August 20, 1789); Brant, *James Madison: Father of the Constitution*, 271; Labunski, *James Madison*, 223–24.

75. *Senate Journal*, 70 (September 3, 1789), 1:70; *Complete Bill of Rights*, 3–6.

76. *House Journal*, 146, in *Complete Bill of Rights*, 6; *Senate Journal*, 142, in *Complete Bill of Rights*, 7–8; Brant, *James Madison: Father of the Constitution*, 271; Brant, "Madison," 16; Labunski, *James Madison*, 239.

77. *Annals*, 1:758–79; see Cord, *Separation of Church and State*, 49, 214.

78. Madison to Robert Walsh, March 2, 1819, in Dreisbach and Hall, *Sacred Rights of Conscience*," 594–95.

79. *Annals*, 1:796.

80. Daniel O. Conkle, "Toward a General Theory of the Establishment Clause," *Northwestern University Law Review* 82 (1988): 1113, 1133–34; Steven D. Smith, *Foreordained Failure: The Quest for a Constitutional Principle of Religious Freedom* (New York: Oxford University Press, 1995), 30; Elk Grove School District v. Newdow, 542 U.S. 1 (2004) (Thomas, J., concurring in the judgment).

81. See Steven K. Green, "Federalism and the Establishment Clause: A Reassessment," *Creighton Law Review* 38 (2005): 761–97.

82. David Ramsay, *An Oration Delivered in St. Michael's Church, before the Inhabitants of South Carolina, on the Fourth of July, 1794, in Commemoration of American Independence* (Charleston, SC: W. P. Young, 1794), 8.

83. Leonard W. Levy, *The Establishment Clause: Religion and the First Amendment* (New York: Macmillan, 1986), 46–51; Curry, *First Freedoms*, 162–92; McLoughlin, *New England Dissent*, 2:610–11.

84. *Annals*, 1:757–59.

85. *Annals*, 1:757–59.

3. The Early National Period

1. Thorpe, *Federal and State Constitutions*, 3100; Frost, *Perfect Freedom*, 74–76; Curry, *First Freedoms*, 222.

2. Thorpe, *Federal and State Constitutions*, 1274 (Kentucky); Thorpe, 3422 (Tennessee); Thorpe, 2910 (Ohio).

3. Jack Nips (John Leland), "The Yankee Spy" (1794), in Hyneman and Lutz, *American Political Writing*, 989; John Leland, "The Connecticut Dissenters' Strong Box," in Sandoz, *Political Sermons*, 1086, 1089, 1094.

4. Ramsay, *An Oration*, 8.

5. Ramsay, *Oration*, 9.

6. Christopher Grasso, *Skepticism and American Faith: From the Revolution to the Civil War* (New York: Oxford University Press, 2018), 25–26; Kerry S. Walters, *Rational Infidels: The American Deists* (Durango, CO: Longwood Academic, 1992), 5–7; Edwin S. Gaustad, *Faith of the Founders* (Waco, TX: Baylor University Press, 2004); Gordon S. Wood, *The Americanization of Benjamin Franklin* (New York: Penguin, 2004), 30; Franklin, *Autobiography*, repr. in *"In God We Trust": The Religious Beliefs and Ideas of the American Founding Fathers*, ed. Norman Cousins (New York: Harper, 1958), 24.

7. Grasso, *Skepticism and American Faith*, 25, 97–106; Eric R. Schlereth, *An Age of Infidels: The Politics of Religious Controversy in the Early United States* (Philadelphia: University of Pennsylvania Press, 2013), 44–76.

8. Thomas Paine, *The Age of Reason* (1794, 1795), in *The Life and Major Writings of Thomas Paine*, ed. Philip S. Foner (New York: Citadel Press, 1974), 498, 469, 477.

9. Gary B. Nash, "The American Clergy and the French Revolution," *William and Mary Quarterly* 22 (1965): 392–422, 403; Charles Beecher, ed., *Autobiography of Lyman Beecher* (New York: Harper, 1864), 1:43; Schlereth, *Age of Infidels*, 49–55.

10. Enos Hitchcock, "An Oration," (1793), in Sandoz, *Political Sermons*, 1180; Jedidiah Morse, *The Present Situation of Other Nations of the World, Contrasted with Our Own* (Boston: Samuel Hall, 1795), 11, 14; Nash, "American Clergy and French Revolution," 394–97.

11. Noah Webster, "The Revolution in France" (1794), in Sandoz, *Political Sermons*, 1253; Nash, "American Clergy and French Revolution," 402–6.

12. Timothy Dwight, "The Duty of Americans, at the Present Crisis," in Sandoz, *Political Sermons*, 1374–75, 1380; Schlereth, *Age of Infidels*, 130–37; Nash, "American Clergy and French Revolution," 397–99.

13. John Smalley, "On the Evils of a Weak Government," in Sandoz, *Political Sermons*, 1438.

14. Nash, "American Clergy and French Revolution," 407–10; Kramnick and Moore, *Godless Constitution*, 88–100; Charles O. Lerche Jr., "Jefferson and the Election of 1800: A Case Study in the Political Smear," *William and Mary Quarterly* 5 (October 1948): 467–91; Fred C. Luebke, "The Origins of Thomas Jefferson's Anti-Clericalism," *Church History* 32 (September 1963): 344–56; Constance B. Schultz, "'Of Bigotry in Politics and Religion:' Jefferson's Religion, the Federalist Press, and the Syllabus," *Virginia Magazine of History and Biography* 91 (1983): 73–91; Frank Lambert, "'God—and a Religious President . . . [or] Jefferson and No God': Campaigning for a Voter-Imposed Religious Test in 1800," *Journal of Church and State* 39 (1997): 769–89.

15. John Ferling, *Adams v. Jefferson: The Tumultuous Election of 1800* (New York: Oxford University Press, 2004); Bernard A. Weisberger, *America Afire: Jefferson, Adams, and the Revolutionary Election of 1800* (New York: William Morrow, 2000).

16. Luebke, "Origins of Thomas Jefferson's Anti-Clericalism," 349; "A Layman," *The Claims of Thomas Jefferson to the Presidency* (Philadelphia: Asbury Dickins, 1800), 29–30.

17. John M. Mason, *The Voice of Warning to Christians on the Ensuing Election* (1800), in *The Complete Works of John M. Mason, D.D.*, ed. Ebenezer Mason (New York: Baker & Scribner, 1849), 541–43, 551–53; William Linn, *Serious Considerations on the Election of a President Addressed to the Citizens of the United States* (Trenton, NJ: Sherman, Mershon & Thomas, 1800), 4, 12, 21–28.

18. Abraham Bishop, *An Oration on the Extent and Power of Political Delusion* (Philadelphia: Mathew Carey, 1800); Noah Webster, *A Rod for the Fool's Back* (Bennington, CT: William Stockwell, 1800), 10.

19. *Gazette of the United States*, October 9, 1800, repr. in *American Aurora*, ed. Richard N. Rosenfeld (New York: St. Martin's, 1997), 864.

20. *New-England Palladium*, September 7, 1800, repr. in Lerche, "Jefferson and the Election of 1800," 474n20.

21. Mason, *Voice of Warning*, 558, 560–61, 570; Linn, *Serious Considerations*, 18, 20, 23, 28.

22. *Gazette of the United States*, August 21, 1798, May 3, 1800, and April 14, 1800, in Rosenfeld, *American Aurora*, 218, 782, 770.

23. Grotius, *Vindication of Thomas Jefferson against the Charges Contained in a Pamphlet Entitled, "Serious Considerations"* (New York: David Denniston, 1800), 17–18, 32, 34; Benjamin Pollard [?], "'Serious Considerations': or the Voice of Warning to Religious Republicans," 12.

24. Pollard, "Serious Considerations," 2, 14; Grotius, *Vindication of Thomas Jefferson*, 40.

25. Grotius, *Vindication of Thomas Jefferson*, 21–22; n.a., *A Test of the Religious Principles of Mr. Jefferson* (Easton, MD: Thomas Perrin Smith, 1800), preface.

26. Tunis Wortman, "A Solemn Address to Christians and Patriots," in Sandoz, *Political Sermons*, 1481–1528, 1488.

27. Wortman, "Solemn Address," 1482, 1489, 1494.

28. Jefferson to Monroe, May 26. 1800, *The Works of Thomas Jefferson*, ed. Paul Leicester Ford (New York: G. P. Putnam's Sons, 1904–05), 9:135–36; Jefferson to Rush, September 23, 1800, in Ford, *Works of Thomas Jefferson*, 9:146–149.

29. Everson, 330 U.S., 15–16.

30. McLoughlin, *New England Dissent*, 2:985–1005; Richard J. Purcell, *Connecticut in Transition, 1775–1818* (Middletown, CT: Wesleyan University Press, 1963), 32–64; James R. Beasley, "Emerging Republicanism and the Standing Order: The Appropriation Act Controversy in Connecticut, 1793–1795," *William and Mary Quarterly* 29 (1972): 587–610.

31. McLoughlin, *New England Dissent*, 2:919, 988; "Letter from Danbury Baptist Association," October 7, 1801, in Dreisbach and Hall, *Sacred Rights of Conscience*, 526.

32. Jefferson to Levi Lincoln, January 1, 1802, in Dreisbach and Hall, *Sacred Rights of Conscience*, 527.

33. McLoughlin, *New England Dissent*, 2:1004–17.

34. Jefferson to Nehemiah Dodge, Ephraim Robbins, and Stephen S. Nelson, January 1, 1802, in Dreisbach and Hall, *Sacred Rights of Conscience*, 528.

35. Robert M. Healey, "Thomas Jefferson's 'Wall': Absolute or Serpentine," *Journal of Church and State* 30 (1988): 441–62.

36. Levy, *The Establishment Clause*, 181–85.

37. Cord, *Separation of Church and State*, 36–46; Daniel L. Dreisbach, "'Sowing Useful Truths and Principles': The Danbury Baptists, Thomas Jefferson, and the 'Wall of Separation,'" *Journal of Church and State* 39 (1997): 455–501, 473–74.

38. Dreisbach, "'Sowing Useful Truths and Principles,'" 471, 477; Vincent Phillip Muñoz, *God and the Founders: Madison, Washington, and Jefferson* (New York: Cambridge University Press, 2009), 77–82; Corwin, "The Supreme Court as National School Board," 14. "[T]he principal importance of the [first] amendment lay in the separation which it effected between the respective jurisdictions of state and nation regarding religion, rather than in its bearing on the question of the separation of church and state."

39. James Huston, "Thomas Jefferson's Letter to the Danbury Baptists: A Controversy Rejoined," *William and Mary Quarterly* 56 (1999): 775–90, 776; Corwin, "Supreme Court as National School Board," 14; Daniel L. Dreisbach, "Thomas Jefferson and the Danbury Baptists Revisited," *William and Mary Quarterly* 56 (1999): 805–16.

40. Robert M. O'Neil, "The 'Wall of Separation' and Thomas Jefferson's Views on Religious Liberty," *William and Mary Quarterly* 56 (1999): 791–94.

41. Isaac Kramnick and R. Laurence Moore, "The Baptists, the Bureau, and the Case of the Missing Lines," *William and Mary Quarterly* 56 (1999): 817–22; Edwin S. Gaustad, "Thomas Jefferson, Danbury Baptists, and 'Eternal Hostility,'" *William and Mary Quarterly* 56 (1999): 801–4; O'Neil, "'Wall of Separation,'" 791–94; Thomas E. Buckley, "Reflections on a Wall," *William and Mary Quarterly* 56 (1999): 795–800; Johann N. Neem, "Beyond the Wall: Reinterpreting Jefferson's Danbury Address," *Journal of the Early Republic* 27 (2007): 139–54.

42. Dreisbach, "'Sowing Useful Truths and Principles,'" 491.

43. Henry A. Washington, ed., *The Writings of Thomas Jefferson*, (Washington, DC: Taylor & Maury, 1854), 8:113–14; Jeremiah S. Black, "Religious Liberty: An Address to the Phrenakosmian Society of Pennsylvania College" (September 17, 1856), in *Essays and Speeches of Jeremiah S. Black*, ed. Chauncy F. Black (New York: D. Appleton, 1883), 53; C. Peter Mcgrath, "Chief Justice Waite and the Twin Relic: Reynolds v. United States," *Vanderbilt Law Review* 18 (1965): 507–43; Reynolds, 98 U.S., 164.

44. William G. McLoughlin, ed., *The American Evangelicals, 1800–1900* (Gloucester, MA: Peter Smith, 1976), 1–27; William G. McLoughlin, *Revivals, Awakenings, and Reform* (Chicago: University of Chicago Press, 1978), 98–140; Paul E. Johnson, *A Shopkeeper's Millennium* (New York: Hill & Wang, 1978); Timothy L. Smith, *Revivalism and Social Reform: American Protestantism on the Eve of the Civil War* (Baltimore: Johns Hopkins University Press, 1980), 15–62.

45. Johnson, *Shopkeeper's Millennium*, 4–5, 109–10.

46. Clifford S. Griffin, *Their Brothers' Keepers: Moral Stewardship in the United Sates, 1800–1865* (New Brunswick, NJ: Rutgers University Press, 1960), 47–49, Mark A. Noll, *America's God: From Jonathan Edwards to Abraham Lincoln* (New York: Oxford University Press, 2002), 208. See also Robert T. Handy, "The Protestant Quest for a Christian America, 1830–1930," *Church History* 22 (1953): 8–20.

47. Robert Baird, *Religion in the United States of America* (Glasgow: Blackie & Son, 1844), 600–603, 606.

48. Muzzy v. Wilkins, 1 Smiths. 1, 10–11 (N.H. 1803).

49. Muzzy v. Wilkins, 12–14.

50. Muzzy v. Wilkins, 9, 11.

51. McLoughlin, *New England Dissent*, 2:880–911; Brian Franklin, "Towns and Toleration: Disestablishment in New Hampshire," in Esbeck and Den Hartog, *Disestablishment and Religious Dissent*, 351–72.

52. Purcell, *Connecticut in Transition*, 195–97; McLoughlin, *New England Dissent*, 2:946; Sidney E. Mead, "Lyman Beecher and Connecticut Orthodoxy's Campaign against the Unitarians, 1819–1826," *Church History* 9 (1940): 218–34. Quote attributed to Abraham Bishop, repr. in Purcell, *Connecticut in Transition*, 191, 202.

53. Beecher, *Autobiography*, 1:261; McLoughlin, *New England Dissent*, 2:915–22.

54. McLoughlin, *New England Dissent*, 2:919–38; Purcell, *Connecticut in Transition*, 33–61.

55. John Leland, "The Rights of Conscience Inalienable," in Sandoz, *Political Sermons*, 1094.

56. Zephaniah Swift, *A System of the Laws of the State of Connecticut* (1795, 1796) (New York: Arno, 1972), 1:136, 141.

57. Swift, *System of the Laws*, 145.

58. Swift, 141, 146.

59. McLoughlin, *New England Dissent*, 2:1006–42; Robert J. Imholt, "Connecticut: A Land of Steady Habits," in Esbeck and Den Hartog, *Disestablishment and Religious Dissent*, 327–50.

60. Lyman Beecher, "The Building of Waste Places," in *Beecher's Works* (Boston: John P. Jewett, 1852), 2:124–26.

61. Beecher, "Building of Waste Places," 126; McLoughlin, *New England Dissent*, 2:1029–33.

62. *American Mercury*, March 19, 1816, 2; *American Mercury*, September 10, 1816, repr. in Purcell, *Connecticut in Transition*, 217; McLoughlin, *New England Dissent*, 2:1032.

63. McLoughlin, *New England Dissent*, 2:1025–62; Purcell, *Connecticut in Transition*, 262–63; Imholt, "Connecticut," 339–44.

64. Beecher, *Autobiography*, quoted in Wilson and Drakeman, *Church and State*, 94–95.

65. Beecher, 94–95.

66. Taylor, *Massachusetts, Colony to Commonwealth*, 128; John D. Cushing, "Notes on Disestablishment in Massachusetts," *William and Mary Quarterly* 26 (April 1969): 169–90, 169–73; Jacob M. Meyer, *Church and State in Massachusetts from 1740 to 1833* (Cleveland: Western Reserve University Press, 1930), 107–8.

67. Meyer, *Church and State in Massachusetts*, 139–43; Cushing, "Notes on Disestablishment," 173–81.

68. Avery v. Tyringham, 3 Mass. 160, 174, 179–80 (1807).

69. McLoughlin, *New England Dissent*, 2:1091–05; Cushing, "Notes on Disestablishment," 185–86.

70. 16 Mass. 488, 502 (1820). See also Meyer, *Church and State in Massachusetts*, 174–76, and McLoughlin, *New England Dissent*, 2:1189–97.

71. Meyer, *Church and State in Massachusetts*, 177; McLoughlin, *New England Dissent*, 2:1196.

72. McLoughlin, *New England Dissent*, 2:1197–98.

73. Meyer, *Church and State in Massachusetts*, 201–2; McLoughlin, *New England Dissent*, 2:1207–62.

74. McLoughlin, *New England Dissent*, 2:1013; Hamburger, *Separation of Church and State*, 163–80.

75. Jefferson to Priestly, March 21, 1801, in Ford, *Works*, 9:216–19; Jefferson to Moses Robinson, March 23, 1801, in Dreisbach and Hall, *Sacred Rights of Conscience*, 516.

76. Jefferson to M. Harrison Smith, August 6, 1816, in Andrew A. Lipscomb, Albert E. Bergh, and Richard Holland Johnston, eds., *Writings of Thomas Jefferson*, (Washington, DC: Thomas Jefferson Memorial Association, 1905), 15:59–61. See also Jefferson to Elbridge Gerry, March 29, 1801, in Ford, *Works*, 9:240–44; Jefferson to Charles Clay, January 29, 1805, in Lipscomb, Bergh, and Johnston, *Writings*, 14:232–34; Jefferson to John Adams, June 15, 1813, in Ford, *Works*, 11:293–97; and Jefferson to William Short, April 13, 1820, in Lipscomb, Bergh, and Johnston, *Writings*, 15:241–48.

77. Much of Jefferson's correspondence about religion is reprinted in Cousins, *"In God We Trust,"* 114–294.

78. Jefferson to Samuel Miller, January 23, 1808, in Ford, *Works*, 11:7–9; Dreisbach, "'Sowing Useful Truths and Principles,'" 477–79.

79. Second Inaugural Address, March 4, 1805, in Dreisbach and Hall, *Sacred Rights of Conscience*, 530.

80. Jefferson to the Baltimore Baptist Association, October 17, 1808, in Cousins, *"In God We Trust,"* 135–36; Jefferson to Charles Clay, January 29, 1815, in Lipscomb, Bergh, and Johnston, *Writings*, 14:232–34.

81. Jefferson to James Smith, December 8, 1822, in Cousins, *"In God We Trust,"* 358–59.

82. Jefferson to Adams, October 28, 1813, in *Adams-Jefferson Letters*, 387–92; Jefferson to Adams, May 4, 1817, in *Adams-Jefferson Letters*, 512–14.

83. O'Neil, "'Wall of Separation,'" 793.

84. Brant, "Madison," 5, 24; Drakeman, "Religion and the Republic: James Madison and the First Amendment," 437–45; Paul J. Weber, "James Madison and Religious Equality: The Perfect Separation," *Review of Politics* 44 (1982): 163–86; Loconte, "Faith and the Founding: The Influence of Religion on the Politics of James Madison," 699–735; Rodney A. Grunes, "James Madison and Religious Freedom," in *James Madison: Philosopher, Founder, and Statesman*, ed. John R. Vile, Willian D. Peterson, and Frank J. Williams (Athens: Ohio University Press, 2008), 105–32; Muñoz, *God and the Founders*, 11–48; Jeffrey Sikkenga, "Government Has No 'Religious Agency': James Madison's Fundamental Principle of Religious Liberty," *American Journal of Political Science* 56 (2012): 745–56.

85. Banning, "James Madison, the Statute for Religious Freedom, and the Crisis of Republican Convictions," 109–10.

86. James Madison, *Memorial and Remonstrance*, in *Founders Constitution*, 5:82, doc. 43.

87. *Federalist Papers*, nos. 10, 51.

88. James Madison, Inaugural Address, March 4, 1809, in *Republic of Letters*, 1561–62.

89. Madison's veto is consistent with Mark McGarvie's thesis that a leading separationist impulse involved the privatization of religious institutions and the removal of their traditional role of providing public services. McGarvie, *One Nation under Law*, 9, 48.

90. Madison's proclamations are reprinted in Dreisbach and Hall, *Sacred Rights of Conscience*, 458–61; Madison to Edward Livingston, July 10, 1822, in Dreisbach and Hall, *Sacred Rights of Conscience*, 596–97; Elizabeth Fleet, "Madison's 'Detached Memoranda,'" *William and Mary Quarterly* 3 (1946): 534–68.

91. Madison to Robert Walsh, March 2, 1819, in Dreisbach and Hall, *Sacred Rights of Conscience*, 594–95.

92. Madison to F. L. Schaeffer, December 3, 1821, in *James Madison on Religious Liberty*, ed. Robert S. Alley (Buffalo, NY: Prometheus, 1985), 82; Madison to Edward Everett, March 19, 1823, in Alley, *James Madison on Religious Liberty*, 83–84; Madison to George Mason, July 14, 1826, in Alley, 85–86; Madison to Edward Livingston, July 10, 1822, in Alley, 82–83; Green, *Second Disestablishment*, 94–96.

93. Jasper Adams, *The Relation of Christianity to Civil Government in the United States* (Charleston: A. E. Miller, 1833), 6–7, 12–13, 15–16; Green, *Second Disestablishment*, 98–100; Daniel L. Dreisbach, *Religion and Politics in the Early Republic* (Lexington: University Press of Kentucky, 1996).

94. Madison to Jasper Adams, September 1833, in Dreisbach and Hall, *Sacred Rights of Conscience*, 612–14.

95. Sidney E. Mead, "Neither Church nor State: Reflections on James Madison's Line of Separation," *Journal of Church and State* 10 (1968): 349–63; Dreisbach, *Religion and Politics in the Early Republic*, 157.

96. Fleet, "Madison's 'Detached Memoranda,'" 554–55; Grunes, "James Madison and Religious Freedom," 115–21.

97. Fleet, "Madison's 'Detached Memoranda,'" 554–56.

98. Fleet, 555, 558–61.

99. Leo Pfeffer, "Madison's 'Detached Memoranda': Then and Now," in *Virginia Statute for Religious Freedom*, 283–307.

4. The Protestant Establishment of the Nineteenth Century

1. Robert T. Handy, *A Christian America*, 2nd ed. (New York: Oxford University Press, 1984); Robert T. Handy, "The Protestant Quest for a Christian America, 1830–1930," *Church History* 22 (1953): 8–20, 12; James Fulton Maclear, "The 'True American Union' of Church and State: The Reconstruction of the Theocratic Tradition," *Church History* 28 (1959): 41–62; Jon Butler, *Awash in a Sea of Faith: Christianizing the American People* (Cambridge, MA: Harvard University Press, 1990), 257–95; Steven K. Green, *The Second Disestablishment: Church and State in Nineteenth-Century America* (New York: Oxford University Press, 2010), 81–103, 173–203; David Sehat, *The Myth of Religious Freedom* (New York: Oxford University Press, 2011).

2. Christopher Grasso, *Skepticism and American Faith* (New York: Oxford University Press, 2018), 153–395; Green, *Second Disestablishment*, 329–85; Phillip Hamburger, *Separation of Church and State* (Cambridge, MA: Harvard University Press, 2002), 342.

3. Alexis de Tocqueville, *Democracy in America*, trans. Henry Reeve (New York: Adlard & Saunders, 1838), 308.

4. Louis Kossuth, *The Future of Nations, in What Consists Its Security: A Lecture Delivered in New York, June 21, 1852* (New York: Fowler & Wells, 1854), 32.

5. Agénor de Gasparin, *The Uprising of a Great People: The United States in 1861* (London: S. Low, 1861), 63–64; Adam G. De Gurowski, *America and Europe* (New York: D. Appleton, 1857), 323.

6. Madison to Edward Livingston, July 10, 1822, in Robert S. Alley, *James Madison on Religious Liberty* (Buffalo, NY: Prometheus, 1985), 82–83.

7. Green, *Second Disestablishment*, 81–118

8. Timothy L. Smith, *Revivalism and Social Reform* (New York: Abington, 1957, 34–44; Ronald G. Walters, *American Reformers 1815–1860* (New York: Hill & Wang, 1978).

9. Clifford S. Griffin, *Their Brothers' Keepers: Moral Stewardship in the United States, 1800–1865* (New Brunswick, NJ: Rutgers University Press, 1960), 34–49; John R. Bodo, *The Protestant Clergy and Public Issues, 1812–1848* (Princeton, NJ: Princeton University Press, 1954), 20.

10. Lyman Beecher, "The Practicability of Suppressing Vice, by Means of Societies Instituted for That Purpose" (1804), in Lyman Beecher, *Lyman Beecher and the Reform of Society* (New York: Arno, 1972), 19–20.

11. Lyman Beecher, "A Reformation of Morals Practicable and Indispensable" (1812), in Beecher, *Lyman Beecher*, 17–19; Beecher, "Practicability of Suppressing Vice," 16–17.

12. Beecher, "Reformation of Morals Practicable and Indispensable," in Beecher, *Lyman Beecher*, 17–19; Lyman Beecher, "Perils of Atheism to Our Nation," in Lyman Beecher, *Works* (Boston: Jewett, 1852–53), 1:138.

13. Robert H. Abzug, *Cosmos Crumbling: American Reform and the Religious Imagination* (New York: Oxford University Press, 1994), 30–56; Handy, *Christian America*, 37–47; Butler, *Awash in a Sea of Faith*, 284–87; Clifford S. Griffin, "Religious Benevolence as Social Control, 1815–1860," *Mississippi Valley Historical Review* 44 (1957): 423–44; Bodo, *Protestant Clergy and Public Issues*, 20.

14. The phrase is Jon Butler's (*Awash in a Sea of Faith*, 225). Alice Felt Tyler, *Freedom's Ferment: Phases of American Social History to 1860* (Minneapolis: University of Minnesota Press, 1944), 47–224.

15. Grasso, *Skepticism and American Faith*, 250–322; Erik R. Schlereth, *An Age of Infidels: The Politics of Religious Controversy in the United States* (Philadelphia: University of Pennsylvania Press, 2013), 171–236; John Lardas Modern, *Secularism in Antebellum America* (Chicago: University of Chicago Press, 2011), 1–47; Leigh Eric Schmidt, *Village Atheists: How America's Unbelievers Made Their Way in a Godly Nation* (Princeton, NJ: Princeton University Press, 2016).

16. Timothy Dwight, *Travels in New England and New York* (London: W. Baynes, 1823), 4:272–73; Lyman Beecher, "The Building of Waste Places" (1814), in *Works*, 2:121–22; Schlereth, *Age of Infidels*, 169–70.

17. Griffin, "Religious Benevolence as Social Control," 425–26, Grasso, *Skepticism and American Faith*, 281–93; Arthur M. Schlesinger Jr., *The Age of Jackson* (New York: Little, Brown, 1945), 136; Bertram Wyatt-Brown, "Prelude to Abolitionism: Sabbatarian Politics and the Rise of the Second Party System," *Journal of American History* 58 (1971): 316–41.

18. Schlesinger, *Age of Jackson*, 351; Albert Post, *Popular Freethought in America, 1825–1850* (New York: Octagon, 1974), 75–120.

19. Lori D. Ginzberg, "'The Hearts of Your Readers Will Shudder': Fanny Wright, Infidelity, and American Freethought," *American Quarterly* 46 (1994): 195–226 (quoting the *Advocate of Moral Reform* [1836]).

20. Beecher, "Perils of Atheism," 1:92–93.

21. Ginzberg, "'Hearts of Your Readers,'" 203; Grasso, *Skepticism and American Faith*, 194–95.

22. Lyman Beecher, "Lectures on Political Atheism, and Kindred Subjects," in *Works*, 1:56–58, 75–76, 117, 125–26; Beecher, "Building of Waste Places," 1:122.

23. Ezra Stiles Ely, *The Duty of Christian Freemen to Elect Christian Rulers* (Philadelphia: n.p., 1828), in Wilson and Drakeman, *Church and State*, 96–100; Schlesinger, *Age of Jackson*, 137; Grasso, *Skepticism and American Faith*, 193–215.

24. "Union of Church and State," *Universalist Magazine*, October 13, 1827, 9; Justus E. Moore, *The Warning of Thomas Jefferson: A Brief Exposition of the Dangers to Be Apprehended to Our Civil and Religious Liberties from Presbyterianism* (Philadelphia: William J. Cunningham, 1844), 33.

25. *The Works of William E. Channing, D.D.* (Boston, 1878), in *Church and State in American History*, 105–9.

26. Schlesinger, *Age of Jackson*, 138.

27. Green, *Second Disestablishment*, 110–18; Richard R. John, "Taking Sabbatarianism Seriously: The Postal System, the Sabbath, and the Transformation of American Political Culture," *Journal of the Early Republic* 10 (Winter 1990): 517–67; James R. Rohrer, "Sunday Mails and the Church-State Theme in Jacksonian America," *Journal of the Early Republic* 7 (1987): 53–74; Wayne E. Fuller, *Morality and the Mail in Nineteenth-Century America* (Urbana: University of Illinois Press, 2003); Timothy Verhoeven, *Secularists, Religion and Government in Nineteenth-Century America* (Basingstoke, UK: Palgrave Macmillan, 2019), 33–62.

28. Meyer, *Church and State in Massachusetts*, 138–39; Beecher, "Practicability of Suppressing Vice," 15; Lyman Beecher, "The Design, Rights and Duties, of Local Churches," in Beecher, *Works* (1819), 207–8; Harmon Kingsbury, *The Sabbath: A Brief History of Laws, Petitions, Remonstrances, and Reports, with Facts, and Arguments, Related to the Christian Sabbath* (New York: Robert Carter, 1840), 59, 45.

29. *American State Papers*, class 7, Post Office Department (Washington, DC: Gales & Seaton, 1832), 44–45; Kingsbury, *Sabbath*, 24–31; John, "Taking Sabbatarianism Seriously," 522–35; Kramnick and Moore, *The Godless Constitution*, 132–34; Wyatt-Brown, "Prelude to Abolitionism," 328–29.

30. *American State Papers*, no. 86, 226–29; Lyman Beecher, *Lectures on Scepticism* (Cincinnati: Corey & Fairbank, 1835), 113–14.

31. John, "Taking Sabbatarianism Seriously," 542–43; Verhoeven, *Secularists, Religion and Government*, 35–37.

32. *American State Papers*, no. 27, 232–33; Kingsbury, *Sabbath*, 38–71; Verhoeven, *Secularists, Religion and Government*, 38–41, and appendix A, 253–54.

33. "Preamble and Resolutions, Adopted at a Meeting of the Citizens of New York, against the Passage of Any Law Prohibiting the Transportation and Opening of the Mail on the Sabbath," February 9, 1829, 20th Cong., 2d sess., S. Doc. 64.

34. Petition from Windham County, Vermont, February 24, 1831, 21st Cong., 2d sess., H. Doc. No. 104; William Addison Blakely, ed. *American State Papers Bearing on*

Sunday Legislation (Washington, DC: Religious Liberty Association, 1911), 277–78; Blakely, *American State Papers*, 278; Verhoeven, *Secularists, Religion and Government*, 45–48.

35. Senate Report on Sunday Mails, Committee on the Post Office and Post Roads, January 19, 1829, 20th Cong., 2nd sess., and House Report on Sunday Mails, Committee on the Post Office and Post Roads, March 4 and 5, 1830, 21st Cong., 1st sess., in Blakely, *American State Papers*, 233–70; Schlesinger, *Age of Jackson*, 139; John, "Taking Sabbatarianism Seriously," 558–60; Rohrer, "Sunday Mails and the Church-State Theme," 66–67; Verhoeven, *Secularists, Religion and Government*, 53–58.

36. Senate Report on Sunday Mails, 234–237; House Report on Sunday Mails, 257.

37. Senate Report on Sunday Mails, 239.

38. House Report on Sunday Mails, 255.

39. Rohrer, "Sunday Mails and the Church-State Theme," 68–69; Schlesinger, *Age of Jackson*, 136–41; Richard J. Carwardine, *Evangelicals and Politics in Antebellum America* (New Haven: Yale University Press, 1993), 61, 66.

40. Schlesinger, *Age of Jackson*, 351–52; Griffin, "Religious Benevolence as Social Control," 427–28; Carwardine, *Evangelicals and Politics*, 76–77

41. Theodore Frelinghuysen, *An Inquiry into the Moral and Religious Character of the American Government* (New York: Wiley & Putnam, 1838), 2–3, 14, 187, 189, 198, 207.

42. Green, *Inventing a Christian America*, 199–241.

43. Robert Baird, *Religion in the United States of America* (Glasgow: Blackie & Son, 1844), 243, 260–61.

44. Stephen Colwell, *The Position of Christianity in the United States* (Philadelphia: Lippincott, Grambo, 1854), 11.

45. B. F. Morris, *Christian Life and Character of the Civil Institutions of the United States* (Philadelphia: George W. Childs, 1864), 248–49.

46. Colwell, *Position of Christianity*, 23–24, 16–17.

47. Kermit L. Hall, *The Magic Mirror: Law in American History* (New York: Oxford University Press, 1989), 247–48.

48. Green, *Second Disestablishment*, 150–54, 160–72; Joseph Story, "Christianity a Part of the Common Law," *American Jurist and Law Magazine* 9 (April 1833): 346–48.

49. People v. Ruggles, 8 Johns. 290 (N.Y. 1811); Updegraph v. Commonwealth, 11 Serg. & Rawle, 394 (Pa. 1824); Commonwealth v. Kneeland, 20 Pick. (37 Mass.) 206, 213 (1836); State v. Chandler, 2 Harr. 553, 555 (Del. 1837).

50. Commonwealth v. Wolf, 3 Serg. & Rawle 48, 49–51 (Pa. 1817); Shover v. State, 10 Ark. 259, 263 (1850); O'Donnell v. Swenney, 5 Ala. 467, 469 (1843); Lindenmuller v. The People, 33 Barb. 548, 568 (1861). See Tim Verhoeven, "In Defense of Civil and Religious Liberty: Anti-Sabbatarianism in the United States before the Civil War," *Church History* 82 (2013): 293–316.

51. City Council of Charleston v. Benjamin, 2 Strob. 508, 511, 521–22, 524–25 (S.C. 1846).

52. Green, *Second Disestablishment*, 205–47.

53. Bloom v. Richards, 2 Ohio St. 387, 390–92, 404 (1853).

54. Ex parte Newman, 9 Cal. 502, 506–7 (1858). Three years later, the California Supreme Court upheld a revised Sunday closing law, declaring that the "primary

object of the legislation . . . is not the promotion of religion." See Ex parte Andrews, 18 Cal. 678, 682–83 (1861).

55. Perry v. Commonwealth, 44 Va. 632, 641–43 (1846).

56. Shaw v. Moore, 49 N.C. 25, 29 (1856); Bush v. Commonwealth, 80 Ky. 244, 249 (1882); Green, *Second Disestablishment*, 214–18.

57. Frank Way, "Religious Disputation and the Civil Courts: Quasi-Establishment and Secular Principles," *Western Political Quarterly* 42 (December 1989): 523–43.

58. Attorney General v. Pearson, 3 Merivale 353 (1817), quoted in Watson v. Jones, 80 U.S. 679, 727 (1872). See Hendrickson v. Shotwell, 1 N.J. Eq. 577 (1832); App v. Lutheran Congregation, 6 Pa. 201 (1847).

59. Watson v. Jones, 80 U.S. 679, 727–29 (1872).

60. Lamb v. Cain, 29 N.E. 13, 21 (Ind. 1891); White Lick Quarterly Meeting of Friends v. White Lick Quarterly Meeting of Friends, 89 Ind. 136, *8 (1886); Chase v. Cheney, 58 Ill. 509, 536 (1871); Pounder v. Ash, 63 N.W. 48, 50 (Neb. 1895).

61. See Steven K. Green, *The Bible, the School, and the Constitution* (New York: Oxford University Press, 2012); Hamburger, *Separation of Church and State*, 201–51, 287–359; J. Spencer Fluhman, *A Peculiar People: Anti-Mormonism and the Making of Religion in Nineteenth-Century America* (Chapel Hill: University of North Carolina Press, 2012); Sarah Barringer Gordon, *The Mormon Question: Polygamy and Constitutional Conflict in Nineteenth-Century America* (Chapel Hill: University of North Carolina Press, 2002).

62. H. G. Good, *A History of American Education* (New York: Macmillan, 1962), 41–43, 110–16; Carl Kaestle, *Pillars of the Republic: Common Schools and American Society* (New York: Hill & Wang, 1983), 13–29; Lawrence A. Cremin, *American Education: The Colonial Experience, 1607–1783* (New York: Harper & Row, 1970), 499–509; Lawrence A. Cremin, *American Education: The National Experience, 1783–1876* (New York: Harper & Row, 1980), 33–44, 107–21; David Nasaw, *Schooled to Order: A Social History of Public Schooling in the United States* (New York: Oxford University Press, 1979), 30, 40; Frederick Rudolph, ed. *Essays on Education in the Early Republic* (Cambridge, MA: Belknap Press of Harvard University, 1965), xvi–xvii.

63. Noah Webster, "On Education of Youth in America" (1790), in Rudolph, *Essays on Education*, 50–51; Samuel Knox, "An Essay on the Best System of Liberal Education" (1799), in Rudolph, *Essays on Education*, 327, 330–33.

64. Kaestle, *Pillars of the Republic*, 13–29; Nasaw, *Schooled to Order*, 29–34.

65. "Moral Education: The Bible in Schools," *Connecticut Common School Journal* (January 1, 1841): 70; Calvin E. Stowe, *The Religious Element in Education* (Boston: William D. Ticknor, 1844), 20–34; "The Bible Essential in Education," *New York Evangelist*, May 17, 1842, 44; Noah Feldman, "Non-sectarianism Reconsidered," *Journal of Law and Politics* 18 (2002): 65–117, 66.

66. Horace Mann, *Twelfth Annual Report* (Boston: Horace B. Fuller, 1848), 116–17; Horace Mann, *Common School Journal* 1 (November, 1838): 14.

67. Feldman, "Non-sectarianism Reconsidered," 80–81.

68. Mann, *Twelfth Annual Report*, 105, 111, 119–21.

69. Sidney E. Mead, *The Lively Experiment* (New York: Harper & Row, 1963), 67; Cubberley, *Readings in Public Education in the United States* (Boston: Houghton Mifflin, 1934), 202–12; "Speech of Bishop John Hughes," in William Oland Bourne, *History of the Public School Society of the City of New York* (New York: William Wood, 1870), 436.

70. Horace Bushnell, "Christianity and the Common Schools," *Connecticut Common School Journal* 2 (1839): 102; Horace Bushnell, "Common Schools" (1853), in *Building Eras in Religion* (New York: Charles Scribner's Sons, 1902), 3:75–76.

71. "The Catholics and the Common Schools," *New Yorker*, February 27, 1841, 10; "The Bible Essential to Education," *New York Evangelist*, May 17, 1842, 13.

72. Ruth Miller Elson, *Guardians of Tradition: American Schoolbooks of the Nineteenth Century* (Lincoln: University of Nebraska Press, 1964).

73. Peter Guilday, ed., *The National Pastorals of the American Hierarchy (1792–1919)* (Washington, DC: National Catholic Welfare League, 1923), 27–28, 134.

74. "The Bible Burning in New York," *New York Observer*, January 14, 1843, 6; John Dowling, *The History of Romanism* (New York: Edward Walker, 1846), 612–13.

75. Ray Allen Billington, *The Protestant Crusade 1800–1860* (New York: Macmillan, 1938), 220–34; Michael Feldberg, *The Philadelphia Riots of 1844: A Study of Ethnic Conflict* (Westport, CT: Greenwood, 1975); Vincent P. Lannie and Bernard C. Diethorn, "For the Honor and Glory of God: The Philadelphia Bible Riots of 1840," *History of Education Quarterly* 8 (September 1968): 44–106.

76. Lyman Beecher, *A Plea for the West* (Cincinnati: Truman & Smith, 1835), 69–70, 75, 78–79; Samuel F. B. Morse, *Foreign Conspiracy against the Liberties of the United States* (New York: Leavitt, Lord, 1835), 52, 57–58; Billington, *Protestant Crusade*, 298–93.

77. Frederick Saunders and Thomas Bangs Thorpe, *A Voice to America, or, The Model Republic, In Glory, or in Fall* (New York: Edward Walker, 1855), 313.

78. Guilday, *National Pastorals*, 26–28, 74, 78, 134, 190–91.

79. Green, *Bible, School, and Constitution*, 45–91.

80. Bourne, *Public School Society*, 52–55, 88–89, 127–30, 139–40; John Webb Pratt, *Religion, Politics, and Diversity: The Church-State Theme in New York History* (Ithaca, NY: Cornell University Press, 1967), 165–68.

81. Massachusetts, St. 1826, ch. 143, § 7 (March 10, 1827); Mann, *Twelfth Annual Report*, 117–19; Paul Goda, "The Historical Background of California's Constitutional Provisions Prohibiting Aid to Sectarian Schools," *California Historical Society Quarterly* 46 (June 1967): 157–71.

82. Thorpe, *Federal and State Constitutions*, 2:1074 (Indiana), 2:1189 (Kansas), 4:1931 (Michigan), 4:1993 (Minnesota), 5:2925 (Ohio), 5:2998 (Oregon), 7:4078–79 (Wisconsin). The Florida Constitution of 1838 and the Kentucky Constitution of 1850 provided that the school funds shall be appropriated in aid of common schools "but for no other purpose." Art. X, sec. 1, Thorpe, 2:677, and art. XI, sec. 1, Thorpe, 3:1311.

83. Charles Henry Clay, ed., *The Oregon Constitution and Proceedings and Debates of the Constitutional Convention of 1857* (Salem, OR: State Printing Department, 1926), 296–308, 305.

84. Clay, *Oregon Constitution*, 302–3.

85. John R. Mulkern, *The Know-Nothing Party in Massachusetts* (Boston: Northeastern University Press, 1990).

86. Harold M. Helfman, "The Cincinnati 'Bible War,' 1869–1870," *Ohio State Archeological and Historical Quarterly* 60 (1951): 369–86; Green, *Bible, School, and Constitution*, 93–135; Robert G. McCloskey, ed., *The Bible in the Public Schools: Arguments*

in the Case of John D. Minor, et al. versus the Board of Education of the City of Cincinnati, et al. (Cincinnati: Robert Clarke, 1870; New York: De Capo, 1964), 369–71.

87. McCloskey, *Bible in the Public Schools*, 396–97, 415.

88. Board of Education v. Minor, 23 Ohio St. 211, 248, 253 (1873).

89. Green, *Bible, School, and Constitution*, 181–86.

90. *New York Tribune*, July 8, 1875, 4.

91. *New York Times*, October 22, 1875, 1; Green, *Bible, School, and Constitution*, 179–99. The full text of the original Blaine Amendment follows: "No State shall make any law respecting an establishment of religion, or prohibiting the free exercise thereof; and no money raised by taxation in any State for the support of public schools, or derived from any public fund thereof, nor any public lands devoted thereto, shall ever be under the control of any religious sect; nor shall any money so raised or lands so devoted be divided between religious sects or denominations" (4 Congressional Record, 5453 [1876]).

92. Green, *Bible, School, and Constitution*, 199–209.

93. William T. Harris, "Division of School Funds," *Atlantic Monthly* (August 1876): 171–84.

94. William W. Patton, *Purely Secular Public Schools. An Address on the Bible and Public Schools* (Chicago: Lakeside, 1876), 10, 17; H. L. Wayland, "The Compulsory Use of the Bible in Schools," *Michigan Teacher* (June 1871): 1–15; Nathaniel Seaver Jr., *The Bible in the Public Schools* (Davenport, IA: Globe Steam, 1872), 8; G. W. Collings, *Bible Reading and Prayer in the Public Schools* (Rockville, IN: Patriot, 1875), 7; Samuel T. Spear, *The Bible in Public Schools* (New York: William G. Martin, 1870), 17–19.

95. Henry Ward Beecher, "The Common School as an Element of National Unity," November 13, 1869, in *The Bible in the Public Schools: Opinions of Individuals and the Press* (New York: J. W. Schermerhorn, 1870), 8–9; Henry Ward Beecher, "Has the State a Right to Establish Common Schools?" December 4, 1869, in *Bible and the Schools*, 23; Henry Ward Beecher, "The School Question," *Christian Union*, January 8, 1870, 16–18.

96. Spear, *Religion and the State*, 18, 51, 117, 22–24, 372.

97. Max Lilienthal, "The Contest for Religious Liberty in Cincinnati; or, the Bible Question," *Jewish Times*, December 1, 1869, in *Bible in Public Schools: Opinions*, 62–71; Naomi W. Cohen, *Jews in Christian America: The Pursuit of Religious Equality* (New York: Oxford University Press, 1992), 79–85.

98. Green, *Bible, School, and Constitution*, 209–23; Steven K. Green, "The Insignificance of the Blaine Amendment," *Brigham Young University Law Review* (2008): 295–333.

99. Upholding Bible reading: McCormick v. Burt, 95 Ill. 263 (1880); Moore v. Monroe, 20 N.W. 475 (Ia. 1884); Hart v. School District of Sharpsville, 2 Lanc. 346 (Pa. Com. Pl. 1885); Nessle v. Hum, 1 Ohio N.P. 140, 142 (1894); Pfeiffer v. Board of Education, 77 N.W. 250, 252 (Mich. 1898); Curran v. White, 22 Pa. C. 201 (1898); Stevenson v. Hanyon, 7 Pa. D. 585 (1898); Billard v. Board of Education, 76 P. 422, 433 (Kan. 1904); Hackett v. Brooksville Graded Sch. Dist., 87 S.W. 792, 794 (Ky. 1905); Church v. Bullock, 109 S.W. 115, 118 (Tex. 1908). Striking Bible reading: State ex rel. Weiss v. District Board of School Dist. No. 8, 44 N.W. 967 (Wis. 1890); State ex rel. Freeman v. Scheve, 91 N.W. 846, 847 (Neb. 1902); State ex rel. Freeman v. Scheve, 93 N.W. 169 (Neb. 1903); People ex rel. Ring v. Board of Education, 92 N.E. 251 (Ill. 1910).

100. William T. Harris, *Report of the Commissioner of Education for the Year 1894–1895* (Washington, DC: Government Printing Office, 1896), 2:1656; "Respecting Establishments of Religion and Free Public Schools," in *In Defense of the Public Schools* (Philadelphia: Aldine, 1888), 95; R. Laurence Moore, "Bible Reading and Nonsectarian Schooling: The Failure of Religious Instruction in Nineteenth-Century Public Education," *Journal of American History* 86 (March 2000): 1581–99.

101. "The Public School Essential to American Institutions," *Universalist Quarterly and General Review* (January 1890): 27–38.

102. William Croswell Doane, "The Roman Catholic Church and the School Fund," *North American Review* (January 1894): 30.

103. "The Mormon Outrages in Salt Lake," *New York Times*, November 21, 1851, 4.

104. Gordon, *Mormon Question*, 19–23; Leonard J. Arrington and Davis Bitton, *The Mormon Experience: A History of the Latter-day Saints* (New York: Vintage Books, 1979), 68–82; Klaus J. Hansen, *Mormonism and the American Experience* (Chicago: University of Chicago Press, 1981), 138–41.

105. Gordon, *Mormon Question*, 94–96; Fluhman, *Peculiar People*, 107.

106. "The Rise and Progress of the Mormon Faith and People," *Southern Literary Messenger* (September 1844): 526–39; "The Mormon Schism," *Workingman's Advocate*, June 22, 1844, 3.

107. Charles J. Peterson, "Mormonism and the Mormons," *Graham's American Monthly Magazine* (May 1851): 531; "War with the Mormons," *New York Times*, May 13, 1857, 4; J. W. Mendenhall, "The Mormon Problem," *Ladies' Repository*, April 1, 1875, 306–13; Orma Linford, "The Mormons and the Law: The Polygamy Cases, Part I," *Utah Law Review* 9 (1964): 308–79.

108. Linford, "Mormons and the Law," 314–17; Edwin Brown Firmage and Richard Collin Mangrum, *Zion in the Courts: A Legal History of the Church of Jesus Christ of Latter-day Saints, 1830–1900* (Urbana: University of Illinois Press, 1988), 148–51.

109. *Reynolds v. United States*, 98 U.S. 145 (1879); Linford, "Mormons and the Law," 331–41; Gordon, *Mormon Question*, 119–45; Firmage and Mangrum, *Zion in the Courts*, 151–56.

110. 98 U.S., 162, 164.

111. 98 U.S., 164, 165, 167.

112. 98 U.S., 163; C. Peter Magrath, "Chief Justice Waite and the Twin Relic: Reynolds v. United States," *Vanderbilt Law Review* 18 (1965): 507–34.

113. 98 U.S., 164; Magrath, "Chief Justice Waite and the Twin Relic," 529–30; Everson, 330 U.S., 16.

114. H.R. Rep. No. 2735, 49th Cong., 1st sess. 5–8 (1886); 17 Cong. Rec. 507 (1886); 18 Cong. Rec. 1900–1903 (1887); Linford, "Mormons and the Law," 326–327; Firmage and Mangrum, *Zion in the Courts*, 197–205.

115. Linford, "Mormons and the Law," 348–50; Arrington and Bitton, *Mormon Experience*, 181–83 Gordon, *Mormon Question*, 147–64.

116. The Late Corporation of the Church of Jesus Christ of Latter-day Saints v. United States, 136 U.S. 1, 49 (1890).

117. John Eaton, "Mormonism as a Religion," *The Independent*, April 16, 1896, 4–5; Linford, "Mormons and the Law," 583–85; Firmage and Mangrum, *Zion in the Courts*, 205.

118. Josiah Strong, *Our Country: Its Possible Future and Its Present Crisis* (New York: Baker & Taylor, 1885, 1891), 98, 100–101.

119. "The Church and the State," *Universalist Quarterly and General Review* (July 1877): 308–21.

120. "Gibbons Answers Sabatier: Cardinal Is for Real Separation of Church and State," *New York Times*, April 24, 1907, 2; Gerald T. Fogarty, "The Holy See, Apostolic Delegates, and the Question of Church-State Relations in the United States," *U.S. Catholic Historian* 12 (1994): 69–89.

121. Clarence Greeley, "The Christian Evolution of a Secular State," *New Englander and Yale Magazine* 51 (October 1889): 275–83.

5. Separation Becomes Constitutional Canon

1. Everson v. Board of Education, 330 U.S. 1 (1947). In *Town of Greece v. Galloway*, Justice Clarence Thomas wrote derisively that "the Everson Court glibly effected a sea change in constitutional law" that "might be explained, although not excused, by the rise of popular conceptions about 'separation of church and state' as an 'American' constitutional right." Town of Greece v. Galloway, 572 U.S. 565, 607n1 (2014) (Thomas, J., concurring).

2. The exception to this is Justice Frankfurter's opinion in *McCollum* the following year in which he discussed the contributions of Horace Mann and President Grant. 333 U.S., 215–19.

3. "Roman Catholics after Public Money Again," *Christian Century*, May 27, 1936, 757; "Threats to Religious Liberty," *Christian Century*, June 21, 1939, 791; "The Church's New Troubles in Spain," *The Nation*, November 18, 1939, 539; *The Nation*, April 6, 1940, 435; "What Southern Baptists Believe," *Washington Herald*, May 13, 1920, 5; *The Menace*, April 20, 1918, 1; *The Menace*, October 26, 1918, 1; *The Menace*, June 28, 1919, 1.

4. Steven K. Green, *The Third Disestablishment: Church, State, and American Culture, 1940–1975* (New York: Oxford University Press, 2019), 301–52.

5. Quoted in Naomi W. Cohen, *Jews in Christian America: The Pursuit of Religious Equality* (New York: Oxford University Press, 1992), 46.

6. D. Philipson, "The Jew as a Liberal Force," *American Jewish Historical Society* (1906): 136–41.

7. Cohen, *Jews in Christian America*, 93–96, 99–100, 105–19; Jonathan D. Sarna, "Christian America or Secular America? The Church-State Dilemma of American Jews," in *Jews in Unsecular America*, ed. Richard J. Neuhaus (Grand Rapids, MI: Eerdmans, 1982), 8–19.

8. Robert T. Handy, *Undermined Establishment: Church-State Relations in America, 1880–1920* (Princeton, NJ: Princeton University Press, 1991), 139–45; George M. Marsden, *Fundamentalism and American Culture* (New York: Oxford University Press, 1980), 135–36; Conrad Henry Moehlman, "The Baptist View of the State," *Church History* 6 (1937): 24–49; "Wants Church Kept Divided from State," *New York Times*, July 5, 1926, 14; "Clergy Ask Church to Eschew Politics," *New York Times*, June 12, 1930, 17.

9. William R. Hutchison, *The Modernist Impulse in American Protestantism* (New York: Oxford University Press, 1982), 145–84.

10. Walter Rauschenbusch, *Christianity and the Social Crisis* (New York: Hodder & Stoughton, 1907), 380.

11. Rauschenbusch, *Christianity and the Social Crisis*, 380.

12. Rauschenbusch, 380; Charles William Eliot, "The Churches and the Prevailing Social Sentiment," *Harvard Theological Review* 6 (October 1913): 397–406; Handy, *Undermined Establishment*, 107–12.

13. Isaac A. Cornelison, *The Relation of Religion to Civil Government in the United States of America* (New York: G. P. Putnam's Sons, 1895), vi, 176, 186; Sanford H. Cobb, *The Rise of Religious Liberty in America* (New York: Cooper Square, 1902), 524–25, 15–16.

14. Thomas M. Cooley, *A Treatise on the Constitutional Limitations* (Boston: Little, Brown, 1868; repr. 1903), 663, 668; Thomas M. Cooley, *General Principles of Constitutional Law* (Boston: Little, Brown, 1880; repr. 1898), 224–25.

15. Henty Campbell Black, *Handbook of American Constitutional Law* (St. Paul, MN: West Publishing, 1897), 389–94.

16. Carl Zollman, *American Civil Church Law* (New York: Columbia University, 1917); Carl Zollman, *Church and School in the American Law* (St. Louis: Concordia, 1918); Carl Zollman, "Religious Liberty in the American Law," *Michigan Law Review* 17 (1919): 355–77; Carl Zollman, "The Constitutional and Legal Status of Religion in Public Education," *Journal of Religion* 2 (1922): 236–44.

17. Bradfield v. Roberts, 175 U.S. 291, 297, 298 (1899).

18. Roberts v. Bradfield, 12 App. D.C. 453, 467 (1898).

19. Quick Bear v. Leupp, 210 U.S. 50, 81 (1908).

20. William M. Halsey, *The Survival of American Innocence: Catholicism in an Era of Disillusionment, 1920–1940* (Notre Dame, IN: University of Notre Dame Press, 1980), 2, 10; Patrick W. Carey, *Catholics in America: A History* (Westport, CT: Praeger, 2004), 79; Thomas T., McAvoy, "American Catholics and the Second World War," *Review of Politics* 6 (April 1944): 131–50.

21. Philip Gleason, "In Search of Unity: American Catholic Thought, 1920–1960," *Catholic Historical Review* 65 (April 1979): 185–205; Halsey, *Survival of American Innocence*, 4, 15.

22. Frederick Joseph Kinsman, *Americanism and Catholicism* (New York: Longmans, Green, 1924), 152, 142–43; Cardinal James Gibbons, "The Church and the Republic," in *A Retrospect of Fifty Years* (Baltimore: John Murphy, 1916), 1:234 (repr. from *North American Review*, March 1909, 321–36).

23. John A. Ryan and Moorhouse F. X. Millar, *The State and the Church* (Washington, DC: National Catholic Welfare Council, 1922), 34, 60; John A. Ryan, "The Catholic Reply to the Opposition," *Current History* (1922): 778–83; Zachary R. Calo, "The Indispensable Basis of Democracy: American Catholicism, the Church-State Debate, and the Soul of American Liberalism, 1920–1929," *Virginia Law Review* 91 (2005): 1037–73.

24. William E. Leuchtenburg, *The Perils of Prosperity, 1914–1932* (Chicago: University of Chicago Press, 1958, 1973), 66–103; Lerond Curry, *Protestant-Catholic Relations in America: World War I through Vatican II* (Lexington: University Press of Kentucky, 1972), 4–5; John Higham, *Strangers in the Land: Patterns of American Nativism, 1860–1925* (New Brunswick, NJ: Rutgers University Press, 1955, 2008), 234–63, 247; Kelly J.

Baker, *Gospel According to the Klan: The KKK's Appeal to Protestant America, 1915–1930* (Lawrence: University Press of Kansas, 2011), 44–47.

25. Higham, *Strangers in the Land*, 286–89; Wyn Craig Wade, *The Fiery Cross: The Ku Klux Klan in America* (New York: Touchstone, 1987), 119–85, 253; Curry, *Protestant-Catholic Relations in America*, 6–11; *The Menace*, August 24, 1918, 1; *The Menace*, October 26, 1918, 1; "Woman Organizer Defends Ku Klux," *New York Times*, September 12, 1921, 12; Philip Hamburger, *Separation of Church and State* (Cambridge: Harvard University Press, 2002), 399–414.

26. "An Open Letter to the Honorable Alfred E. Smith," *Atlantic Monthly* 139 (April 1927): 540–49.

27. Alfred E. Smith, "Catholic and Patriot: Governor Smith Replies," *Atlantic Monthly* 139 (May 1927): 728; Edmund A. Moore, *A Catholic Runs for President: The Campaign of 1928* (New York: Ronald Press, 1956), 77–79; Curry, *Protestant-Catholic Relations in America*, 14.

28. "The Religious Issues," *Christian Century*, October 18, 1928, 1251–53; Curry, *Protestant-Catholic Relations in America*, 15–19; Moore, *Catholic Runs for President*, 196–99; James H. Smylie, "The Roman Catholic Church, the State and Al Smith," *Church History* 29 (September 1960): 321–43; Robert Moats Miller, "A Footnote to the Role of the Protestant Churches in the Election of 1928," *Church History* 25 (June 1956): 145–59.

29. John C. Bennett, "After Liberalism—What?," *Christian Century*, November 8, 1933, 1403–6; Robert T. Handy, "The American Religious Depression, 1925–1935," *Church History* 29 (March 1960): 3–16; Halsey, *Survival of American Innocence*, 4–5; Donald B. Meyer, *The Protestant Search for Political Realism, 1919–1941* (Berkeley: University of California Press, 1960).

30. "Should Protestantism Be Catholic-Conscious?," *Christian Century*, May 26, 1937, 670–72; Handy, *Undermined Establishment*, 190.

31. "Decency and Censorship," *Christian Century*, July 29, 1936, 1030–32; "Vatican over Hollywood," *The Nation*, July 11, 1936, 33.

32. George Seldes, *The Catholic Crisis* (New York: Julian Messer, 1939); Carey, *Catholics in America*, 90; John P. Diggins, "American Catholics and Italian Fascism," *Journal of Contemporary History* 2 (1967): 51–68; "Spanish Hierarchy Is Denounced Here," *New York Times*, October 4, 1937, 1, 12; John T. McGreevy, "Thinking on One's Own: Catholicism in the American Intellectual Imagination, 1928–1960," *Journal of American History* 84 (June 1997): 97–131.

33. "Catholic Schools and Public Money," *Yale Law Journal* 50 (March 1941): 917–27; "Educators Assail Church-School Aid," *New York Times*, February 28, 1938, 17.

34. McGreevy, "Thinking on One's Own," 97–131; Emma Long, *The Church-State Debate: Religion, Education and the Establishment Clause in Post War America* (London: Continuum, 2012), 12–13.

35. John Mulder and Marvin Comisky, "Jehovah's Witnesses Mold Constitutional Law," *Bill of Rights Review* 2 (1941–42): 262–68; Victor W. Rotnem and F. G. Folsom Jr., "Recent Restrictions upon Religious Liberty," *American Political Science Review* 36 (1942): 1053–68; Shawn Francis Peters, *Judging Jehovah's Witnesses: Religious Persecution and the Dawn of the Rights Revolution* (Lawrence: University Press of Kansas, 2000).

36. Jones v. City of Opelika, 316 U.S. 584, 597–99 (1942); West Virginia State Board of Education v. Barnette, 319 U.S. 624, 653–55 (1943) (Frankfurter, J., dissenting).

37. "Catholic Schools and Public Money," 917–27; Cochran v. Louisiana State Board of Education, 281 U.S. 370, 374–75 (1930). *Cochran* was decided on due process grounds rather than under the Establishment Clause.

38. Everson v. Board of Education, 44 A.2d 333 (N.J. 1945).

39. Brief of Junior Order of United American Mechanics, 2; Brief of the General Conference of Seventh-day Adventists et al., 2, 7; Brief of ACLU, 4, 8–12.

40. Daryl R. Fair, "The *Everson* Case in the Context of New Jersey Politics," in *Everson Revisited: Religion, Education, and Law at the Crossroads*, ed. Jo Renée Formicola and Hubert Morken (Lantham, MD: Rowan & Littlefield, 1998), 1–21; Christine L. Compston, "The Serpentine Wall: Judicial Decision Making in Supreme Court Cases Involving Aid to Sectarian Schools" (PhD diss., University of New Hampshire, 1986), 59–60; Reinhold Niebuhr, "Church and State in America," *Christianity and Crisis*, December 15, 1941, repr. in Reinhold Niebuhr, *Essays in Applied Christianity* (New York: Living Age Books, 1959), 84–87.

41. Brief of the National Council of Catholic Men and the National Council of Catholic Women, 13–14, 21–35.

42. Donald L. Drakeman, "*Everson v. Board of Education* and the Quest for the Historical Establishment Clause," *American Journal of Legal History* 49 (2007): 119–68; Jo Renée Formicola, "*Everson* Revisited: "This Is Not . . . Just a Little Case over Bus Fares," *Polity* 28 (Fall 1995): 49–66.

43. Everson, 330 U.S., 16–18; Roger K. Newman, *Hugo Black: A Biography* (New York: Pantheon, 1994), 363–64.

44. Everson, 330 U.S., 31–32 (Rutledge, J., dissenting); Everson, 330 U.S., 26 (Jackson, J., dissenting).

45. Del Dickson, ed., *The Supreme Court in Conference* (New York: Oxford University Press, 2001), 400–401; Drakeman, "*Everson v. Board of Education*," 132–33; Compston, "Serpentine Wall," 110–14.

46. Hugo Black Papers (hereafter cited as HB), Library of Congress, box 285, folders 2–3; Drakeman, "*Everson v. Board of Education*," 139–40; Compston, "Serpentine Wall," 69–72.

47. Multiple drafts of the opinion are contained in Wiley Rutledge Papers, Library of Congress, box 143, folders 8–12, and box 144, folders 1, 3–7; HB, box 285, folders 2–3; Everson, 330 U.S., 33–34 (Rutledge, J., dissenting); Drakeman, "*Everson v. Board of Education*," 140; Newman, *Hugo Black*, 362; John M. Ferren, *Salt of the Earth, Conscience of the Court: The Story of Justice Wiley Rutledge* (Chapel Hill: University of North Carolina Press, 2004), 264–66.

48. "High Court Backs State Right to Run Parochial Buses," *New York Times*, February 11, 1947, 1, 31; "Religion: Edge of the Wedge?," *Time*, March 3, 1947; Ferren, *Salt of the Earth*, 266.

49. "Now Will Protestants Awake?," *Christian Century*, February 26, 1947, 262–64; "Baptists Hit Ruling on Catholic Schools," *New York Times*, February 12, 1947, 27.

50. "Cushing Stresses Parents' Rights," *New York Times*, April 10, 1947, 18; J. M. O'Neill, "Church, Schools, and the Constitution," *Commentary* (June 1947): 562–70;

James M. O'Neill, *Religion and Education under the Constitution* (New York: Harper & Bros., 1949); James M. O'Neill, *Catholic and American Freedom* (New York: Harper & Bros., 1952).

51. Note, "Tracing the 'Wall': Religion in the Public School System," *Yale Law Journal* (1948): 1114–22; Richard Dierenfield, *Religion in American Public Schools* (St. Paul, MN: Public Affairs, 1962), 75–82; "School Time Voted for Church Study," *New York Times*, November 14, 1940, 1.

52. McCollum, 330 U.S., 209, 211–12.

53. McCollum, 330 U.S., 212–32 (Frankfurter, J.).

54. "Ruling on Religion by Court Scored," *New York Times*, July 25, 1948, 8; "Banning Religion in School Assailed," *New York Times*, September 12, 1948, 57.

55. "Church's Teaching Held Endangered," *New York Times*, June 13, 1948, 50; "Catholic Bishops Hit Supreme Court," *New York Times*, November 21, 1948, 1, 63; "Releasing the Time," *Commonweal*, March 26, 1948, 581–82; Winfrid Parsons, *The First Freedom: Considerations of Church and State in the United States* (New York: Declan X. McMullen, 1948), ix.

56. "Supreme Court Bans Released Time," *Christian Century*, March 17, 1948, 294; "The Champaign Case, *Christian Century*, April 7, 1948, 308–9; "Public Schools Can Teach Religion!," *Christian Century*, April 28, 1948, 374–76; "Salvaging Released Time," *Christian Century*, May 5, 1948, 405–6.

57. "Three Faiths File Brief for Released Time," *New York Times*, June 17, 1948, 27; "Protestant Leaders on Church-State Cooperation," *America*, June 26, 1948, 278; *Christianity and Crisis* 8 (1948): 90; Charles C. Brown, *Niebuhr and His Age* (Philadelphia: Trinity Press International, 1992), 204–5; K. Healan Gaston, *Imagining Judeo-Christian America* (Chicago: University of Chicago Press, 2019), 204–9.

58. John Courtney Murray, "Law or Prepossessions," *Law and Contemporary Problems* 14 (1949): 23–43.

59. Murray, "Law or Prepossessions," 32.

60. "New Body Demands Church Separation," *New York Times*, January 12, 1948, 1, 12; "Protestants United Issue Manifesto," *Christian Century*, January 21, 1948, 68–69, 79–82; Green, *Third Disestablishment*, 128–33, 150–63.

61. Gaston, *Imagining Judeo-Christian America*, 122–24.

62. Robert S. Ellwood, *The Fifties Spiritual Marketplace: American Religion in a Decade of Conflict* (New Brunswick, NJ: Rutgers University Press, 1997), 9, 45–101; Mark Silk, *Spiritual Politics: Religion and America since World War II* (New York: Simon & Schuster, 1988), 54–69, 87–107; William Petersen, "Religious Statistics in the United States," *Journal for the Scientific Study of Religion*, 1 (1962): 165–78; Gaston, *Imagining Judeo-Christian America*, 153–84.

63. Zorach v. Clauson, 343 U.S. 306, 312, 313–14 (1952).

64. Zorach, 316–18 (Black, J., dissenting).

65. "Final Stamp Noted on Released Time," *New York Times*, April 29, 1952, 23; "Time Off for Religion," *New York Times*, April 30, 1952, 26; "Released Time," *The Nation*, May 10, 1952; "Religious Education and the Constitution," *America*, May 17, 1952, 195–97; "The Court Concurs," *Christian Century*, May 14, 1952, 582–83; "The Constitution and Released Time," *Columbia Law Review* (1952): 1033–39.

66. Dickson, *Supreme Court in Conference*, 404–6. In *Doremus v. Board of Education* (342 U.S. 492 [1952]), the Court dismissed a challenge to public-school Bible reading on the basis that the plaintiff lacked standing to mount a challenge to the practice.

6. Separation's Apex and Decline

1. McGowan v. Maryland, 366 U.S. 420, 431–45 (1961); Two Guys from Harrison-Allentown v. McGinley, 366 U.S. 582, 592–98 (1961); Braunfeld v. Brown, 366 U.S. 599 (1961); Gallagher v. Crown Kosher Super Market, 366 U.S. 616 (1961); Torcaso v. Watkins, 367 U.S. 488 (1961). Anthony Lewis, "High Court Backs States' Blue Laws," *New York Times*, May 30, 1961, 1.

2. Torcaso, 367 U.S., 492–96.

3. "Kennedy Opposed Church-State Tie," *New York Times*, February 17, 1959, 1, 19; "Party's Debate on Kennedy Takes Note of Catholic Vote," *New York Times*, January 3, 1960, 1; Shaun A. Casey, *The Making of a Catholic President* (New York: Oxford University Press, 2009), 22–23, 27–28; Steven K. Green, *Third Disestablishment: Church, State, and American Culture, 1940–1975* (New York: Oxford University Press, 2019), 220–48.

4. "Political Pots Begin to Boil," *Christian Century*, January 13, 1960, 37–38; "Bigotry or Smear?," *Christianity Today*, February 1, 1960, 20.

5. Casey, *Making of a Catholic President*, 105, 119, 132–33; "Anti-Catholic View Found Widespread in Parts of South," *New York Times*, September 4, 1960, 1; Randall Balmer, *God in the White House* (San Francisco: HarperOne, 2008), 22–23; Axel R. Schafer, *Piety and Public Funding: Evangelicals and the State in Modern America* (Philadelphia: University of Pennsylvania Press, 2012), 134–38.

6. "Protestant Unit Wary on Kennedy," *New York Times*, September 8, 1960, 1; "Protestant Groups' Statements," *New York Times*, September 8, 1960, 25; "'Protestant Underworld' Cited as Source of Attack on Kennedy," *New York Times*, September 11, 1960, 69; "Text of Statement on Religious Issue," *New York Times*, September 16, 1960, 18; Casey, *Making of a Catholic President*, 98–99, 123–26, 136–44.

7. "Kennedy Assures Texas Ministers of Independence," *New York Times*, September 13, 1960, 1; "Transcript of Kennedy Talk to Ministers and Questions and Answers," *New York Times*, September 13, 1960, 22; Theodore H. White, *The Making of the President, 1960* (New York: Athenaeum, 1961), 284–86, 426–30.

8. "Anti-Catholic Groups Closely Cooperate in Mail Campaign to Defeat Kennedy," *New York Times*, October 17, 1960, 24; "Religious Effect Not Nationwide," *New York Times*, November 11, 1960; 23; Peter Kihss, "Kennedy's Faith Said to Cut Vote," *New York Times*, November 23, 1960, 13; Louis H. Bean, "Why Kennedy Won," *The Nation*, November 26, 1960, 408–10; Green, *Third Disestablishment*, 244–48.

9. "Daily Prayer in All Schools Is Urged by State's Regents," *New York Times*, December 1, 1951, 1, 6; "State Board Favors Prayer in New York Schools," *Christian Century*, December 19, 1951, 1452; Engel v. Vitale, 191 N.Y.S.2d 453, aff'd, 11 App. Div. 2d 340, aff'd, 176 N.E.2d 579 (1961); Bruce J. Dierenfield, *The Battle over School Prayer* (Lawrence: University Press of Kansas, 2007), 67–70, 86–118.

10. Engel v. Vitale, 370 U.S. 421, 424, 430 (1962).

11. Engel, 370 U.S., 430–31.

12. Engel, 434–35, 425.

13. "The Prayer Ruling," *New York Times*, July 1, 1962, 113.

14. Hugo Black Papers, box 354, folder 3, Library of Congress, n.d.; Del Dickson, ed., *The Supreme Court in Conference* (New York: Oxford University Press, 2001), 424; Dierenfield, *Battle over School Prayer*, 127–33.

15. Engel, 370 U.S., 445–46 (Stewart, J., dissenting); Corinna Barrett Lain, "God, Civic Virtue, and the American Way: Reconstructing *Engel*," *Stanford Law Review* 67 (March 2015): 479–555.

16. "Supreme Court Outlaws Official School Prayers in Regents Case Decision," *New York Times*, June 26, 1962, 1; "Supreme Court Prayer Ban: Where Will It Lead?," *Christianity Today*, July 20, 1962, 25; "Tempest over School Prayer Ban," *Christianity Today*, July 20, 1962, 46; Stuart Nagel and Robert Erikson, "Editorial Reaction to Supreme Court Decisions on Church and State," *Public Opinion Quarterly* 30 (Winter 1966): 647–55.

17. "The Regents' Prayer Decision," *Christianity and Crisis*, July 23, 1962, 125–26.

18. "Court Again under Fire," *New York Times*, July 1, 1962, 114; "Opinion of the Week: Prayers in School," *New York Times*, July 1, 1962, 113; "Both Houses Get Bills to Lift Ban on School Prayer," *New York Times*, June 27, 1962, 1.

19. "Ruling on Prayer Upheld by Rabbis," *New York Times*, July 1, 1962, 48; "What Churchmen Are Saying," *Christianity Today*, August 8, 1962, 25; "Prayer Still Legal in Public Schools," *Christian Century*, July 4, 1962, 832–33; "Politics of Prayer Stir the Nation," *Christian Century*, July 11, 1962, 856.

20. "Supreme Court Prayer Ban: Where Will It Lead?," *Christianity Today*, July 20, 1962, 25; "Church-State Separation: A Serpentine Wall?" *Christianity Today*, July 20, 1962, 29; "Bible Reading in the Public Schools," *Christianity Today*, March 1, 1963, 42–43.

21. Murray v. Curlett, 179 A.2d 698, 701–3 (Md. 1962); School District of Abington Township v. Schempp, 374 U.S. 203 (1963).

22. "Is the Supreme Court on Trial?," *Christianity Today*, March 1, 1963, 28; "Court Weighs Religious Exercises," *Christianity Today*, March 15, 1963, 31.

23. Schempp, 374 U.S., 212–13, 222, 225.

24. Schempp, 216–21.

25. Schempp, 309, 312 (Stewart, J., dissenting).

26. "Churches Divided, with Most in Favor," *New York Times*, June 18, 1963, 1, 29; "Response to Bible-Prayer Readings," *Christianity Today*, July 5, 1963, 47; "The Meaning of the Supreme Court Decision," *Christianity Today*, July 5, 1963, 29; "The Court Decides Wisely," *Christian Century*, July 3, 1963, 851–52; "School Prayer and Beyond," *Christianity and Crisis*, June 24, 1963, 113–14; George R. La Noue, "The Supreme Court's New Frontier between Religion and the Public Schools," *Phi Delta Kappan* 45 (December 1963): 123–27.

27. "Prayer Hearing Begins in House," *New York Times*, April 23, 1964, 14; John Herbert Laubach, *School Prayers: Congress, the Courts, and the Public* (Washington, DC: Public Affairs, 1969), 1–69; "On School Prayer Amendment," *Congressional Quarterly* 22 (May 1, 1964): 881–85; "Congress and the School Prayer Decisions," *Congressional Digest* (November 1964): 257–88; Donald E. Boles, *The Bible, Religion, and the Public Schools* (Ames: Iowa State University Press, 1965), 298–330.

28. "Dirksen to Press Campaign for Amendment on Prayer," *New York Times*, May 6, 1966, 28; "Witnesses Score Prayer Proposal," *New York Times*, August 2, 1966,

23; "Clergymen Divided on School Prayers," *New York Times*, August 6, 1966, 10; Laubach, *School Prayers*, 141–50.

29. Green, *Third Disestablishment*, 301–3.

30. Boles, *Bible, Religion, and Public Schools*, 298–330; Joe Edward Barnhart, *The Southern Baptist Holy War* (Austin, TX: Texas Monthly Press, 1986).

31. Harold D. Hammett, "Separation of Church and State: By One Wall or Two?," *Journal of Church and State* 7 (1965): 190–206; Steven D. Smith, "Constitutional Divide: The Transformative Significance of the School Prayer Decisions," *Pepperdine Law Review* 38 (2011): 945–1020; Robert Boston, *Why the Religious Right Is Wrong about Separation of Church and State* (Buffalo, NY: Prometheus Books, 1993), 16–17.

32. Paul Blanshard, *American Freedom and Catholic Power* (Boston: Beacon, 1949); Una M. Cadegan, "Guardians of Democracy or Cultural Storm Troopers? American Catholics and the Control of Popular Media, 1934–1966," *Catholic Historical Review* 87 (April 2001), 252–82.

33. See, generally, Lerond Curry, *Protestant-Catholic Relations in America: World War I through Vatican II* (Lexington: University Press of Kentucky, 1972); George A. Kizer, "Federal Aid to Education: 1945–1963," *History of Education Quarterly* (1970): 84–102, and Emma Long, *The Church-State Debate: Religion, Education and the Establishment Clause in Post War America* (London: Continuum, 2012), 24–26. A confessional state is one that officially practices one religion and encourages its citizens to adhere to that faith.

34. James W. Guthrie, "A Political Case History: Passage of ESEA," *Phi Delta Kappan* 49 (February 1968): 302–6; Philip Meranto, *The Politics of Federal Aid to Education in 1965* (Syracuse, NY: Syracuse University Press, 1967); Harvey Kantor, "Social Reform and the State: ESEA and Federal Education Policy in the 1960s," *American Journal of Education* 100 (November 1991): 47–83.

35. "Religion and Race," *Christian Century*, January 30, 1963, 133–35; "National Council Action on Race," *Christianity and Crisis*, July 8, 1963, 131–32; James F. Findlay, *Church People in the Struggle: The National Council of Churches and the Black Freedom Movement, 1950–1970* (New York: Oxford University Press, 1993), 32–34.

36. Dean M. Kelley, "Beyond Separation of Church and State," *Journal of Church and State* 5 (1963): 181–98.

37. "Separation and Interaction of Church and State, National Council of Churches," *Journal of Church and State* 6 (1964): 147–53.

38. Franklin H. Littell, *From State Church to Pluralism* (Garden City, NY: Doubleday, 1962); Thomas G. Sanders, *Protestant Concepts of Church and State* (New York: Holt, Rinehart and Winston, 1964), 230–49; Philip Wogaman, "The Changing Role of Government and the Myth of Separation," *Journal of Church and State* 5 (1963): 61–76; Philip Wogaman, *Protestant Faith and Religious Liberty* (Nashville, TN: Abingdon, 1967), 42–60.

39. Wilber G. Katz, "Freedom of Religion and State Neutrality," *University of Chicago Law Review* 20 (Spring 1953): 426–40; Dallin H. Oaks, *The Wall between Church and State* (Chicago: University of Chicago Press, 1963), 2–3; Mark De Wolfe Howe, *The Garden and the Wilderness: Religion and Government in American Constitutional History* (Chicago: University of Chicago Press, 1965), 6–19.

40. Dierenfield, *Religion in American Public Schools*, 49–52.

41. Board of Education v. Allen, 392 U.S. 236, 242–44, 247–48 (1968).

42. Allen, 251, 254 (Black, J., dissenting).

43. "Book Aid to Church Pupils Upheld by Supreme Court," *New York Times*, June 11, 1968, 1; "Court's Textbook Ruling Hailed by Church School Officials, Deplored by Liberties Groups," *New York Times*, June 11, 1968, 38; "Retreat on Church Schools," *New York Times*, June 12, 1968, 46.

44. Walz v. Tax Commission, 397 U.S. 664, 668–76 (1970).

45. Richard E. Morgan, "The Establishment Clause and Sectarian Schools: A Final Installment?," *Supreme Court Review* (1973): 57–97, 65.

46. In between the two cases, the Court decided *Epperson v. Arkansas*, which struck down an Arkansas statute prohibiting the teaching of evolution in state schools. Justice Abe Fortas held that the statute violated the Establishment Clause by favoring "a particular [religious] dogma" about human origins. Fortas cited *McCollum*, repeating that the justices there had declared that using school property for religious purposes breached "the 'wall of separation' which, according to Jefferson, the First Amendment was intended to erect between church and state." However, the phrase was not incorporated into the reasoning of Fortas's opinion. Epperson v. Arkansas, 292 U.S. 97, 106 (1968).

47. Lemon v. Kurtzman, 403 U.S. 602 (1971); Tilton v. Richardson, 403 U.S. 672 (1971). A companion case to Lemon was DiCenso v. Robinson, 403 U.S. 602 (1971).

48. Lemon, 403 U.S., 612–13, 614.

49. Dickson, *Supreme Court in Conference*, 410–12; Donald A. Giannella, "Lemon and Tilton: The Bitter and the Sweet of Church-State Entanglement," *Supreme Court Review* (1971): 147–200.

50. Norman Redlich, "The Separation of Church and State: The Burger Court's Tortuous Journey," in *The Burger Years*, ed. Herman Swartz (New York: Viking, 1987), 56–91; Earl M. Maltz, *The Chief Justiceship of Warren Burger, 1969–1986* (Columbia: University of South Carolina Press, 2000), 166–75.

51. Brusca v. State Board of Education, 405 U.S. 1050 (1972); Levitt v. PEARL, 413 U.S. 472 (1973); Sloan v. Lemon, 413 U.S. 825 (1973); PEARL v. Nyquist, 413 U.S. 756 (1973); Hunt v. McNair, 413 U.S. 734 (1973); Wheeler v. Barrera, 417 U.S. 402 (1974); Meek v. Pittenger, 421 U.S. 349 (1975); Roemer v. Board of Public Works, 426 U.S. 736 (1976); Long, *Church-State Debate*, 57–60.

52. Morgan, "Establishment Clause and Sectarian Schools," 57; "Private School Aid in State Upset by Supreme Court," *New York Times*, June 26, 1973, 1; "The Court Reverses a Trend," *New York Times*, July 1, 1973, 149.

53. Wolman v. Walter, 433 U.S. 229 (1977); PEARL v. Regan, 444 U.S. 646 (1980); Bowen v. Kendrick, 487 U.S. 589 (1988).

54. Mueller v. Allen, 463 U.S. 388 (1983); Witters v. Washington Commission for the Blind, 474 U.S. 481 (1986).

55. Aguilar v. Felton, 473 U.S. 402 (1985); Grand Rapids School District v. Ball, 473 U.S. 373, 390 (1985).

56. Wallace v. Jaffree, 472 U.S., 107 (Rehnquist, dissenting); Ball, 473 U.S., 401 (Rehnquist, J., dissenting); Bowen v. Kendrick, 487 U.S. 589 (1988); Zobrest v. Catalina Foothills School District, 509 U.S. 1 (1993); Rosenberger v. University of Virginia, 515 U.S. 819 (1995); Agostini v. Felton, 521 U.S. 203 (1997); Mitchell v. Helms, 530 U.S. 793

(2000); Zelman v. Simmons-Harris, 536 U.S. 639 (2002); Espinoza v. Montana Department of Revenue, 140 S. Ct. 2246 (2020).

57. Stone v. Graham, 449 U.S. 39 (1980); Wallace v. Jaffree, 472 U.S. 38 (1985); Edwards v. Aguillard, 482 U.S. 578 (1987); Lee v. Weisman, 505 U.S. 507 (1992); Santa Fe School District v. Doe, 530 U.S. 290 (2000).

58. Wallace, 472 U.S., 53n37.

59. Board of Education v. Mergens, 496 U.S. 226 (1990); Lamb's Chapel v. Center Morishes Union School District, 508 U.S. 384 (1993); Good New Club v. Milford Central School, 533 U.S. 98, 116n6 (2001).

60. Lynch v. Donnelly, 465 U.S. 668, 673 (1984).

61. Van Orden v. Perry, 545 U.S. 677, 683 (2005).

62. Van Orden, 698 (Breyer, J., concurring).

63. Van Orden, 709, 730 (Stevens, J., dissenting).

64. Van Orden, 709n4.

65. Rosenberger, 515 U.S., 855, 856 (Thomas, J., concurring); Town of Greece v. Galloway, 572 U.S. 565, 607n1 (2014) (Thomas, J., concurring).

66. Zelman, 536 U.S., 732 (Breyer, J., dissenting); Rosenberger, 515 U.S., 881n7 (Souter, J., dissenting).

67. Trinity Lutheran Church, 137 S. Ct., 2027.

68. American Legion v. American Humanist Association, 139 S. Ct. 2067 (2019); American Legion, 2091 (Breyer, J. concurring).

69. American Legion, 2105 (Ginsburg, J., dissenting).

70. American Legion, 2095 (Thomas, J., concurring in the judgment).

71. McCreary County v. American Civil Liberties Union, 545 U.S. 844, 882 (O'Connor, J., concurring).

Conclusion

1. Philip E. Hammond, "The Shifting Meaning of a 'Wall of Separation,'" *Sociological Analysis* 42 (Autumn 1981): 227–34; Edwin S. Gaustad, "Thomas Jefferson, Danbury Baptists, and 'Eternal Hostility,'" *William and Mary Quarterly* 56 (1999): 801–4.

2. Jones v. Wolf, 443 U.S. 595 (1979); Hosanna–Tabor Evangelical Lutheran Church v. EEOC, 565 U.S. 171 (2012); Our Lady of Guadalupe School v. Morrissey-Berru, 140 S. Ct. 2049 (2020).

3. Lee v. Weisman, 505 U.S. 507, 600–601 (1992) (Blackmun, J., concurring); Lee, 625–26 (Souter, J., concurring).

4. Good News Club v. Milford Central School, 533 U.S., 113 (2001).

5. Lynch v. Donnelly, 465 U.S. 668 (1984); Greece v. Galloway, 572 U.S. 565 (2014); Van Orden v. Perry, 545 U.S. 677 (2005); American Legion v. American Humanist Association, 139 S. Ct. 2067 (2019). See Steven K. Green, "The Supreme Court's Ahistorical Religion Clause Historicism," *Baylor Law Review* 73 (Fall 2021).

6. Witters v. Washington Department of Services for the Blind, 474 U.S. 481 (1986); Bowen v. Kendrick, 487 U.S. 589 (1988); Mitchell v. Helms, 530 U.S. 793; Zelman v. Simmons-Harris, 536 U.S. 639 (2000); Trinity Lutheran Church v. Comer, 137 S. Ct. 2012 (2017); Espinoza v. Montana Department of Revenue, 140 S. Ct. 2246, 2260–61 (2020).

7. "How Religious Commitment Varies by Country among People of All Ages," Pew Research Center on Religion and Public Life, June 13, 2018, https://www.pewforum.org/2018/06/13/how-religious-commitment-varies-by-country-among-people-of-all-ages/.

8. Ira C. Lupu and Robert W. Tuttle, *Secular Government, Religious People* (Grand Rapids, MI: Eerdmans, 2014).

9. David Sehat, *The Myth of American Religious Freedom* (New York: Oxford University Press, 2011), 4–5.

10. Lemon v. Kurtzman, 403 U.S. 602, 612–13, 614 (1971).

Index

www.ingramcontent.com/pod-product-compliance
Lightning Source LLC
Chambersburg PA
CBHW021548270826
50534CB00014B/267/J
* 9 7 8 1 5 0 1 7 6 2 0 6 2 *